BOUNDLESS REALM
Deep Explorations Inside Disney's Haunted Mansion

FOXX NOLTE

INKLINGWOOD PRESS

© 2020 Foxx Nolte

FIRST EDITION
Published by Inklingwood Press

No part of this publication may be reproduced, distributed, or transmitted in any form or by any means, including photocopying, recording, or other electronic or mechanic methods, without the prior written permission of the publisher, except for brief quotations for critical, educational, and non-commercial uses permitted by copyright law.

This book is not associated with The Walt Disney Company. Quotations and images used throughout this book either have permission to be used or are used under Fair Use for educational and research purposes. Various nomenclature including theme park names, land names, attraction names, and intellectual property is copyright its respective owner.

Although every precaution has been taken to verify the accuracy of the information contained herein, no responsibility is assumed for any errors or omissions, and no liability is assumed for damages that may result from the use of this information.

"The bourgeois interior of the 1860s to the 1890s - with gigantic sideboards distended with carvings, the sunless corners where potted palms sit, the balcony embattled behind its balustrade, and the long corridors with their singing gas flames - fittingly houses only the corpse."
 - Walter Benjamin, One-Way Street

"Over the years Disney repeated to his animators: "Make it read!" Meaning, make the action distinct and recognizable. No contradictions, no ambiguities."
 - Bob Thomas, Walt Disney:
   An American Original

CONTENTS

FOREWORD BY JEFF KURTTI 1
SOME WORDS BEFORE 3
PART I: A HOUSE BY A RIVER 9
   1. WARNING SHADOWS 10
   2. SQUARES AND PLAZAS 29
   3. HISTORY AND THE HAUNTED MANSION 38
   4. DEATH AND DECLINE 49
   5. UP OR DOWN? 53
   6. A LIGHT IN THE ATTIC 61
   7. THE OLD HOUSE AND THE SEA 66
PART II: THIS OLD DARK HOUSE 73
   1. A COLD WELCOME 75
   2. THE STRETCH ROOM 88
   3. THE GREAT HALL 102

4. THE WATCHFUL EYES 117
5. PRICELESS FLAT EDITIONS 128
6. ENTR'ACTE: THE GRAND STAIRS 141
7. DOWN THE DARK HALL 153
8. TIME VORTEX 162
9. INTERMEZZO: RESCUE CIRCLE 179
10. FURIOSO: DANCE MACABRE 188
11. THE ATTIC: HINGE 201
12. THE GREAT INDOORS 220
13. OUT OF THE GRAVE 242
14. THESES ON THE HAUNTED MANSION 260

PART III: APPENDICES 263
   APPENDIX A: HUMAN AND ANIMAL IMAGERY 264
   APPENDIX B: PHANTOM MANOR 269
   APPENDIX C: MARC, CLAUDE, AND THE MANSION 283
   APPENDIX D: THE SINISTER ELEVEN 292
   APPENDIX E: FOUR OTHER HAUNTED MANSIONS 306
NOTES 329

FOREWORD BY JEFF KURTTI

In the lexicon of Disney, there are several familiar moods: music, magic, family, happy endings. Oh, and one more. Terror.

None of the rest of it works without the critical element of fear. Without sorrow, joy is empty; without peril, triumph has no meaning. Walt Disney seems to have had a deep understanding of the dark side of life that he used to heighten the heroism in his works. When creating his stories for animation, live-action films, television, and even Disneyland, Walt Disney was fearless about using fear as a primary element.

From Mickey's early nemesis Pete to the terpsichorean undead of *Skeleton Dance*; from the various witches and stepmothers of classic animation, to the dark, accursed deity Chernabog, to the Headless Horseman; Disney culture is rife with fright. Walt knew that peril is necessary in building compelling storytelling.

Frank Thomas and Ollie Johnston wrote in their classic 1993 book *The Disney Villain*, "When we would see his face screwed up, eyes half closed, trying to figure out what villainous act would do the most harm, we felt he had experienced much of that from bullies in his own childhood. He certainly met much villainy throughout his life. The greater his success, the more conflict he encountered as others tried to take it away from him."

Walt's Midwestern childhood was no doubt infused with family ghosts stories, spooky rural legends, and campfire tales of hauntings and bewitchment. Most towns had a "haunted house," a deserted farmhouse or abandoned town home that was the subject of whispers and unease.

It's no surprise that when Disneyland was being designed, Disney Legend Harper Goff's earliest renderings of Main Street, U.S.A. featured just such a haunted house.

When Disneyland opened, the villains of Walt's animated features were ported over into the Fantasyland "dark rides" based upon those stories - Captain Hook menaces Peter Pan in Never Land to this day, and the Wicked Queen transforms into a haggard peddler woman to threaten Snow White. In 1983, a new Pinocchio attraction brought the little wooden boy's nemeses to dimensional life, from Foulfellow and Gideon to Stromboli and Monstro the Whale. Each of them has a propelling story element: the peril of the hero and the Guest as the surrogate.

When Walt's "haunted house" finally opened at Disneyland a few years after his passing, it's interesting to note that it takes a strange viewpoint on fear—an eerie tour of a dusty and long-abandoned house begins subtly, on "the trail of the tingling spine," and progresses apace, growing in its tempo and thematic temperament to a frenetic, but *comedic* climax in the graveyard—with the visitors to this strange mansion themselves acting as the fulcrum between comedy and creepiness.

More than anything, and beyond the clinical necessity of conflict in creating compelling stories, Walt's "final fright," perhaps more than any other of his works, reveals his attitude about fear—that being scared can be really fun.

"Walt said once, 'What I understand about kids that nobody else understands, is that they think it's delicious to be frightened," Walt's friend and the star of *Mary Poppins*, Dick Van Dyke, recalled. "Kids love to be scared. They love ghost stories.' And he always put the witch or something in there, to give them that delicious goose bump. He knew."

JEFF KURTTI is the most prolific nonfiction legacy author in Disney history, with more than 40 volumes to his credit over 25 years. A leading authority on The Walt Disney Company, its founder, and its history, he is also a writer-director of award-winning documentary content, and a respected public speaker. For several years, he worked for Walt Disney Imagineering, the theme park design division of The Walt Disney Company, and then for the Corporate Special Projects department of Disney. Since 1995, Kurtti has enjoyed a career as an author, writer, and consultant in the motion picture, theater, and themed design industries, including as creative director, content consultant, and media producer for The Walt Disney Family Museum in San Francisco.

SOME WORDS BEFORE

If it can be believed, there was a time when it was not terribly fashionable to like the *Haunted Mansion*. In the past twenty years, the attraction has graduated from tradition to cultural institution, and I have been there to see it. After fifty years it and its older sister *Pirates of the Caribbean* have finally begun to approach something resembling respectability - the two default examples for those who want to hold up the craft of the themed show as something that could be called **Art**. Yet there was a point in time where not only the *Haunted Mansion*, but the entire institution of the kind of sensibility which it represented seemed to be sitting on crumbling foundations.

It began in 1989, with the opening of the Disney-MGM Studios in Orlando. Here was Disney's first direct attack on their competition - their answer to the kind of amped-up thrill experiences Universal Studios Florida was building just up Interstate 4. Here was a Disney theme park for the 90s: it was loud, it was self-aware, and seemingly every other show ignited a fireball. For a company which previously only got about as intense as *Space Mountain*, sending the creature from *Alien* after riders was a new level of fright.

It was the first era of in-your-face, and the public loved it. *Body Wars* shot you through the chambers of a human heart - riders saw red for hours afterwards. *Honey, I Shrunk the Audience* bounced, jostled, and sprayed water on its audience. *Alien Encounter* had a nasty bug lick your neck. The queues for these short, thrill-based rides climbed while classically imaginative, gentle attractions like *World of Motion* and *Horizons* seemed empty.

Then came the closures. Attractions which had seemed popular, like *20,000 Leagues Under the Sea*, closed for refurbishment and never returned. One day the Fantasyland submarine ride had a full queue, the next it was gone. *Horizons*, left to flounder without a sponsor, closed and sat there unused. *World of Motion* closed. *Journey into Imagination* closed. *Mr. Toad's Wild*

Ride, the busiest and most popular of the Fantasyland dark rides, closed.

These were not minor attractions. Some losses, like *Horizons* and *Journey into Imagination*, tore a hole in the heart of their parks which can still be felt to this day. *The Enchanted Tiki Room: Under New Management* rubbed salt into fresh wounds by openly mocking guests who enjoyed Walt Disney's original show. *Mr. Toad's Wild Ride* promoted protests and newspaper coverage - "Save Toad" remains a potent catchphrase, even today. It really did seem as if Disney was determined to close or rework every last classic attraction in the park.

Meanwhile, over in Paris, Euro Disneyland did not open with a *Haunted Mansion* - they had *Phantom Manor*, a darker, dramatically different take on the same material. Rumors, fed by the rashes of closures and "edgy" reboots, began to swirl that Disney was planning on converting the *Haunted Mansion* into *Phantom Manor*. Those of us who were longtime fans began to brace for the worst.

In that growing darkness, a bunch of geeks on the internet lit a candle. People began to talk about the *Haunted Mansion* - not as some antiquated seventies spook show, but as a rich source of fascinations. How were the effects done? How does the ride fit inside that big house? Who were the ghosts? What does it mean?

From forums and trivia websites, communities began to form exclusively devoted to that weirdest of Disney attractions. People wanted to know more about this ride - in an era when Disney still liked to explain away Yale Gracey's ingenious effects as holograms, or real ghosts.

The internet was still new - graphical web browsing barely five years old - and so real videos were impossible. Some of us traded VHS tapes through mail (!) of 10 or 12 home videos of the ride. In the absence of details, and with fans thousands of miles away from Disneyland or Walt Disney World, the internet filled with discussion, speculation, and lore.

Many of those early research efforts and discussions formed the basis for the rich mythology that surrounds the attraction. It wasn't manufactured by Disney; like an urban legend, everyone made it happen all at once. The light from that candle grew, and something bigger than all of us was happening. We were going to save the attraction by making everyone else obsessed with it, too.

I was a *Haunted Mansion* kid. I was there with them, postulating, theorizing, obsessing over those precious few photos of the inside of the place that existed. I created my first *Haunted Mansion* website in Microsoft Publisher when I was fourteen. My mother bought me a magazine on HTML, and I taught myself how to create websites just to add mine to the fray. When I visited Walt Disney World in 1999, I burned through five or six disposable cameras taking flash photos inside the ride. The Cast Members let me stay aboard the ride - on one day I believed I logged about two dozen rides. I'm sure I was intolerable - everyone is when they're that young. Now I'm just glad I created the documentation that I did, because in some cases it is all that still exists.

The tidal pull of the *Haunted Mansion* eventually dragged me south to Florida. It took me only a few weeks to get a job at Walt Disney World. The drive from my college campus to Disney was nearly an hour, but I didn't care. All I could think about was that now, I could ride the *Haunted Mansion... whenever I wanted.*

To my credit, I resisted actually working at the attraction for a long time, and once I did finally take the plunge, I was immediately reassured of the wisdom in my reticence. I hated the job; the tedium, the exhaustion of walking the belts all day, the pressure of moving groups through the first rooms of the house. My temperament was better suited to the slow chug of the Riverboat around Tom Sawyer Island. But there was one real advantage to working the *Haunted Mansion*, and that was that *I was working the Haunted Mansion.*

In the old days before Disney computerized every theme park job and sucked much of the fun of working there out of it, those of us in Ad/Lib - that's Adventureland-Liberty Square Operations - had such a thing as a "Bucket". This was an assigned job for when there was nothing else that needed to be done, and was so called because you went to the supply closet, got an empty 5 gallon bucket and a pair of pickers, and rode thru the Mansion, picking up trash on the floor and putting it in the bucket. I was really good at Buckets, and I did them a lot. When I wasn't hoping to do a Bucket, I was often getting in a ride car anyway, loudly announcing I was going to check "Show Quality". I spent as much time riding, instead of working, the Mansion as possible.

And then, of course, I had access to the ride itself - the vast winding basements, backdoors, and obscure corners of my childhood obsession. I climbed up to catwalks, wriggled beneath churning Doombuggies (nearly electrocuting myself in the process), peeked through holes in the sets to watch the cars go by, dug through dusty piles of paper, and moved set dressing to places I saw fit. I spent a lot of time in that old house on the hill.

When this book was first developing, it was originally going to be something of a reminisce; having been on the Mansion more times in my life than most people, I was imagining a slim book full of funny stories and juicy backstage gossip. But the trouble is, *I* was the one writing it, and my own sensibilities are about as far from juicy backstage gossip as you can get. In time, many of the stories were pared out, and the book took shape. What originally began as a memoir turned into a thesis - but then so does everything I write, anyway.

What this book is not, however, is a historical overview of the *Haunted Mansion*; indeed, **my specific *Haunted Mansion*** sits amongst the wilds of the Florida swamps, not the growing garden nestled inside the freeways of Southern California.

The creative development of the attraction is another story, and another house, and indeed **a story that has been told well before**. I am not striving for a primer text on the attraction, but for something more specific, more personal - more weird.

All are welcome, but entry comes with a caveat: I will be assuming that you, the reader, are already familiar with the basics of the *Haunted Mansion*. I will not stop for an extended discussion of how the Ballroom effect is accomplished, nor will I introduce the key players behind the creation of the *Haunted Mansion* one by one. This book is less narrative than it is an enthusiast's tour. We will be investigating rooms, discussing designs, and taking a wide ranging overview of what could be termed the "cultural footprint" occupied by the *Haunted Mansion*.

Thankfully there are two extremely comprehensive books already in print which act as Haunted Mansion primers: *The Haunted Mansion: Imagineering A Disney Classic* by Jason Surrell, and *The Unauthorized Story of Disney's Haunted Mansion* by Jeff Baham. Either is fully recommended for those first starting their personal journey through the *Haunted Mansion*.

This attraction has meant so much to so many. This book is a short (!) attempt to explain what it has meant to *me*.

PART I: A HOUSE BY A RIVER

1. WARNING SHADOWS

By midnight moons, o'er moistening dews,
In habit for the chase arrayed;
The hunter still the deer pursues,
The hunter and the deer, a shade!
- Philip Freneau, *The Indian Burial Ground*

Deep at the root of American culture is a strong and abiding morbidity.

We may have inherited it from our Puritan ancestors, who unloaded off the boat facing death or starvation and saw in the tractless American wilderness the Devil crouched behind every tree and rock. There is something distinctly morbid in the Puritan twin obsessions of sex and death, in the impulse to see on every plate of food, every human interaction a potential ticket to Hell.

Americans invented their own Yankee brand of horror. The horror tales of the English isles are animated by abandoned rectories and haunted castles, paintings that change to reveal horrible truths and old gold coins buried in the woods. In contrast, the Germanic, continental horror tradition is that of daily life being manipulated and overcome by sinister, outside forces beyond control. In Asia, hell is other people, with curses, revenges, and broken promises animating their specters like clockwork gorillas lurching after doomed prey.

The American horror concept which resonates most strongly through the national character is the Bad Place.[1] The notion that perfectly innocent looking locales could harbor horrible secrets, like Wendigos stalking our ancestral forests or curses streaming out of ancient Indian burial grounds. It is only in America that the notion that houses became haunted because they were built on rotten or cursed earth reached its full Gothic flower.

The abiding suspicion that the dark gods of ancient, pre-Christian religions stalk our continent may have descended from those Puritans, who created Bad Places of their own and gave them names to match - names which are still with us. Connecticut alone has The Devil's Kitchen, The Devil's Drip-Pan, The Devil's Hop-Yard, The Devil's Den, and Satan's Kingdom. Maine has a Devil's Footprint. Maybe, just maybe, those old Puritans were right.

Morbidity is everywhere right from the start of what we recognize as uniquely American literature. In 1787, the year of the signing of the Constitution, Philip Freneau published *The Indian Burial Ground*, memorializing the early American terror of the howling, pre-Christian wilderness. Freneau himself, a contemporary of James Madison, also composed *The House of Night* in 1779, a lurid dream narrative involving a cemeteries, haunted forests and a visit with Death incarnate which strongly prefigures the Gothic. In later ages, Mark Twain imagined Injun Joe lost, screaming forever in the caverns, and the bloated corpse of Huck Finn's father floating dead in his houseboat.

An early proponent of American mythologizing, Washington Irving created folk tales of ghosts and magic out of the whole cloth of the American character so accurately they do not feel like pastiche. Herman Melville turned his pursuit of the whale *Moby Dick* into a supernatural horror story of the open sea, a fatal reckoning with the inhuman, untamable power which brought life to the New World.

Meanwhile, in Europe, a new genre of lurid and romantic mysteries was being minted, inspired by Wapole's *The Castle of Otranto*. *Otranto* doesn't seem to have gotten much traction in the new United States, but Ann Radcliffe, author of *The Mysteries of Udolpho*, was incredibly popular. These new "Gothic" novels, inspired by the ancient crumbling stone castles they were often set in, combined family curses and lost treasure with sensationalistic melodrama and were the trash romance novels of their era. Originating in England, thanks to authors such as Friedrich von Schiller and E.T.A. Hoffmann, the "Gothic" novel also became known as a "Germanic" novel, the term having slipped from "Gothic" to "Goth" in the intervening years.

Decades later in the United States, two authors now closely allied with the horror tradition launched a "second wave" of

Radcliffe-inspired gothic novels, as a reaction and redefinition of an old concept as much as a participant in the earlier cycle. This is why Edgar Allan Poe's first published story, *Metzengerstein*, is subtitled "In Imitation of the German", just as Mary Shelley titled her *Frankenstein* with a Germanic-sounding name to alert readers to the horrifying content within.

Hawthorne's *The House of Seven Gables* unified the notions of poisoned earth and poisoned lives, building his seven gabled house on land confiscated from a woman executed for witchcraft. Madness and death plagued the house and haunted the guilty conscience of the family within. Edgar Allan Poe united the Puritan terrors of the Bad Place, Sex, and Death in *The Fall of the House of Usher*, a gothic mansion which literally sits on a fault line representing the unhealthy, morbid, and incestuous impulses of its benighted inhabitants. Poe's emphasis on terror and horror, especially in pieces like "*The Pit and the Pendulum*" or "*The Facts In The Case of M. Valdemar*", essentially invented the terror tale subgenre.

In 1841, just two years after the publication of *The Fall of the House of Usher*, P.T. Barnum opened Barnum's American Museum in New York, a gigantic and permanent freak show and cabinet of curiosities. There was, naturally, a bar in its basement. Barnum and Poe guided America through our own native national tragedy - the Civil War - and once it was over, Barnum's American Museum immolated in 1865,[2] like Nosferatu caught in the morning sun. But as always, success breeds imitation, and in the wake of Barnum's massive show, "Dime Museums" sprouted in urban centers up and down the east coast, offering frauds, disfigurements, and illusions. The very term "dime museum" prefigures a coming entertainment intended for the illiterate, urban, often immigrant masses - the Nickelodeon.

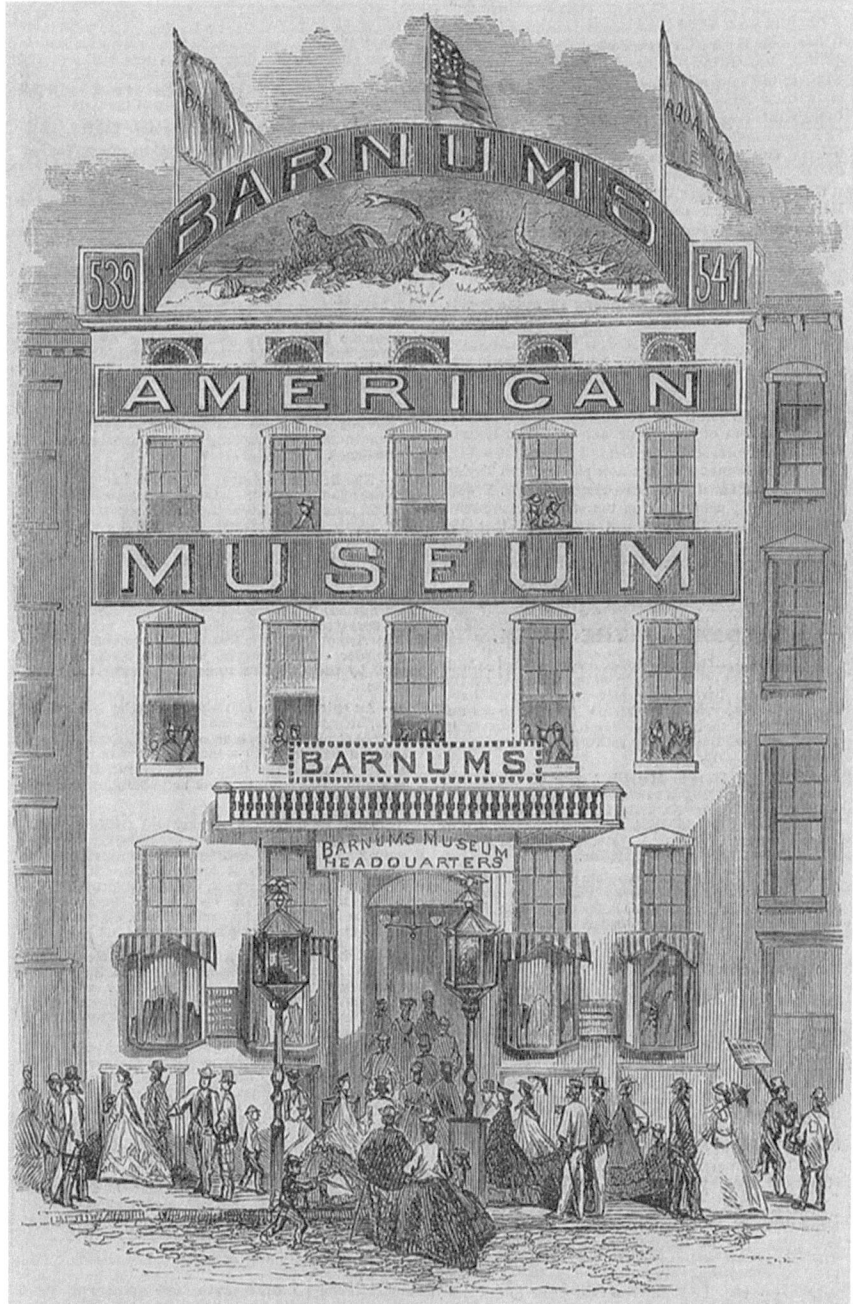

BARNUM'S NEW AMERICAN MUSEUM, NO. 539 & 541 BROADWAY, N. Y., BETWEEN SPRING AND PRINCE STREETS.

Amusement parks and motion pictures were born at the same cultural moment.

Cinema, of course, is French - no matter how much Thomas Edison wanted to convince the American people otherwise. The amusement park, however, is truly all-American, and the starting pistol was the World's Columbian Exposition, better known as the 1893 Chicago World's Fair.

The industrial revolution, which had caused so much misery in American cities and repeatedly crashed the economy, had by then advanced to the point that mansions and smaller dwellings could be decorated with as much old-world elegance as the finest pre-modern examples. Such developments as the band saw and cutting die meant that elaborate visual ornamentation was cheaper than ever before, which had led to increasing ornamentation on and in American homes. Of course, that same saw and die could carve wood into gilt extravagances to whirl and twirl on a carousel.

The amusement park naturally gravitated to its dark twin, the dime museum and circus sideshow. The horrors of the human body could now be experienced just steps away from physical thrills which were once impossible to experience. The amusement park allowed patrons to survive experiences which previously would have proved fatal - falling from great heights in roller coasters, going down waterfalls in boats at the Shoot-the-Chutes, or riding out of control horses at the Steeplechase. These nicely complemented the whirling wheels of light - the carousels and Ferris wheels - which so strongly resemble turning wheels of chance and fate. The Tunnel of Love even offered an opportunity to get a little romance into the night. In its fullest flower, the amusement park is a ritual opportunity to face down death and mutilation - and survive.

Yet these sorts of experiences had been pushing towards what was not yet known as the "cinematic" for some time. In the same way that today one may go to a State Fair and ride a Scrambler ride hauled in on a truck, cinema got its start in vaudeville houses and carnivals, a novelty carried from place to place by traveling showmen. The reason for this retrospectively bizarre arrangement is due to the fact that many of these showmen had previously been exhibiting Magic Lantern shows, a sort of primitive warning tremor of cinema.

Magic Lantern is an art of another era, emerging at a time when the United States did not yet even exist. The point of these Magic Lantern shows, of course, was to terrify, and as they became more sophisticated, the results could become, for their era, startling. Ghosts, devils, and dancing skeletons could appear. Several operators began to overlay multiple magic lantern projections over the top of each other, with one lantern mobile, pushed back and forth to cause images to grow or shrink on the screen; when synchronized to music or sound effects, these illusions could be quite effective. They were called Phantasmagorias, and the height of their popularity was 1820, not 1920. Phantasmagorias danced in the dreams of E.A. Poe.

But just as the Magic Lantern eventually became the cinema, the cinema also became the amusement park, their identities as purveyors of the fantastic indelibly intertwined for generations. There were Hale's Tours, a sort of Edwardian premonition of a simulator ride accomplished with a motion picture screen and a rocking room. Even more to the point was the famous *Trip to the Moon* attraction designed by Fred Thompson, which combined magic lantern effects, actors, a gigantic rocking ship, and papier-mâché sets to bring visitors to the Lunar surface and encounter "the king of the moon". Not to be outdone, Portland's Lewis and Clark Exposition in 1905 included a Haunted Castle, where skeletons danced and shimmied and ghosts appeared.

Simulteaneously, just at the interregnum where American popular culture splits off into the Modern, the Fun House was created. Gigantic temples of anarchy where repressed Edwardians could thumb their noses at authority, the original Fun Houses, especially the *Pavilion of Fun* at Coney Island, were DeSadeian three ring circuses of absurdity where patrons were the performers. Outrageously long slides, rolling rooms, mirror mazes, and spinning discs sent patrons scurrying and flying. Clowns patrolled balconies armed with electrical wands to shock unwary passerby. Women's

No. 171 Pub. by I. Stern, Brooklyn, N. Y LUNA PARK, CONEY ISLAND.

skirts were blown upwards by blasts of compressed air. As the Fun House evolved, they became linear walkthrough experiences, sending patrons through ancient Arabic cities or Chinese slums.

Then came the Great War in 1914, and things changed forever. America suddenly became a world leader, uniquely positioned by economic chance and American aggressiveness to spread their version of popular culture far and wide. The leading French film companies collapsed at the start of the war in 1914, and a new little Western colony called Hollywood - where motion picture producers had fled to escape the long legal arm of Thomas Edison - swooped in to fill the breach.

By the end of the war, the American economy and film industry were ascendant, and Europe was sending home a steady stream of war heroes who were no longer mentally or physically complete. Advances in medical technology saved the lives of many men who would have died in previous conflicts, and suddenly American cities were filled with veterans of the kind never seen in human history - missing legs, lower bodies, noses, eyes, faces.[3] America was suddenly filled with the type of "human oddity" previously only seen in sideshows.

The Great War kicked into high gear the burgeoning American horror literature genre. Pulp magazines such as *Weird Tales* and *Amazing Stories* flooded American newsstands, bringing with them the dark gods of the universe as imaged by H. P. Lovecraft, the first American fiction writer to truly synthesize popular literature with the Bad Place. Lovecraft inspired legions of imitators such as Robert Bloch, who would go on to write *Psycho*, and initiated the great American wave of horror fiction, leading directly to Shirley Jackson and Stephen King.

The Great War also invented the horror film. Just as the great triptych of nineteenth century horror novels were European - Bram Stoker's *Dracula*, Mary Shelley's *Frankenstein*, and Robert Louis Stevenson's *The Strange Case of Dr. Jekyll and Mr. Hyde* - Europe's decimated population and ravaged cities were the perfect stew to incubate a new genre.

The Cabinet of Dr. Caligari, from 1919, welded the weirdness of the European carnival to a transparent war parable and a visual style guaranteed to offend people - Expressionism. *Nosferatu*, following in 1922, depicted a pastoral Germany of the 18th century being attacked by a malignant plague carrier from the uncivilized East. *Nosferatu* was conceived, designed and produced by Albin Grau - a genuine occultist - as an attempt to bring occultism to the motion picture screen. Grau's next picture, *Warning Shadows*, was even weirder, and directed by an American.

Americans scoffed at the horribleness of these European imports. A combination of cultural insularity, Puritanism and war-motivated racism caused a riot in Los Angeles to protest the showing of *Cabinet of Dr. Caligari*. But truthfully, the horrors of these European films are **obvious** - vampires, dagger-wielding somnambulists, dopplegangers, and reanimated clay golems are clearly bad news.

In actuality, the truly disturbing films from the silent era are all American.

While the morals brigade were clucking their tongues over the decadence of these European art pictures, America was cultivating her own home-grown horrors. Lon Chaney had risen to prominence in the years following the end of hostilities, and by 1922 was one of America's biggest box office attractions. Lon Chaney's films are hard to classify as horror movies, exactly, not in the way that *Nosferatu* is *identifiably* a horror movie. Chaney specialized in lurid melodramas and unhinged potboilers of the kind not seen since.

Lon Chaney's stock characterization was that of the suffering outsider. While the Jazz Age roared, Chaney wept. His characters were separated from American society by racial heritage, physical deformity, or mental illness. Chaney became famous portraying life's cataclysmic losers. In the classic Chaney roles - *The Hunchback of Notre Dame*, *The Phantom of the Opera*, *The Unholy Three* - Chaney is a demonic lover who suffers horribly for his love. Many films ended with him sending the girl away to live life with her "normal" boyfriend. This is very similar to the poignant endings of many Charlie Chaplin films, where the homeless drifter falls in love with a girl and lets her go.

The surface optimism of the 1920s concealed darker undercurrents operating in the society, undercurrents exposed in popular art of the day. The foxtrot and jitterbug could not stave away the Puritanical feeling that the wolf was already at the door.

Broadway enjoyed a vogue for mystery melodramas starting in 1920. The original play was *The Bat*, by Mary Roberts Rinehart and Avery Hopwood. Set in a rambling Long Island mansion, the house is invaded by a caped criminal - The Bat - who has just knocked over a bank. The inhabitants of the house try to survive the night as The Bat murders them one by one. For twelve years, suspense thrillers of this type became normal stage attractions - including, in 1927, a drawing room shudderer called *Dracula*.

This cycle of horror plays begat the first truly native American horror pictures when they began to be adapted for the screen starting in 1925 - the "Old Dark House" genre.

The Monster, from 1925, was the first of these, starring Lon Chaney and an electric chair in an okay spin on Poe's *The System of Doctor Tarr and Professor Fether*. *The Bat* followed in 1926, and its success begat a deluge: *The Cat and the Canary* (1927), *The Haunted House* (1928), *The Gorilla* (1927), *The Last Warning* (1929), *The Bat Whispers* (1930), *Seven Footprints to Satan* (1928), and more.

These pictures generally involved a large cast of characters in a scary old house where bodies keep turning up and the apparently supernatural events turn out to be the machinations of mortals, out for inheritance money or hidden gold. By the 1930s, long before Nancy Drew or Scooby Doo, these tropes were sufficiently well known enough to be parodied in films like *Doctor X* (1932).

Audiences had good reason to seek out horror pictures as the 20s crashed and the Great Depression began, and Universal filmed the most salacious and successful shockers yet: *Dracula* and *Frankenstein*. Suddenly, every major studio in town had to have shockers that out-did each other in horribleness: *The Mask of Fu Manchu* (1932) featured torture scenes, *The Mystery of the Wax Museum* (1933) included facial disfigurement. A man's mouth is sewn shut in *Murders in the Zoo* (1933). *Island of Lost Souls* (1932) has a very kinky Dr. Moreau using mad surgery to turn beasts into men — without anesthetics, their inhuman screams echoing across the island.

Just a few years before, in the final days of the Jazz Age, the final component of America's great Carnival of Horrors came into being. Leon Cassidy, a former silent film pianist, got the idea to run a bumper car through a darkened room on a track. The resulting ride through pitch darkness was intended to be a sort of Tunnel of Love deluxe. The twists and turns inspired a name - *The Pretzel* - and it stuck. While the public was thrilling to Lon Chaney in *West of Zanzibar*, the dark ride was born.[4]

The earliest version of *The Pretzel* was a stark, haunted experience. Inside the darkened room, the Pretzel cars would spark as they turned corners, providing the only visual stimulation in the ride. Occasionally, cars would roll over levers in the floor, raising and then dropping iron rods onto cymbals, making ball bearings roll through a tilting metal box, or send a chain of cowbells ringing. The ride was intensely suspenseful, as patrons kept expecting the car to crash!

But it was really Chicago ride operator and designer Harry Traver who took the idea of the Pretzel ride and ran with it. He filed a nearly identical patent for a single rail ride car in 1932 and began opening his successful *Laff in the Dark* rides.

If the original Pretzel rides were austere in comparison, Henry Travers was intent on running his riders through a hellish gauntlet of non sequiturs. Bulldogs barked, lions pounced, lightning struck the ground, ghouls rose from behind gravestones, mules kicked their hind legs, and Al Jolson danced. As the Travers-style dark rides became increasingly popular, earlier Pretzel ride operators began installing black boxed "stunts" to scare riders. Trips through the *Laff in the Dark*, *The Witches' Castle*, and the *Pirate's Cove* increasingly resembled frenzied fever dream trips through the American unconscious.

It is not a coincidence that the amusement park and film industries went through transformative experiences together, trailing hand in hand like dark twins mirroring the unconscious desires of a burgeoning American working class. Films and amusement parks were budget priced vacations, cheap retreats for a class of hardworking men and women. They were people who voted with their money and they voted, in 1895, 1914, 1927, and 1931 for new and novel experiences that scared the tar out of them. It is a minor glory of the dark ride that it was born in working class neighborhoods away from the taste makers in New York and Los Angeles, in places like New Jersey, Philadelphia, and Chicago.

Walt Disney was part of this cultural moment for the macabre, as well.

While Al Jolson talked, Lon Chaney scared, and Leon Cassidy laid Pretzel tracks, Walt Disney took a gamble on a cartoon called *Steamboat Willie*. The early Mickey Mouse cartoons take place in a strange, American vernacular landscape of barns, split rail fences, hicks, and nakedly unsuppressed impulses. In *The Shindig* (1930), Clarabelle Cow lounges naked on a sofa. Later in the cartoon, Mickey gets slapped when he reaches over to pat Minnie's backside once too often. In *Plane Crazy* (1928), Mickey builds an airplane and gets Minnie up in the plane to attempt to molest her. Minnie belts Mickey, jumps out of the plane, and uses her underwear as a parachute.[5] These cartoons represent frankly carnal impulses, as aggressively and surreally American as a ride through the *Laff in the Dark*.

Walt Disney's chief animator, Ub Iwerks, created perhaps his masterpiece with *The Skeleton Dance*, a cartoon which combines unnerving imagery with a playful tone. Flatly rejected by several distributors for "gruesomeness", *Skeleton Dance* doesn't so much kid the horror craze as much as it *participates* in it.

The skeletons, especially in shots where they approach and retreat from the audience, are sufficiently unnerving to cause even adult viewers to recoil in their seats. It's one of the great morbid images of the zeitgeist. Along with *Dracula* silently emerging from his crypt in Transylvania and the Monster in *Frankenstein* pitifully reaching for sunlight, Walt Disney gave us skeletons, linked hands, prancing in a moonlit graveyard in a circle. The *Skeleton Dance* seems to mock and synthesize the end of the Jazz Age just as America was sliding into the Great Depression. And Walt Disney learned that juxtaposing morbidity with comedy was as sure a tactic as comic pratfalls.

1933's *The Mad Doctor*, a wildly inventive parody of the Hollywood horror cycle, pits Mickey against Doctor XXX in an attempt to save Pluto. One of the most effective Mickey shorts before the switch to color, *The Mad Doctor* also features a frightening spider-skeleton, a suspenseful build and release, looming shadows, and a coffin clock.[6]

There's no shortage of hallucinatory and potentially frightening imagery in the Silly Symphonies, but the Disney affinity for terror reached no purer expression than in *Snow White and the Seven Dwarfs*. *Snow White*, more than any other Disney film, resembles a roller coaster in the way it plunges audiences through laughter, terror, grief, and joy.

Snow White's Wicked Queen is a figure from a Grand Guignol play in a costume taken direct from the 1935 adventure film *SHE*. All icy reserve and cunning in the first half of the film, once the Wicked Queen turns into the Witch she suddenly becomes a villain from a vaudeville act. In a performance twist likely borrowed from Frederich March's funny but scary monster in the 1932 *Dr. Jekyll and Mr. Hyde*, the zest and relish of her villainy as she torments the bones of a starved prisoner is even more hair-raising for being so amusing. You have to look to Ernest Thesiger in *The Bride of Frankenstein* to find a horror film performance that devours more scenery.

But the true dark heart not only of the film, but the entire Disney horror canon, is Snow White's flight through the forest. Originally begun with a more restrained approach,[7] Walt and his team added superimposed faces and eyes and a terrifying montage of horrors as the sequence builds. The little princess twists and twists before collapsing in terror, recalling Lillian Gish's agony as the abused urchin in *Broken Blossoms* (1919). This is one for the canon; it's up there with the "synthetic flesh" sequence in *Doctor X* (1932) and the House of Pain segments in *Island of Lost Souls* (1932) as the most upsetting shock sequences in 1930s cinema.

The Dr. Jekyll aspects of The Wicked Queen, and the obvious reference to the 1932 *Jekyll and Hyde* film as she drinks the magic potion and the room around her begins to spin, points towards the memorable horror scenes in *Pinocchio* (1940). Pinocchio is a film of delicate beauty and joy, but it's the gauntlet of horrors that stays with viewers, a lasting and even despairing reminder of what can happen when you step out of the warmth of the toy shop.

Although Walt never quite went further with his efforts to bring genuine horror scenes to the screen than he did in his first two feature films, the entire initial run of five key film classics - *Snow White, Pinocchio, Fantasia, Dumbo,* and *Bambi* - stand apart from all other Disney films in their emotional intensity, and those emotions include fear. There's the specters flying direct at the screen in the "Night on Bald Mountain" sequence and the rather frightening pink elephant hallucinations of *Dumbo*, often ignored in modern Disney appreciations in favor of the far tamer Heffalumps and Woozles from *Winnie-the-Pooh and the Honey Tree*. Animated but unused in *Bambi* was a shot of Bambi's mother falling over dead.[8]

In the full flower of his greatest ambition, Walt understood that children not only had a great need, but a great ability to be frightened. And he played fair with them: the world may be full of traps, Pleasure Islands and dark forests, and adversaries may be terrifying, but the impact of seeing Snow White revive is all the keener for having felt the grief for her so potently. Later Disney films would never require their heroes to earn their happy ending so thoroughly.

Snow White and the Seven Dwarfs, in particular, deserves its place in the horror pantheon, alongside *King Kong* and *Frankenstein*. The British Board of Film Censors had complained bitterly to Hollywood studios about the rising tide of shock pictures. Following Universal's *The Raven* in 1935, they announced they would no longer be looking at pictures of this type, effectively banning horror in Britain.

The Film Censors initially gave *Snow White* an "A" certificate, the equivalent of a modern "R" rating. Disney appealed the decision, trimming a skeleton scene with the witch and trimming back other scary scenes. Local exhibitors served up the film with no warnings attached, inadvertently terrifying an entire generation of English children.

In Italy, Benito Mussolini had banned all horror films outright,[9] and presumably had not given *Snow White* a very close look due to its animated nature. The flight through the forest lingered with an entire generation of children who did not even know that films could contain such shocks. When these same children grew up and started making films of their own during the horror boom of the 1960s, the old images reappear, in Mario Bava's *Black Sunday* (1960) and *Twitch of the Death Nerve* (1971). Dario Argento's *Suspiria* (1977) is essentially a stealth remake of the Disney *Snow White*, reconfiguring a flight through a dark forest, an isolated house, lurid color, and a witch into a new horror fantasia.

Walt Disney's final filmic horror show, *The Adventures of Ichabod and Mr. Toad* (1949), starts as a straight comedy and introduces sinister suggestions, before blossoming into pure suspense and exploding into a slapstick chase. No Disney product so fully exploits the hazy line between laughing and screaming as *The Legend of Sleepy Hollow*, which manages to pivot effortlessly from blood-chilling suspense to comedy hijinx so repeatedly it leaves audiences disoriented and thrilled. It's this sequence which, more than any other, resembles an amusement park dark ride - *Laff in the*

Dark. There may be no more perfect combination of the comic and the sinister than those four words.

And so it would be entirely natural that upon branching out into the amusement park form - America's symbolic dance of death - that Walt Disney would resurrect and refashion the *Laff in the Dark* and create its most sophisticated, most complex form yet: Disneyland.

For the 1950s, a decade so concerned with wholesomeness and appropriateness, Walt Disney got rid of the skeevy ride operators and replaced them with smiling, well groomed young people. Walt closed the beer tent in favor of the Coke corner. He organized the attractions into broad categories supported by architecture, color, and landscaping. And he brought the dark ride outdoors, inventing the "scenic cruise", subsequently copied by smaller amusement park operators for generations.

But he did not blunt the morbidity at the core of the amusement park formula; that he kept. So while Disneyland may have been cleaner and safer than the amusement park, the areas where the morbid material came out were that much sharper for the contrast.

There was *Snow White's Adventures*, which ran park guests through the gauntlet that had haunted so many Depression-era children, ensuring the primal trauma of the dark forest lived on. If *Snow White's Adventures* took and elaborated the "boo" aspects of the *Laff in the Dark*, *Mr. Toad's Wild Ride* elaborated the helpless, out of control qualities. A light hearted spin through the English countryside abruptly took a nasty turn as riders faced down an oncoming locomotive, ending up in a comedy version of Hell. *Alice in Wonderland* accented the nightmarish quality of the feature, offering upside down rooms and pouncing flowers. Even the benign *Peter Pan's Flight* was not free from images inducing vertigo and leering skulls.

Disneyland - and later Magic Kingdom - are two of the greatest collections of morbid material in American history: call it Walt's American Museum. Death and mortality hang over the heads of the children it entertains and enlightens.

Adventureland offers skulls on sticks as an early warning of the encampment of cannibals on the *Jungle Cruise*. A dinosaur skeleton pokes out of the red rocks of Frontierland. A tattered corpse steers a ghost ship in *Pirates of the Caribbean*. Dinosaurs battle to the death above erupting lava in the *Primeval World*. *Flight to the Moon* in Tomorrowland encouraged gruesome contemplation by cheerfully, scientifically offering the information that without spacesuits, the blood of astronauts would "literally boil". In Frontierland, a blazing settler's cabin included the lurid detail of its inhabitant's corpse pierced with an arrow. This was presented as part of the "*hard facts that have created America*" promised by Walt's dedication, but really it's just another manifestation of the latent American morbidity roiling under the surface. As seen from a miniature steamboat called the Mark Twain, one can imagine Sam Clemens seeing this scene and approving of it enthusiastically.

Just as the dark twins of cinema and the amusement park guided Americans through the terrors of the 20th century, offering even darker alternatives to their modern lives, Disneyland was a colorful panorama of American popular culture, including its darkest mythology.

The *Haunted Mansion* is Disneyland's depository for these ancient gods of darkness, comically thumbing their noses at the surface optimism of the nuclear family. And while the *Haunted Mansion* is nothing less than the most rigorously conceived, carefully executed *Laff in the Dark* ever created, it meets the standard of Walter Benjamin's "major work": it did not establish, but it *did* abolish the genre.

And so it is appropriate that the two most obvious inspirations for the tone of Walt's house of horrors came from two movies, established from the earliest designs by Ken Anderson for the show in the 50s: Universal's *The Cat and the Canary*, and Disney's *Legend of Sleepy Hollow*. Andersen made the connection clear by having monstrous hands emerging from secret panels as in *Cat*, and the headless horseman galloping past the house, seen through a picture window under a full moon.

As the 1950s faded and the 1960s roiled with changing culture, television Monster hosts like Vampiria and Zacherley punned their way through midnight movies. Over in Burbank, not far from the television soundstages, the ultimate haunted house with the ultimate "Ghost Host" would take shape in the halls of WED Enterprises. Like Zacherley, he was armed with an army of ghoulish puns and would lord over one final gothic dance of death.

The *Haunted Mansion* opened on August 9, 1969 at Disneyland. Guests driving down to Disneyland that hot morning may have had their radios tuned to the news and heard of another landmark event in horror history that very same day: the discovery of the Sharon Tate murders in Los Angeles.

As the public awareness of the Manson family atrocities raised the profile of the serial killer and the Vietnam War sent home young men no longer physically or mentally sound, the American horror landscape shifted. No longer would the creaky old dark house be the iconography of horror; the 1970s gave us Leatherface, Michael Myers, and Jason Vorhees. Ted Bundy became a household name. Simultaneously, Disneyland and, soon, Magic Kingdom were putting traditional amusement parks and boardwalks out of business.

Perched on the tipping point between Modern and Post-Modern horrors, the *Haunted Mansion* is the end of the line for American Gothic; the final, triumphant scare chord at the end of the reign of the *Pretzel* and the *Laff in the Dark* as a uniquely American institution.

End of the line; step out to your left, please.

2. SQUARES AND PLAZAS

Haunted Mansions lurk deep inside theme parks, and this is as it should be.

Think of how inappropriate it would be to pass through the park turnstiles and see a creepy old house beckoning you inside right away - like any old Pretzel or *Laff in the Dark* off any amusement park midway. No, it's crucial that we must first pass through themed areas celebrating an optimistic, golden past - the gingerbread finery of Main Street, the filigreed clapboard of Frontierland, or the lacy trim of old New Orleans before we hit the place where that optimism somehow went all wrong.

Disney theme parks are reassuringly orderly, carefully crafted environments. Bricks meet neatly, facades are fresh painted, and every element is designed to be visually pleasing and harmonious. Yet the attractions are different - they represent untamed regions where no return is guaranteed - as in the *Jungle Cruise*, the *Matterhorn*, or *Big Thunder Mountain*. They represent magic portals into other worlds, as in *Alice in Wonderland* and *Pirates of the Caribbean*. And they represent places where mystery and dislogic reign, as in the *Tower of Terror* and *Indiana Jones Adventure*. Disney attractions are places of danger where the order and safety of the rest of the park breaks down.

The *Haunted Mansion* is the grandest example of these. It looks innocent on the outside, and originally, before there were aged bricks, silly tombstones, mystery hearses, and spooky music, the only thing differentiating these particular houses from any other impressive architectural specimens inside the parks was a simple sign near the front: "**Haunted Mansion**".

The *Haunted Mansion* is the equivalent of those houses that evil rumors swirled around in your own hometown. It could be anything from a cemetery where the creepy statue of the angel is said to bleed, or an old gutted road that you're warned to stay away from.

2. Squares and Plazas

From that moment on, that place was marked forever, and you'd look at it every day as you passed hoping, but not hoping, to catch a glimpse of something monstrous in its shadows.

Inside Disneyland and Magic Kingdom, that's the dynamic that the *Haunted Mansion* creates. It sits there, an invisible sign sitting on it like a shroud: "Haunted Mansion Here!" Its arrival in your life is drearily anticipated from the moment your foot makes contact with the tarmac on Main Street, USA.

There's basically three directions from which one can approach the *Haunted Mansion* at Magic Kingdom. One of these we can excuse from the discussion immediately, which is to enter Fantasyland, turn left, and then head down the hill into Liberty Square. From this direction, the Mansion is hidden - you have to stop and look behind you to see it.

The other two options require you to pass through a themed gauntlet. Option one, from the central plaza, is to head directly through Liberty Square and turn right at the riverboat landing. The more dramatic method is to proceed into Adventureland, use the Veranda Breezeway past the bathrooms, and emerge alongside the Rivers of America. From this view, the *Haunted Mansion* is most dramatically posed: composed between Aunt Polly's on Tom Sawyer Island and the Riverboat, it seems impossibly tall and impossibly distant, lording over its little stretch of the river. The effect is genuinely spooky, and it draws you forward like a magnet: "wouldn't you like to find out what's in here?"

At the time that the Magic Kingdom was built, Liberty Square was an old idea. It had been announced for Disneyland back in the late 1950s, sitting off Main Street. It still fills this role admirably well positioned off the Florida Main Street, as if everybody's hometown suddenly surged back in time to the "Days of '76".

I'd argue this is the reason why, for Magic Kingdom, WED Enterprises - the theme park design team - created an eastern seaboard boomtown in the style of, say, an Atlantic City or Saratoga Springs, New York instead of Disneyland's midwestern small town.

Liberty Square feels faintly, suspiciously like it's what Main Street *replaced.*

Liberty Square is simple, yet deceptively complex. It consists of three subsections, each with different styles and meanings. The area immediately off the hub is a cluster of Colonial buildings, which is the true "square". Organized around the central *Hall of Presidents*, which visually recalls - but is not a copy of - Independence Hall in Philadelphia, citified facades representing the Boston, New York, and Philadelphia of the colonial revolution sit nearby. Across the way, a chain of Federal facades, originally housing Olde World Antiques, give way to the rough stonework of the more rural area, in a space which once housed the Johnny Tremain Silversmith. A string of charming Colonial cottage facades rest behind the area's other central feature, the Liberty Tree, a gigantic oak which represents the rallying area on the village green of many American revolutionary towns. A white-columned riverboat landing sits at the back of the area.

From the colonial village, you can head north or south, and if we do, then the theme changes subtly.

A turn south, towards Frontierland, represents the leaving of the original thirteen colonies and heading westward. On the southern side of the Liberty Tree and the colonial village sits a colonial tavern - the Liberty Tree Tavern - which can be perhaps located in Virginia or North Carolina, as represented by its Grecian Revival white columns. Past that sits the Diamond Horseshoe - a citified blue and white clapboard trim saloon. The Diamond Horseshoe represents St. Louis, the Gateway to the West, and Frontierland is right beyond it, over a short bridge. A stream runs under the bridge, and it's called "The Little Mississippi".

If we head north from the riverboat landing we head upstate, out of the heart of the battle for independence as represented by Philadelphia house-fronts and a pocket reproduction of the Capitol House of Williamsburg. We pass the Columbia Harbour House, which could be any coastal Boston, Nantucket, or New Bedford sailor's inn, and the Yankee Trader, a seaport shop, where we approach the *Haunted Mansion* at last.

2. SQUARES AND PLAZAS

Liberty Square is a fantasy location, a shifting, kaleidoscopic view of the colonial east, yet it also has an actual, comprehensible geographic layout to it. We enter, like the Dutch settlers, near upstate New York and head towards Philadelphia. As we head north or south from the central colonial village, we head north or south geographically through not only the United States, but through the history of the United States.

In other words, time passes as we head north towards the *Haunted Mansion* and south towards Frontierland. Liberty Square and Frontierland themselves form a sort of ultra-land, ringing Tom Sawyer Island and the wilderness beyond, which is a comprehensive view of the United States.

Here, in miniature, is myth and superstition, the old South, George Washington, Abraham Lincoln, food, hospitality, the Mississippi, Mark Twain and Tom Sawyer, the Br'er Rabbit tales, cowboys, indians, vaudeville, and gold. It's an entire self-contained America theme park inside the Magic Kingdom.

I call this the "River District" and it is centered on the Rivers of America, but the river itself has a shifting meaning depending on where you are standing. For example, when you're in the central colonial village, the river is actually invisible.

Unlike at Disneyland, Tokyo Disneyland, and Disneyland Paris, Liberty Square doesn't sit flush with its Rivers of America, but a good fifteen feet above it. The riverboat landing is quite tall, and carefully designed to block your view of the riverboat from inside the colonial village. Unlike at Disneyland, the riverboat actually loads from the middle deck via a bridge, and unloads from the bottom deck. You aren't *meant* to see it when you're standing near the *Hall of Presidents*.

As you head south towards Frontierland - spiritually moving west - the pedestrian pathway physically dips down to allow the river to come into view. Of course, by heading south we are allowing the riverboat itself to be seen, which is appropriate since the geography tells us we are now in the southern colonies and heading towards Mark Twain's Mississippi. And, just on cue, structures become

visible on Tom Sawyer Island - Harper's Mill and Aunt Polly's - in a Midwest United States architectural style.

This is one of WED's most remarkable magic tricks, and almost nobody sees it. They hide an entire riverboat and river, and then pull them out of their hat only when it's most thematically appropriate. It's a Manifest Destiny that you accomplish on foot.

What do we learn, then, while heading north?

If the architecture and presence of the riverboat cues us to understand that we are heading towards the center of the country as we head south, then heading north seems to reveal a coastal space.

What do we make of the Columbia Harbour House? In 1971, this restaurant was not open - it would have to wait until mid 1972 until it was complete - but circa 1971 promotional materials call the forthcoming restaurant "The Nantucket Harbour House". Nantucket and New Bedford were the colonial center for the American whaling industry, a fact commemorated on the exterior facade by a mural of whalers. Anyone who's read *Moby Dick* will feel right at home in the Columbia Harbour House, for it resembles nothing so less than the whaling inn described in the first chapters of the book.

Why did its name change to the Columbia Harbour House, then? This is especially puzzling in that there is no such place in the United States as "Columbia Harbor".

It's because the Magic Kingdom was actually slated to receive a *Columbia* sailing ship.[10] In 1971, the river's big boat was a duplicate of the *Mark Twain* at Disneyland, called the *Admiral Joe Fowler*. Early models of the park show a sailing ship circling the Rivers of America, likely a duplicate of the *Columbia* which is still in use at Disneyland.

The ship that actually appeared in 1973 was yet another river boat - called the *Richard F. Irvine*. Yet, in 1972, the *Columbia*'s arrival was anticipated by changing the name of its adjacent restaurant!

I think Disney changed the vessel because of the lessons they learned in operating the Magic Kingdom in its first two years. To begin with, the park was much hotter than the California-based company had anticipated - and much wetter. Attractions which were open air at Disneyland, like the *Mad Tea Party*, had been duplicated verbatim in Orlando, only to turn into baking sheets in the Florida sun, or rain barrels which had to be mopped out constantly. Most queues at Disneyland are also open-air, and this had been replicated at Walt Disney World, to disastrous effect. Anybody who's stood outside in Orlando at 2 pm on a hot day can tell you what a bad idea this is.

And so, shade structures began to sprout up all over Magic Kingdom in early 1972. The *Haunted Mansion*'s signature green entry canopy appeared at this time. So did a merciful roof over the *Mad Tea Party*. The *Jungle Cruise* sprouted an entire adjacent building. And, with new rides like *Pirates of the Caribbean* and *Space Mountain*, WED had learned their lesson, and built extensive, air conditioned queues.

The other thing Imagineering discovered is that they really needed to expand the park quickly. Theater attractions like *The Hall of Presidents* and *Country Bear Jamboree* had out-of-control queues that filled up pedestrian space. It's not difficult to see why Disney axed the *Columbia* in favor of another three-decker riverboat; the *Columbia* holds only 300 guests on an exposed deck while the *Mark Twain* can accommodate over 800.

At the time, Richard "Dick" Irvine was in charge of WED Enterprises. Did he order the change and, if so, is that why they named the boat after him? Regardless, in 1980 the *Admiral Joe Fowler* was irreparably damaged in drydock. It was cut into pieces and the salvageable parts were used in the construction of Tokyo Disneyland's *Mark Twain*. The *Richard F. Irvine* was re-named the *Liberty Belle* in 1996 and remains a design unique to the Magic Kingdom.

This does mean that the north part of Liberty Square lost its "mascot" vessel, although the Columbia Harbour House's name has remained unchanged. In a way, it's a nice idea - a riverboat for Frontierland and the sailing ship for Liberty Square - but this means that the "coastal" atmosphere WED Enterprises was going for is a little oblique.

Where is the *Haunted Mansion*?

Old theories place it on the Hudson River, in upper New York state. This theory is appealing because of the house's proximity to the Rivers of America and spiritual affinity with Sleepy Hollow, the rural hamlet made famous in Washington Irving's *The Legend of Sleepy Hollow*. But let's not be so fast!

Consider the theming of the surrounding area. The structure which sits nearest the *Haunted Mansion* is currently the remains of the boarding area of the *Mike Fink Keel Boats*, done in a rustic shingle-sided "Cape Cod" style. The colors and architecture of the surrounding area seem to beg for a coastal, not riverside, atmosphere.

Indeed were the widow's walks, the nautical lanterns in the Keel Boats queue, and the callout for a "Columbia Harbour" not already dead giveaways, WED Enterprises left hints in their terminology of the area's features itself.

The entirety of Liberty Square is bounded on the river side with an extensive slate wall - slate supposedly quarried from a pit near Williamsburg, Virginia. One of the most impressive architectural features of the Magic Kingdom, it stretches from the *Mansion*'s front doors nearly to Frontierland. Thanks to old training documents we know that the Imagineers called it the "sea wall".

This is confirmation, then, that the *Haunted Mansion* is not an inland riverside haunt but sits overlooking the restless Atlantic Ocean in the tradition of horror films like *The Midnight Mystery* and *Doctor X*. Picture it perched high on a cliff over some storm-tossed jagged rocks, the bitter salt wind whipping its leaden windows, a shadowy figure seen from time to time walking its catwalks when a storm is rolling in from the east. It's a seaside horror mansion, probably owned by a long-dead sea captain, as these things always are.

The house is placed far enough away from the other structures in the fairly compact Magic Kingdom to suggest a splendid isolation, and I'd suggest we think of it as a day's ride from anywhere - north of Boston, north of anything, perched in the best Poe tradition in a particular desolate stretch of countryside. It's the worst place to get caught for the night, so of course we *must* go inside.

3. HISTORY AND THE HAUNTED MANSION

So what *kind* of house are we talking about?
If you ask guests in the park at any time, you're likely to find that even they don't know. It is referred to as the Haunted Castle, The Haunted Palace, The Haunted House, The Ghost House, Grandfather's Mansion,[11] and any other number of variants.

The kicker is that Disney themselves don't seem to know much better. A brief overview of official promotional copy reveals such descriptions as:

> *High on a bluff overlooking the river is the gloomy granite Haunted Mansion, foreboding home of 999 restless ghouls, goblins and ghosts "dying" to meet you.* (Walt Disney World, A Pictorial Souvenir, 1977, pg. 21)

> *In almost every colonial town there was one old house scarcely noticed by day but carefully avoided by night. It was always ramshackle, seemingly abandoned, and thoroughly rumored to be... a Haunted Mansion. Liberty Square's Haunted Mansion is just as foreboding. A peculiar chill shivers through you, the hairs on your neck stand straight up, and you feel someone is watching as you hasten past the family plot...* (A Dream Called Walt Disney World, souvenir VHS, 1980)

> *Not far from the Hall of Presidents is a residence designed to scare up some early American fantasy and folklore. High on a bluff overlooking the Rivers of America, the stone-faced "Haunted Mansion" presents the ominous spectre of a Dutch manor house from the Hudson River Valley. It's an architectural style perhaps best*

3. HISTORY AND THE HAUNTED MANSION

described as early Edgar Allan Poe. (Walt Disney World: The First Decade, 1981, pg. 86)

Those who expect to get the daylights scared out of them inside this big old house, modeled on those built by the Dutch in the Hudson River Valley in the 18th century, will be a tad disappointed. (Steve Birnbaum Brings You the Best of Walt Disney World, 1983, pg. 82)

While the exterior of the Disneyland mansion is that of a light, graceful, filigreed antebellum plantation house, the Florida mansion is brooding - almost architecturally menacing - dark brick and stone Gothic, reminiscent of the great Mansions of the Hudson River Valley. (Jeff Kurtti, Since the World Began, 1996, pg. 61)

This geographical shift led Imagineers to New York's lower Hudson River Valley, the ancestral home of Sleepy Hollow and the Headless Horseman, and they were inspired by the region's stately old manor houses in which English, Dutch, and German settlers would gather around the campfire and spin tales of the supernatural such as those by Washington Irving. (Jason Surrell, The Haunted Mansion From the Magic Kingdom to the Movies, 2003 1st edition, pg. 37)

    Like a pearl growing over the decades, you can see each writer adding their own gloss to basically bad information. To me, "early Edgar Allan Poe" is probably the most accurate, both in time and location and the implicit understanding that the architecture is a fantasy. But it's a *culturally specific* fantasy, one tied in with the Victorians, and if we look in the right places it is possible to unpack it.

I've already voiced my contention, borne out by the design of the architecture around the house, that the *Haunted Mansion* is a seaside, not a riverside house. But I'd give a lot to find out where this idea came from of it being a "Dutch Gothic" Mansion.

These words are so dominant in the conceptual framework of the *Haunted Mansion* that few bother to question what they really mean. After all, it sounds evocative - as evocative as the house itself - and it makes good historical logic.

The Dutch were the first to colonize the area currently known as New York. It's also generally known that the Hudson, besides being home to Washington Irving's Sleepy Hollow, is dotted with old stone mansions. So it's a romantic idea that the *Haunted Mansion* is old - *so old* it predates even the United States - perched in some rolling hill hidden away north of New York, perhaps not far from a road Ichabod Crane once traveled.

Except that this fantasy conflates unrelated periods and events.

It's *true* that the Dutch colonized the Hudson, but that's what it was: a colony. Nobody was in a position to build a permanent stone mansion. And furthermore, what we're talking about is seventeenth century, six hundred years after anybody would be inclined to build an actual Gothic structure. Actual examples of Dutch-era colonial architecture still exist in the United States, but if you seek these out what you're going to be seeing is farmhouses - rambling wooden things.

And if you actually do go looking for examples of Dutch Gothic, what you're going to find is churches - churches in the Netherlands, built in the twelfth or thirteenth centuries. But the *Haunted Mansion* is not *Dutch* Gothic. The *Haunted Mansion* is not a cathedral. It's *Victorian* Gothic.

Now, actual examples of stone mansions do line the Hudson, and they are, largely, Victorian-to-early-twentieth-century houses; country houses built for the Rockefellers and the Vanderbilts of the age - escapes from the sooty city for the new captains of industry. However, this does not mean that the *Mansion* should be thought of on the Hudson just because similar real life houses are there. Just as in our modern era, whatever architecture is popular may be found elsewhere. Besides, if WED wanted us to think of the *Mansion* as being on the Hudson, why didn't they group it with the other architecture in Liberty Square that's *actually* Dutch and *actually located* on the Hudson?

That's right, the first structure which faces us as we enter Liberty Square from the Hub is Dutch Colonial in style. *Sleepy Hollow Refreshments* is modeled on Sunnyside, a country cottage built by Washington Irving. Irving, being a nineteenth century man, was taken with the romance of the bygone age and so drew on the area's local history to create his fantasy of a Dutch mansion. He even put the date "1656" on the side of the house as a joke on the fact that his manor house was a fake, confusing generations of tourists.

WED placed their Sunnyside replica facing the Hub across the way from the side of Olde World Antiques, housed in a Federal facade, so that the two dominant early architectural styles of the New World were the first seen while entering Liberty Square on the left and right. So if the *Haunted Mansion* is Hudson River, why isn't architecture like that grouped near it? Because everything about its placement in Liberty Square points towards oceanside.

If we follow the lead of the actual Victorian brick mansions on the Hudson, however, we will find a thread and can trace it back to where the confusion began. The whole thing started with Sir Walter Scott, back in the Old World.

It starts shortly before the Victorian era began, with the publication of *Ivanhoe* in 1820. Walter Scott in general, and *Ivanhoe* in particular, was amongst the first novels to really be read on both sides of the Atlantic, and Scott cooked up a romantic vision of knights of old and chivalry with a liberal seasoning of historical fact to make it all seem more credible. Scott did his job well; modern readers often have to be cautioned that *Ivanhoe* is a novel of historical fantasy, not fact.

Then, in 1830, Scott really did it by starting construction on his estate in Scotland - Abbotsford. Filled with antiques and bits of architecture rescued from crumbling manor houses around Scotland, incorporating stones from local medieval ruins, and patched together with the latest in modern millwork and conveniences, Abbotsford was an up to date house that looked as though it belonged to some fantasy of the fourteenth century.

Their minds filled with Sir Walter's medieval fantasies and the example of his glorious fake castle, the Victorians decided that they, too, would live like kings. The Industrial Revolution made it possible. You no longer needed to hire an artisan to lovingly hand paint your interior walls - a stencil and a low cost laborer could produce the same effect. Plaster moulds could cover ceilings instead of woodwork, and paint could disguise their factory origin. Furniture could be covered in once impossible scrollwork and detail thanks to the mechanical bevel and modern mitre-saw.

Even those upper and burgeoning middle classes who did not share dreams of a medieval life were increasingly making over their large whitewashed, minimally decorated Georgian interiors to take advantage of the new craze for ornamentation. Everyone went crazy for decorations, even on such previously unattended-to surfaces such as the rear walls of fireplaces.

And because all this furniture was so modern, so new, a lingering fear amongst many homemakers was that it would simply fall apart if exposed to too much light and air. The answer was to cover every window in heavy, light-blocking draperies and curtains so that once airy white rooms were now shrouded in perpetual gloom.

I probably don't need to alert you that we now have all of the elements of our *Haunted Mansion* in place. The *Haunted Mansion* is not a Dutch Gothic anything, it's a Gothic **Revival Castellated** Manor.

Gothic Revival, responding to the craze for anything medieval, made available cement and plaster imitations of eleventh century gothic traceries which could be judiciously applied to any country house or mansion to turn it into a medieval-style castle. Thus, what was then called the "Castellated" style. This is why the

3. HISTORY AND THE HAUNTED MANSION

Haunted Mansion is built out of mass-produced red bricks instead of the hand-carved stones of real medieval castles.

We now know[12] that Imagineer David Mumford accidentally identified the book which sat in the Imagineering reference library and guided the overall design of the *Haunted Mansion* - *Decorative Art of Victoria's Era*, by Frances Lichten.[13]

We know this is the book because it includes a very large photograph of the Shipley-Lydecker Mansion in Baltimore, which was the basis for Sam McKim's famous painting of the Disneyland *Haunted Mansion* - identical in style, architectural detail, and even angle.

On page 59 of the Lichten book is an engraving of a "Castellated" mansion which is unambiguously the source of the Florida facade, and directly above it is this passage where Mrs. Lichten offers insight into the Castellated style:

> *Despite the scarcity of good architects, the taste for the new fashion developed quickly in the United States, and by the 1830's there were many examples of the style. The Gothic was thought to be particularly well suited to the American countryside - a region characterized by the "wilder, romantic and more picturesque country where the hand of man has been only partially laid on the forest. This type of terrain," says A. J. Downing, the greatest American arbiter of architectural taste in the first half of the eighteenth century, "supplies the appropriate background for a style which sprang up among the rocks and fastness of Northern Europe." Mr. Downing's affection for the Gothic was responsible for innumerable example of the Old English cottage, and of residences of the Castellated style, as the domestic specimens imitative of castles were then called. Like mushrooms, they popped up on every hill in the more cultivated regions of the country, for country estates were then a fashionable*

indulgence, and the Gothic, the only style then considered appropriate for rural living.

In 1836, a traveler, describing his initial train ride on New Jersey's first railroad, indicates the early flowering of the taste: "Our ride to Philadelphia over the Camden and Amboy Railroad and up the beautiful Delaware was truly delightful, especially the latter. New and beautiful scenes continually opened to view - with fine country seats, built in imitation of Gothic castles, with towers and battlements standing amid a fine growth of trees of every kind...

In 1837, New York architect Alexander Jackson Davis published a pamphlet called *Rural Residences*, outlining the aims of the taste of his era:

The bald and uninteresting aspect of our houses must be obvious to every traveller; and to those who are familiar with the picturesque Cottages and Villas of England, it is positively painful to witness here the wasteful and tasteless expenditure of money in building. Defects are felt, however, not only in the style of the house but in the want of connexion [sic] with its site, — in the absence of appropriate offices,— well disposed trees, shrubbery, and vines, — which accessories give an inviting and habitable air to the place.

The Greek Temple form, perfect in itself, and well adapted as it is to public edifices, and even to town mansions, is inappropriate for country residences, and yet it is the only style ever attempted in our more costly habitations. The English collegiate style, is for many reasons to be preferred. It admits of greater variety both of plan and outline; — is susceptible of additions from time to time, while its bay windows, oriels,

3. History and The Haunted Mansion

turrets, and chimney shafts, give a pictorial effect to the elevation.

The principal object aimed at in these designs has been to give as much character to the exteriors as possible; — should they answer in any degree the purposes for which they were projected, the architect may submit, at a future period, designs for more expensive structures.

Below an engraving of a Gothic Castellated mansion, Davis writes of his "English Collegiate residence":

The design is irregular, and suited to scenery of a picturesque character, and to an eminence commanding an extensive prospect. The dimensions are 60 feet in front by 30 feet in depth; and the side 50 feet by 20 feet, forming an L like figure, as in the plan. The octagon tower is 50 feet high; the turrets, one on each angle of the front, 37 feet, and the battlement 32 feet.

Davis quoted a price of $12,000 for a version "built of split stone, or brick, stuccoed, with cut stone trimmings and the upper part of the prospect tower of wood". $12,000 in 1837 was the equivalent of more than $300,000 today.

Later, in *Decorative Art of Victoria's Era,* Lichten may have inspired the *Haunted Mansion's* early landscape design, which included a stately rose garden, as well as the wrought iron terraces which cover the house and grounds:

> As the nineteenth century moved into its sixth decade, the craze for the Victorian Gothic house must have reached its utmost in absurdity, for we find it dealt with by the writers of the day. James Russell Lowell accepted the challenge offered his pen by the sight of a ridiculous wooden castle, set on an unshaded, mathematically squared lawn patterned with flower-beds of equal geometric perfection.

> [...]

> Designers for [wrought iron] brought out patterns calculated to attract the eye of the romantically inclined. No longer need the owner of a new Gothic mansion enclose his velvety lawn with anything so commonplace as a white picket fence. Now he could purchase fanciful wrought iron traceries, as Gothic in detail, if not material, as that of the most ornamental of ancient stone or wood carvings. As additional medieval garnish, the foundry men stood ready to supply porches and verandas patterned in formal Gothic trefoils or quatrefoils, as well as garden pavilions - the latter affairs being frivolous counterfeits of the flamboyant traceries of a cathedral window. Over these lacy structures, the Victorian maidens coaxed vines to grow, to simulate the antique arbors of their sentimental

reveries. And if the solemn English ivy, accustomed to a support of honest stone, refused to clamber over a deceitful edifice of iron, the light-minded native vines were found to be more accommodating and made quite as satisfactory if less poetically evocative green draperies.

And so, we may safely say that the *Haunted Mansion* is a country house. If we like, it possibly predates the Gothic Revival trend which began in earnest in the mid-nineteenth century. It has been clad in a then-fashionable style which sought to turn it into a medieval fantasy house out of the writings of Sir Walter Scott.

To the designers of Magic Kingdom, here was a great find: an architecture which was firmly planted in the era of the Victorian horror mansion, which could be one-hundred percent American while simultaneously evoking the old world of Europe and knights on horseback. A world evoked in... Fantasyland, right around the corner.

It's the perfect transition between the old world and the new, between history and fantasy, created by the wasteful romanticism and exuberance of its long-dead inhabitants. As Lichen notes in the final paragraphs of her chapter on the Gothic Revival, it's become to modern eyes the perfect horror dreamscape:

> *Many examples of the Victorian Gothic residence are extant, both in city and country districts: the substantial stone and stucco mansion as well as the wooden farmhouse and cottage, their eaves still supporting the remnants of the once-so-fashionable edging of wooden lace. Where the battlemented stucco castle stands deserted, once trim trees and shrubs crowd the jungle-thick, and push exploring fingers through broken windows of many-colored glass. In the dark of the moon, fog drifts about the ruined toy-like turrets. Morayama's or Arzelia's bower is given over entirely to bats and rubble, and the thrust of strong vines has pushed apart iron traceries.*
>
> *In truth the decaying structure conveys to the present-day observer the same sense of horror and mystery that the medieval ruin conveyed to the popular mind. Lacking the patina which the mellowing touch of time and nature give to the ruins of the middle ages, the abandoned Victorian Gothic domicile, its shoddy fabric disintegrating before one's eyes, has today become the artistic and literary symbol of "the haunted house.* [14]

4. DEATH AND DECLINE

Given all of this historical background, I'm confident in dating the *Haunted Mansion*'s imagined construction to 1840 or 1850. In our minds, it *may*[15] be a renovated Georgian mansion or include elements of older structures; the stone base it sits on appears to be made of a different sort of rock, which has always struck this viewer as an evocative touch included in many reported haunted house stories.

The facade of the *Haunted Mansion* which faces the river is almost certainly not the formal entrance side, which in our imagination is "out back" somewhere, perhaps past the old graveyard in the woods. It was common for Georgian and Victorian houses to have two faces, one for business and one for leisure. The leisure side invariably faced some sort of pictorial view; in our minds, the ocean. The large brick structure that the queue passes through on their way to the door is not a crypt but a porte cochere, a covered area where horses and carriages would pull up to access the house for social events. Everything about the *Haunted Manson* from its layout to its style indicates that it was intended to be a social showplace of the greatest possible impact.

The inspirational architectural engraving as it appears in Francis Lichten's book descends from an 1847 publication by A.J. Downing, exactly the sort of book which sought to popularize the Gothic Revival. Called *Cottage Residences: Or, a series of designs for rural cottages and cottage villas, and their gardens and grounds. Adapted to North America*, this book identifies our mystery house as belonging to Mr. Joel Rathbone of Albany, NY, and includes a floor plan, showing a rear entrance facing away from the estate gardens and a winding side porch.

Rear view of Mr. Rathbone's house, inspiration for The Haunted Mansion

Built by Alexander Jackson Davis for Mr. Rathbone in 1840, in his book Downing enthuses:

> The villa, now completed, is undoubtably one of the finest specimens of the Gothic, or pointed style of architecture, in this country. Although the whole composition evinces unity of feeling, there is as much variety of feature as we ever remember to have seen introduced successfully in a villa; indeed, perhaps, a greater variety of windows, gables and buttresses, than could be introduced in a building of that size to good effect, were it not supported by the corresponding intricacy and variety of the trees and foliage around it, which here are in admirable keeping with the picturesque outlines of the edifice.[27]

So what happened between the Haunted Mansion being a lively social hub and becoming a retirement home for ghosts?

4. Death and Decline

The Victorians were a morbid folk. They were the first generation of people to face down a world which was changing faster than they could comprehend it - each decade brought new horrors of war, modernization, massive deprivation, and class warfare. If we imagine our house as being built circa 1850, then the Civil War and hundreds of thousands of American men dead is right around the corner.

Yet if the Victorians were the first people in the Western world to suffer through modernization, they did not yet reap all of the benefits of it. Their cities still had open sewers for streets and hot water was a luxury. This still was an era when you could take sick and die without medicine being able to help you, and living in a world rapidly modernizing and rushing headlong into violent destruction, the Victorians developed some very queer notions.

They feared sunlight as unhealthy, and as a result very strange beauty standards began to emerge. Women who were dying of consumption - what we today call tuberculosis - were considered extremely sexually attractive, with their dark, sunken eyes and white, nearly translucent skin.

With an entire generation of men wiped out in a bloody war, Victorians coped by believing they were the first generation to contact the dead, and Spiritualists were born. Other, more traditional religions shared space with table tipping and spirit rapping, manifest in the cross-stitch mottoes which filled Victorian households, peering down from "rustic" frames employing passerby with "God Bless this House" and "Home Is Where the Heart Is".

The love of treacly melodrama, lofty sentiment, and a perhaps justified fear of the wider world combined to make the Victorians a perfect fit for the arrival of the supernatural. If Bram Stoker had not invented Count Dracula, he would have arrived anyway under a different name. There's never been a better group of people to become the poster children for the spooky. But even if they hadn't done such an excellent job themselves, the economy would have sealed their fate anyway.

It was an era of economic freefall. There was an economic rebound after the war, but the party ended in May 1873 with the collapse of the Vienna Stock Exchange. This triggered an international panic. Railroads in the U.S. were operating on borrowed money and began to fold, dragging down the companies that owned them and the banks that financed them. Factories closed, workers were laid off, and tens of thousands of businesses closed.

The economy had recovered by 1893 just in time for another panic, and this one was even worse. Then there was a bank panic in 1886, and finally another panic in 1907. That's 35 years of economic chaos and uncertainty.

Just as in our own time, the real estate and housing business was particularly hard hit. The Industrial Revolution and the greatly increased manufacturing output during the war had made elaborate Victorian-style houses cheaper than ever to build, and the periods between panics were punctuated with bursts of construction activity in areas not previously considered suitable for development. When the economy tanked these new houses defaulted, or their banks closed. The countryside was dotted with abandoned, decaying wooden hulks of high Victorian elegance. It seems that every small town had one. It was in this 35 year period that the Victorian mansion was permanently fixed in the popular imagination as the *very embodiment* of the haunted house.

I've always thought that the family plot by the door, and the uniformity of style across them, was a strong implication that the family that lived in the big house all died off pretty rapidly. This charming tableau has since been expanded into a huge whimsical cemetery, which admittedly opens the door for different interpretations. Were they all taken one after another, perhaps with only one Gracey left in the big old place at last, wandering the halls alone while the ghosts began to bleed out of the woodwork?

In truth, however, the *Haunted Mansion* does not offer us many hints. The great power of the ride is that it suggests *leagues* more than it shows. Practically every scene offers visual input of imagistic power and internal logic but which has no larger context outside itself. Our brains labor overtime to trace links where they may not truthfully exist. It's the theme park equivalent of a Rorschach test.

5. UP OR DOWN?

The discovery of the Castellated style is fortunate, because Imagineering nearly ended up with a very different house. That in itself is interesting because the design of the Disneyland *Haunted Mansion* facade was never really in dispute. Walt got what he wanted. And after he was gone, the elements that went into it were suddenly and inevitably drawn together, like driftwood to the eye of a whirlpool.

Yes, you can find abandoned concepts here or there, but most of the main ideas the design team had were developed and used. But then we come to the look of the facade in Florida, and suddenly we see a total reversal of direction. It's one of the only total reconceptions in the history of the ride, and it's worth exploring.

The initial plan for the *Haunted Mansion* in Liberty Square was to be a large Federal-style house of Jeffersonian symmetry sitting roughly at the same spot. It would have been a square, red brick house with two wings, a slate roof, widow's walks, round windows, dormers, and a large veranda covering the whole front. Sloping pathways would have led through a front lawn to the ticket structures, and the whole thing was to be surrounded by a big iron gate.

The unused original facade

In other words, it was supposed to be nearly the same queue system that Disneyland opened with in 1969. A porch used as a holding area, with the queue routed either directly inside the house on slow days or through a side yard on busy days. And, as you may have guessed with that kind of queue setup, there was expected to be an elevator system to bring guests from the foyer down to the load area.

There still are major aesthetic benefits to the way Disneyland runs their queue and manages their facade. There's a tactile pleasure in being able to touch and be near the house you're about to enter that you can't get at Walt Disney World, with its remote castle on the hill.

And, given the fact that the *Haunted Mansion* had finally opened after ten years of development turnaround, logically you'd want to simply repeat as much of what you had achieved as possible when asked to rebuild the ride elsewhere.

Construction began in force on the Magic Kingdom in 1969, just as the Disneyland *Haunted Mansion*'s interior was being manufactured and put in place. The cement foundation pad for the attraction was poured simultaneously with the pad for *it's a small world* and the start of construction on the Utilidor, the underground tunnels which run underneath Magic Kingdom. The show building went up next, and by most accounts the show itself was arriving via freight and being installed by early 1970. Tony Baxter remembers[16] that by October 1970, a full year ahead of schedule, the *Haunted Mansion* was complete and the doors were locked, awaiting fall 1971.

You can see all of this in historical photographs of the construction of Magic Kingdom: when Main Street was nothing but dirt, the *Haunted Mansion* show building looms in the background. What you'll also see is that the "Mansion" itself, i.e. the facade, didn't start really going up until mid 1970, which would be when the interior was being built. In a neat bit of synchronicity, this means that the Florida *Haunted Mansion* was built in the exact opposite order of the California *Haunted Mansion* - ride first, then the house.

5. Up or Down?

Construction blueprints in libraries and private collections show that the version of the *Haunted Manson* designed to use elevators lasted until around about late 1969, and the earliest blueprints I've found for the facade which actually was built date from March 1970. Disney changed their minds while the ride was being built.

I've heard all sorts of rumors about why the elevators were replaced with rooms that rise up. Many maintain that it was because of Florida's high water table. I can safely say that this is nonsense, because it disregards the fact that the whole of Magic Kingdom was built to circumvent the water table. The Utilidor was built above ground level, and the entire park was buried in dirt.

Generally, it can be said that those attractions on the south side of Magic Kingdom sit at lower elevation than those on the north side. *Jungle Cruise* sits in a sunken courtyard. You go down a drop to get into *Pirates of the Caribbean*. I think this is the whole reason they situated *Haunted Mansion* on the north side of the park to begin with: they wanted to situate it high enough to allow room for elevator shafts.

But the real thing that puts the lie to the old water table theory is that Magic Kingdom opened with *two* operating Otis elevator lifts identical in make and model to those used at Disneyland's *Haunted Mansion*. They weren't used in attractions, but for shows - one at Fantasy Faire stage in Fantasyland, and the other at Tomorrowland Terrace. These were Magic Kingdom's equivalent of the famous "rising bandstand" at Disneyland's Tomorrowland.

Did the two elevators intended for *Haunted Mansion* get redistributed to the concert venues? Are we looking at a budget cut?

Or perhaps the facade was re-designed to accommodate a larger queue? The opening of the *Haunted Mansion* in 1969 prompted a frenzied month at Disneyland in the weeks leading up to the return to school. At the same time, The Magic Kingdom's design was continually being revised to accommodate ever-larger crowd predictions through 1968 and 1969.[17] Although the revised facade arrangement for the *Haunted Mansion* did result in greatly increased room for switchbacks outside, why would reworking the queue be the reason for re-engineering an entire special effect which was installed and working?

Maybe they didn't trust the elevator?

In David Koenig's *More Mouse Tales*, Koenig cites information he culled from an interview with Cast Member "Haught":[18]

> The [Haunted Mansion] finally opened six years later, then briefly closed. To lower guests so they can walk underneath the railroad tracks to the main show building, the Haunted Mansion uses a pair of elevators. But, about six months after the ride opened, the elevators stopped going down. Somehow, water had seeped into the elevator pits and caused the lift mechanism to fail. By putting green dye in the water, repair workers were able to trace its source to the

5. UP OR DOWN? 57

Rivers of America. Maintenance pumped the entire river, then resealed the elevator pits.

Six months after August 1969 puts us exactly in February 1970, which is slightly *before* the facade of the Florida ride was redesigned to ditch the elevators. If this is a coincidence, it's one that strains credulity. Sadly, I have no information to back up this story - nothing in *Disneyland Line*, nothing in Los Angeles area newspapers, and most of the memorandum of that era was long ago destroyed.

Originally, the Rivers of America at Disneyland were lined with mud. Today, they are lined with concrete, and I don't know when the concrete came in - whether in 1970 or some later date. The Magic Kingdom's river has *always* been concrete, and I'm going to assume that it was the intent from the start, as Florida's sandy soil would likely have sucked up any clay lining Disney would've put down.

What's interesting about the elevator version of the attraction is how many marks it has left on the final version of the ride. Careful examination of colored elevations of the Federal version of the house shows that the arrangement of foyer and Stretch Rooms would have been identical: two Stretch Rooms side by side with a foyer in front of and between them. The Federal-style facade even had two cupolas on top of the house suggesting where each Stretch Room would have gone.

In other words, the planned layout was simply transposed down onto ground level when the elevators were cut. The Florida *Haunted Mansion* facade is really an ingenious case of form following function; in this case; the form was already determined by an aborted elevator configuration.

The Florida facade is actually very tiny; only large enough to accommodate the Stretch Rooms. The foyer area is disguised as a stone pedestal that the house sits on, and it's buried in dirt on two sides. The *Mansion* itself is really just a tiny wrap that conceals the empty space that the dual Stretch Rooms are hauled up into.

The current entrance door to the *Haunted Mansion* is even in the exact same spot - it's simply changed so it faces west instead of south. What's interesting is that the placement of this door in a darkened antechamber next to the main foyer area shows just how little the layout was altered. Disneyland has always allowed a little bit of daylight into their foyer, although as far as I can tell the shade structure enclosing the porch around the door has always been there to mitigate it somewhat. This is not a problem because there are no special effects in Disneyland's foyer.

Florida seems to have always had the Aging Man effect intended for a fireplace between the two Stretch Rooms, and daylight would very much compromise the effect if the foyer were arranged similarly to Disneyland's. This goes double for a facade built up on a man-made hill in the harsh Florida sun, where rays could easily enter in the afternoon. Walt Disney World's door ended up being buried between hills, facing west behind a stand of trees, making that short hallway somewhat unnecessary, but it remains to this day - a small echo of what was once intended.

Once past the Stretch Room scene, more evidence of the tampered layout can be found. It's no big secret that the Disneyland Stretch Rooms move much further than the Walt Disney World Stretch Rooms, and even allowing for a raised facade on a hill, the elevator arrangement would have unloaded at a lower level than the current Load Area. Is the reason the first three scenes of the ride are situated on a slope because they were designed to sit on a single, level floor - much like the second floor of the existing Disneyland Mansion - and had to be changed?

The Library has a huge chandelier that's anchored to a wall with a thin wire to appear to hang straight down in a room that's situated on an angle, which is a weird choice to make if you don't have to make it. The cars move down a long slope, pass the piano, and immediately go up a huge staircase. That isn't a logical layout to choose unless circumstances demanded it. Are we seeing the remnant of a compensation for a design that had to be rapidly changed?

My guess is yes. It makes a lot of sense to simply repeat the elevators, and the fact that the Magic Kingdom's *Haunted Mansion* interior was being manufactured in December 1969 shows that WED was fully expecting to simply push another *Mansion* out and be done with it.

And yet the facade was undoubtedly improved by the mix-up. Until WED was forced by unknown circumstances to reconsider their approach, the plan was for a conceptual twin of the Disneyland *Haunted Mansion*: a big, old house in the style of the area it was situated in. When Claude Coats went back to the well and discovered the Castellated style, he unearthed with it a mountain of historical connections and spooky associations. These not only made the *Haunted Mansion* a fertile transition into Fantasyland, making the claim that the ride represented the meeting point of history and folklore possible, but changed the groundwork for how we think of the ride. The style is historically valid, while remaining a total gothic fantasy.

So instead of a *Haunted Mansion* which looks pleasant enough on the outside but which holds darkness within, it becomes a house which seems wrong, bizarre, insane from the start. The stonework becomes daggers, the windows become eyes. The wings of the house inch towards you like dead, reaching hands.

Even in the days when the exterior was trim and stately and the bricks were not yet aged, it was the kind of place which dared you to come inside. Disneyland's *Haunted Mansion* played on fears that the worst horrors could wait inside the friendliest looking house, but the Florida house was the archetypal Bad Place from the start: dropped out of your dreams and into reality. It's the haunted house *par excellence*.

6. A LIGHT IN THE ATTIC

You are a bold and courageous person, afraid of nothing. High on a hilltop near your home there stands a dilapidated old mansion. Some say the place is haunted, but you don't believe in such myths.

One dark and stormy night, a light appears in the top-most window in the tower of the old house. You decide to investigate -- and you never return.
- Chilling, Thrilling Sounds of the Haunted House

    I think it's often easier to think of the *Haunted Mansion* as an index of "things you'd expect to see in a haunted house" than anything else. The hoariest old clichés are all trotted out, but *funny*, they don't seem so hoary anymore when they're happening to you, do they?
    The final grace note in the design of *Haunted Mansion* facade is an effect which is rarely spotted, which is of course the best kind. It's the kind of haunted house cliché which should be funny when you see it, but isn't. It's a light which moves from window to window in the old house.
    Nightfall has always been a different time in Disney theme parks. The energy and bombast of the daylight hours gives way to a dreamily pastoral effect, only heightened by the twinkling lights in the trees and, often, the emptied, darker corners of the streets. One reason why the *Haunted Mansion*'s moving light effect is not more famous is because, no doubt, it was broken for many years, entirely forgotten. But there's fewer people around in these well-trod places at night, too, and perhaps even if they were around, few would ever see it.
    For one thing, perhaps the best way to see the effect is to glimpse it accidentally - *is that a flash of light in the upper window?*

Since the effect does not repeat with regularity, if you barely glimpse it you'd have to stand around for a very long time to see it again. That little hook would become etched in your mind, adding to the associative power of the *Haunted Mansion*: it's not a real haunted house, but then why am I seeing things?

And perhaps this is why so many eyewitness accounts of the effect make it out to be much more than it is. People describe a glowing orb that bounces faintly along before vanishing. Others say it's a light which is extinguished by a black shape. As with nearly everything else in the *Haunted Mansion*, what they think they're seeing and what they're really seeing could not be farther apart.

The mechanism which creates the moving light is basically a cylinder made out of sheet metal. There's a light bulb up inside it, and a jagged hole cut in the side of the cylinder. A motor rotates the cylinder.

When the mechanism it at rest, the hole in the cylinder is facing away from the window. When activated, the cylinder rotates a full circle once before triggering an electrical relay to the next cylinder. The "dark shape" some report seeing in the window just before the light goes out is actually the jagged edge of the hole the light is shining out of.

At Magic Kingdom, that's all there is to it. The seven windows the traveling light may be seen in are all dimly illuminated at all times. That's because the light bulbs aren't rigged to turn off between cycles. A close observer may notice in each window facing the river a small black shape may be seen just at the bottom of the window. That's the actual moving light mechanism you're looking at. When you don't see the glow moving past each window, the cylinder is facing away from the window and shining on a piece of black cloth tacked up on the inside window frame.

There's about three feet between the black cloth and the back of the upper portion of the Stretch Room. If the cloth were to fall down in one of the windows, you'd see wood timber framing sliding up and down on rails!

Disneyland's *Haunted Mansion* has a slightly more sophisticated setup, in that their "traveling light" effect cannot be seen while the mechanism is at rest. The ground floor windows of the Disneyland *Mansion*, the ones you can stand right next to and touch, all have the same basic window treatment: behind the glass is a dark green shade. In some cases, the shade doesn't go all the way down and a bit of lacy material may be seen just beyond it. The upstairs windows have the shades too, but they're pulled almost all the way up, so that lace curtains may be seen through the glass. The traveling light fixtures sit right behind this lace drop.

Disneyland has five of them. The effect is supposed to begin at the front of the house, facing the Rivers of America. It's then supposed to travel left, passing the second front-facing window, then reappearing around the side of the house, passing three more windows in sequence and ending at a second floor window nearest the railroad tracks.

I've only ever seen it in this last window in person, and the light seemed to move very slowly. After moving from right to left, it moved back from left to right, as if the sequence was supposed to reverse itself.

The Magic Kingdom moving light effect has seven lights to Disneyland's five. Besides the four front-facing windows, the two side windows above the entrance door and the Conservatory also has the effect. The Conservatory effect is the most spectacular and may be seen from across the Rivers of America.

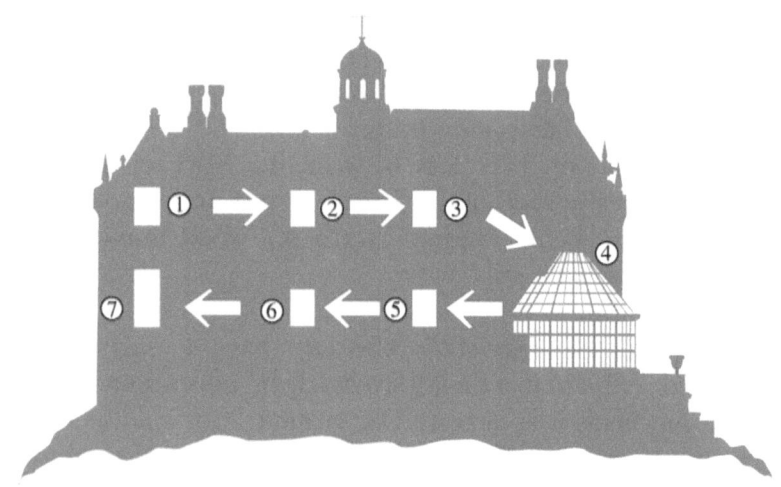

When it's working properly, this is what you're supposed to see: the light appears in the top, side window of the house, facing out towards *Big Thunder Mountain*. It travels to the right, where it appears to pass the top two windows facing the river. There's a pause, then the light appears in the Conservatory, sweeping from right to left (and illuminating dead plants climbing the interior walls of the Conservatory, a nice touch often unnoticed). It then passes the bottom two windows moving left and ends in the far side window, one floor below where it started.

The relays, however, aren't that reliable, and all seven must be in working order to get the full effect. The one that almost always works is the Conservatory, which is the big one. The four on the bottom floor tend to work more frequently than the three on the top floor, for no other reason than that the top ones must be serviced while hanging off a ladder. The whole sequence is supposed to trigger when the Stretch Room on the right side finishes its show and resets, meaning you're supposed to see the full thing every 7 minutes or so. But what you get more often is a smattering of windows where lights may be seen passing at different times. In some ways it may actually be better - *scarier* that way, with a longer wait for each light, making it more likely for a sighting to be happenstance.[20]

Tokyo Disneyland's *Haunted Mansion* was outfitted with the moving light effect. Several of their windows were refurbished in the early 90s with a new look, so I have no idea if it survived that process.

Interestingly, Disneyland Paris actually does use it on the facade of *Phantom Manor*. One window on each of the three visible sides of the house has the light effect installed inside, and the one facing the exit actually has a mock-up figure of the Phantom peering out. As the light passes it silhouettes him - a very nice touch.

Disneyland's version of the effect is probably the most refined and subtle - any view of it would be a view through the layers of wrought iron, glass, and lace, and given all of those obstructions the effect is likely to be extremely unnerving. But of course the effect *doesn't actually operate* at Disneyland, and hasn't for nearly a generation. The moving light still restlessly paces the house in Liberty Square, and may it burn on for generations yet to come.

7. THE OLD HOUSE AND THE SEA

Sea captains, their decaying old mansions, and the ocean are bound tightly into the American imagination. And why not; America was, in her earliest generations, primarily a seagoing nation. Long before the Dutch, Spanish, French, and English arrived to exploit the new world, ancient Vikings, Celts, and Norsemen made the journey seeking gold or copper, leaving behind the various pre-Christian "mystery sites" which still dot New England. One of these primitive buried stone huts in Vermont has inscriptions on its walls in Ogham, a Medieval Celtic alphabet. The inscription could be translated as "*Precincts of the Gods of The Land Beyond the Sunset*".[21]

Later inhabitants arrived in boats and made their fortunes aboard boats, too. While the southern states pioneered crop growing, New England specialized in fishing, shipping, and whaling, and a great many men became rich by living off the ocean. Sea captains were America's original aristocracy.

The concept of the ghost captain may descend from the mythology of the ghost ship, which really got started in earnest in the mid eighteenth century, right about the time the colonies first began to really think about revolution.

Stories of the *Flying Dutchman*, the classic ghost ship, began to be recorded in the late eighteenth century, but almost certainly existed as ocean-going lore before that. Coleridge's *The Rime of the Ancient Mariner* appeared nearly at the same time, and similar stories about doomed sea men and ships followed in the early ninetieth century, contributed by such authors as Sir Walter Scott, Washington Irving, and Edgar Allan Poe. These stories are only called "Romances" because the words necessary to describe weird fiction - what today we'd call fantastical or horror fiction - did not as yet exist.

It's easy to imagine how the stately stone mansions of sea captains, so often vacated of human life while the men were away at sea, whipped with salt winds and often perched high to overlook their ocean, gave rise to folklore of a supernatural bent.

Vermont folklorist Joseph Citro tells a ripper about a Maine sea captain who, pushed past the edge by a nagging wife, beat her to death with a hammer then concealed the body inside the living room floor underneath a carpet. Later residents of the house complained of a large bump underneath the living room carpet which seemingly would appear at random...[22]

Stories like this can be found all through the coastal regions of the country. Marc Davis himself had lived in Galveston, Texas,[23] which is still a place where rumors of Captain Kidd's buried gold swirl. And so, logically, when a *Haunted Mansion* was announced for a New Orleans area of Disneyland, early Disneyland designer Ken Anderson had his house be haunted by a former sea captain - possibly a pirate![24]

The notion of the *Haunted Mansion* as a former sea captain's residence floated around in the ether of the attraction without gaining much ground. Fresh off *Pirates of the Caribbean*, Marc Davis drew various pirates and sea captains for possible inclusion in the attraction, but most of these concepts were dead ends. Or were they?

I've already demonstrated that WED Enterprises went to some lengths to create a seaside horror mansion for the Florida *Haunted Mansion*, and besides a slightly stronger regional character given the house, the main remnant of the concept seems to be the large, menacing portrait of a dead sea captain inside the house. It may or may not be just another detail, but I have my own theory about the old house and the sea.

Marc Davis was, amongst his more colorful habits, an extraordinarily well read man. In designing the *Haunted Mansion*, he was unique among the many people who had worked on the attraction in looking to history and mythology to draw in ideas for Disneyland's ghost house.

For a point of reference, let us consider the Magic Kingdom Rivers of America. Unique to Florida, different spots along the river have floating beacons with location names affixed. These beacons are actually described, absolutely verbatim, in Mark Twain's *Life on the Mississippi*, including several names which are actually *used* at Magic Kingdom.[25]

Similarly, Tom Sawyer Island goes several steps beyond the Disneyland original and actually reproduces locations from the book, including Joe Harper's father's grist mill and Muff Potter's fishing pond. The Injun Joe's Cave attraction carefully references areas of the cave Twain actually wrote about, including faces in the rocks and areas where guests may scare each other by jumping out from behind stalactites.

Both attractions were designed by Marc Davis during the planning stages of Magic Kingdom, and in both cases Marc seems likely to have cracked open Twain's books and annotated passages he could use. This sort of approach is wholly in keeping with the studious culture of creativity and research cultivated by Walt Disney, first at the animation studio and later at WED.

The ultimate American novel about the supernatural and the ocean is Herman Melville's *Moby Dick*. Melville's great accomplishment was to present the ocean as a malevolent supernatural force that dooms men who abuse it. The white whale is described as a thundering god of terrifying power, and Ahab's quest to destroy it is a mission that is not divinely sanctioned. How the book arrives at this metaphorical level from a naturalistic beginning is one of the most remarkable texts in American letters.

Moby Dick was published in 1851, but it was not a success and remained more or less underground for seventy years, until the 1920s, when its complex, non-traditional form and heavily metaphoric style were just right for a world fresh from the Great War. Almost at once it was acclaimed as the greatest American novel on a great, typically American subject - and even better, it had been rescued from obscurity. Marc Davis had been born in 1913, and he grew up as a creative child in a cultural environment where Melville's novel was suddenly embraced as a national treasure.

7. THE OLD HOUSE AND THE SEA

Besides being an animator, ride designer, teacher, and collector of primitive art, in all of that Davis found time to be an accomplished fine artist, executing canvases in an abstract, vivid palette. Besides nudes, he painted a series of boldly expressionistic canvases in the 1950s on *Moby Dick*. His 1952 piece "Ahab's Nightmare", showing a sailing vessel bisected by numerous red-eyes whales, looks like a predecessor to his "Ghost Ship" changing portrait.

Davis seems to have thought the same thing himself, because that seems directly inspired by *Moby Dick*. Davis originally painted it as a six-image sequence, starting with the ship at sail, then caught in the doldrums, then an ocean storm, and finally as a sailing wreck, St. Elmo's Fire glowing between the barren mastheads, spewing ghosts in all directions.

Chapter 119 of *Moby Dick*, The Candles, occurs immediately before the whale is spotted and the chase begins. St.

Elmo's Fire is a genuine electrical phenomena similar to ball lightning, and in the book it is the moment where the sailors aboard the Pequod realize that their voyage is doomed and that Ahab will stop at nothing to catch the whale. It's a powerful moment in the book, where the symbology of the book's conception of the open sea as a supernatural force comes together with the narrative in a moment of frightening foreboding.

Davis' Melville-inflected changing portrait was given a sequel of sorts in the Florida *Haunted Mansion*, where the ship now sits wrecked on rocks in the background of the portrait of the dead sea captain.

Does the curse of the ocean lay on this place, as it laid on the Pequod and the church in New Bedford? These themes may only be a distant, unconscious echo in the Magic Kingdom, but I believe they survived, and may help us understand something about the *Haunted Mansion* and Liberty Square.

What does everything in the north end of Liberty Square tell us about the *Haunted Mansion*? This unity would have been much stronger had the *Columbia* Sailing Ship been built as planned, visually unifying everything, but let's look at what we have in that area. We have a port, a large vessel, and a loading dock. Atop the loading dock of the *Liberty Belle* is a widow's walk, a rotating beacon, and sailing ship weathervane - another hint of the coastal atmosphere. Nearby there's the Columbia Harbour House, themed to a sailor's inn and tavern.

Across the way is the shop that was once known as The Yankee Trader, and it's connected to the Columbia Harbour House through an elevated walkway, implying some sort of relationship. A spring 1973 Magic Kingdom map lists this shop as "Yankee Pedlar Gourmet Culinary Aids" and indicates that the store sells "exotic spices" - spice being, of course, the reason why sailing and taxing routes opened in the first place.

Everything is connected if we imagine that same riverboat landing with a sailing ship in it. Now we have a ship, the port it ties up at, the inn where the sailors drink and sleep, and a store where goods brought in on the ship are sold. And there's the big house where the captain lives, or lived.

I call this the "Liberty Square Triangle". All of these structures on the north side of the land are bound together in a highly profitable cycle of exploitation of the sea.

Is this why the *Haunted Mansion* is haunted? Did the offended gods of the ocean come home to roost and destroy the inhabitants of the spooky old house on the hill, or is it only an old superstition?

Mind you, I don't believe that this was **consciously decided and planned**, although perhaps I could be convinced if, for example, Marc Davis had intervened in the theming of the Columbia Harbour House.[26]

But I do believe that good ideas can jump from one mind to the next, not remarked on but implicitly understood. These ideas cycle through the history of the *Haunted Mansion* like a doomed echo, and perhaps all it took was a spooky old house with a widow's walk along the roof to bring to mind cursed sea captains and the power of the ocean.

But if not, it's an amazing coincidence that in the second floor of the Columbia Harbour House, right in the overpass where the Harbour House connects to the shop, there's a notice pinned to the wall. It calls for all willing and able men to board a whaling ship at Pier No. 9 - signed Captain Ahab.

PART II: THIS OLD DARK HOUSE

The Haunted Mansion is a badly flawed ride, if only for the smug and supercilious treatment is bestows on ghosts, just because they are dead. Even so, it is surely one of the most skillful, sophisticated and engrossing spatial sequences on the planet.

It is useful to see the ride as a progression from outside the event, where the observer and observed are at some distance, to the inside, where the observer, mind and body, has entered into the observed, so that it finally envelops him and even at the end makes an attempt to enter him" - Charles Moore, The City Observed: Los Angeles - A Guide To Its Architecture and Landscapes

1. A COLD WELCOME

Why do we enter the *Haunted Mansion*?

Like all of the best material at Disneyland, the *Mansion* taps deep into subconscious longings and desires in our pop cultural makeup. The best of these are nonspecific: the desire to return to a simpler time (Main Street, USA), the desire to see a real working old-fashioned steamboat, or sail with buccaneers, or climb a mountain. These are timeless, culturally nonspecific desires, which could belong to any era but which belong, at Disneyland and Magic Kingdom, to the American midcentury and the unique personality of Walt Disney.

Disneyland gets to us in ways the most intellectual and guarded cannot anticipate because, while some go in expecting tinsel and sawdust, it reaches deep down inside us and pulls out of us indulgences we never could admit to. Like movies and museums, it lets us see and do things which would otherwise require extraordinary sums of time and money. And, as eloquently phrased in *The Magnificent Ambersons*, in these times the faster we're carried, the less time we have to spare. Places which make us forget, even for a twelve hour span, become sacred.

There was once a time when every town had a haunted house or two; my town in Connecticut had two of them, and they were right across the street from each other. The obvious one was a gigantic crumbling mill, with red sideboards peeling off exposed structural timbers and windows which were once rectangles but had sunk to uneven trapezoids. It was old, pre-revolutionary war, and it was built without a foundation, so that the undulations of the earth below it had bowed and broken what was once a salt-box rectangle into uneven, crooked lines. It was rumored that ghosts lurked on the upper floors.[1]

The other haunted house was of the more typical variety for middle America: a modern one-floor ranch built into the side of a hill with a partially exposed basement level. For a long time the house sat empty, windows shuttered, in a yard littered with trash. It was abandoned, I was furtively told on the bus to and from elementary school, because a husband had murdered his wife with an axe inside it and buried her body in the rear yard. Most of the ghost stories I was told as a child one way or another involved axe murders, because that's how first graders like them.

And so I passed these two haunted houses several times a day for years, my bored face pressed against the school bus window, ever on the lookout for fleeting phantom figures passing broken windows in the old mill or perhaps horrible screams coming from the axe murder house. And I entertained fantasies of going into these forbidden places and having terrifying adventures amongst the ghosts, just like every kid in every town with a haunted house across America.

With the *Haunted Mansion*, Disney built the ultimate childhood dare. If some in my school would dare each other to run up to the old mill and peer in its windows, Walt Disney built a beautiful Mansion, stocked it with ghosts, and left the door open.

You experience the *Haunted Mansion* the same way you experience childhood "haunted houses": it sits there overhanging the river, looking a bit creepy, if totally innocent, on the outside. It's located centrally, so you see and pass it multiple times during the course of your day inside the theme park, wondering all the while what could be inside it. If you ride the riverboat, the captain takes time to point it out, explain that it's haunted, and offer a story or two about strange events that are said to occur inside. The *Haunted Mansion* is an urban legend even inside its own fabricated "town".

This, at least partially, accounts for some of the extraordinary imaginative power of the *Mansion*; it's eerily similar to "real" haunted houses from your own childhood, and thus, even if subconsciously, a great pleasure comes from conquering your old fear, venturing inside, and surviving to tell the tale.

In fact, compared to other Disney attractions, the *Haunted Mansion* requires us to make very few imaginative leaps. We need

1. A Cold Welcome 77

not pretend that we have travelled back in time, or have the power to fly, or are trained astronauts. The entire attraction takes place inside a real, solid house which we examine while waiting to enter it. We move methodically through the house, entering on the ground floor and proceeding level by level until we reach the Attic. Not visible from the main path but out behind the house is a public cemetery which we will discover upon escaping the house through an attic window. This fictional cemetery is physically situated in such a way relative to the house that we understand it's "out back" somewhere. We are even shown that the ghosts can warp our perception of the house's interior, allowing it to seem larger on the inside than it is on the outside. The *only* leap of faith we need to make is that, for the next twenty minutes at least, ghosts are real.

As for us, we're nobody but ourselves, and the time is either now or perhaps when you were a child - and this distinction is irrelevant for many kids who experience it every day. While a modern Disney attraction is always sure to give you a role to play - you're a recruit, a deep sea diver, or a specialist - you cannot hide your essential self from the *Haunted Mansion*. You are yourself, and you enter because you want to. This is why so many children freak out at the prospect of entering the old house - it's a very real nightmare in their regular life actually coming true. But ghosts aren't real - are they?

For those of us who think maybe they are, the distinction between the *Haunted Mansion* and a *potential* reality has now entirely collapsed. One possibility is something we don't expect to happen and the other is something we allow to happen by stepping inside.

And so here we are, waiting in that brick-lined trough leading to the closed, heavy double doors. Off to the left, a small cemetery passes the time with morbid humor obituaries. Somewhere off in the distance, a wolf howls. Here we are, staring down the gun barrel of something that would have terrified us as children. The doors open, and the perfect dream state begins.

Those wolf howls did terrify me as a child. My parents brought me to the *Monster Sound Show* at Disney-MGM Studios so I could understand that the howls were only a sound effect, but that's not why they scared me. I knew they were manufactured, in the vague way that most children know that the things at Disney aren't real. What scared me was their relentless starkness. Much of the Magic Kingdom is filled with music, sound, and color, but waiting to enter the *Haunted Mansion* quiets down even the yahoo contingent. You're stuck there in comparative silence with some graves, yourself, and a lonely howl rising over a scene of mortality. You're given plenty of time to think about your decision to go inside.

Although I do not know if the *Haunted Mansion*'s bend in the river which the riverboat scoots past has always been named 'Howling Dog Bend', I can say with some authority that the sound effect of the howling dog was not installed until 1973.[2] This minor effect seems an especially salient part of my childhood, especially in the old days, when the wolf howl itself was much louder and could be heard through all of Frontierland and Liberty Square. The house, backed into a remote corner, would not allow itself to be forgotten, even when you were not nearby.

The moment when the approach to the house was finally made, the ominous howling only grew louder - climaxed by the long, silent wait by the front doors near the family cemetery, punctuated only by those unearthly howls. It was not until years later that I finally spotted the skeleton hound inside the attraction which made the sounds!

Although I'm sure anyone raised on the Disneyland version would consider the howls to be an especially bizarre, unnecessary gothic touch, I always thought, conversely, it to be weird - nigh-unimaginable - that Disneyland's *Haunted Mansion* did not emit unearthly howls. "*How would anybody know that this was the Haunted Mansion?*" I wondered.

By the late-90s, in the depths of my greatest enchantment with the *Mansion*, I once found myself late at night out on the boat dock of the Grand Floridian. The Magic Kingdom had closed early, as it did in those days, and I stood out there on the water for a long time considering the train station perched along the lagoon and the castle poking out of the trees. Then, very faintly, I heard the wolf howl. I strained and could hear it again. The wind must have been just right because I stood out there in the wet Florida night straining across the abyss to hear my house off in the distance.

It was the first time I ever entertained the possibility that the ride missed me as much as I missed it.

Comedy gravestones are nothing unique or special to the *Haunted Mansion*. Anyone who's been to a Lions Club or 4H haunted house has likely walked past their share of tombstones which say things like "DRACULA" and "I TOLD YOU I WAS

SICK". What's interesting about the *Haunted Mansion* tombstones, besides the unusually high quality of their gallows humor, is their status as WED Enterprises in-jokes.

These tombstones are usually presented as "credits" for those involved in the *Haunted Mansion*, which is not strictly true. Or at least, as not strictly true as it can be considering that WED and MAPO, in 1971, consisted of less than 100 people.

When the Disneyland *Haunted Mansion* opened in 1969, its original set of eight gravestones *were* specifically dedicated to those in WED who helped design the *Mansion* in key creative roles. Generally, the graves at Walt Disney World pay a wider tribute to those in higher and more diverse fields at Imagineering.

Since we now know that Disneyland's eight gravestones were displaced by a queue expansion by mid-1970, it's possible that those in administrative and project management positions at WED requested their own tombstones between the opening of the two attractions, otherwise it seems like a weirdly dissimilar group of people.

Dear Departed Grandpa Marc - Marc Davis, obviously. Marc wasn't much older than anyone else in WED at the time, not even Atencio, so this is likely a joke at the expense of the serious, paternalistic attitude he took on the job. See how one of your peers responds to being called "grandpa" next time you're at work! It's fun!

Brother Claude - the flower at the top of this tombstone, as well as the multiple puns on "plant" and "sod" strongly suggests that X was trying to link Claude to gardening for some reason. It could've been a joke on his gentle demeanor, or maybe X was thinking of Coats's distinctive leaf designs which appeared in his fine art (as well as three attractions he was lead designer on: *Snow White's Adventures*, *Mickey Mouse Revue* and *If You Had Wings*).

A Man Named Martin - for some time I suspected this was a reference to Bill Martin, supervising architect for the entire Magic Kingdom... and yet, that reference to "the lights went out" seemed so

1. A Cold Welcome

strongly to suggest a lighting designer. The Man Named Martin is actually Bud Martin, who was an assistant to Yale Gracey and who probably lit the interior of the Florida Mansion.

Uncle Myall - Chuck Myall was Bill Martin's right-hand man during the Walt Disney World project. Both of their names appear on all of the construction blueprints for the Magic Kingdom, and Chuck went on to become Director of WED East.

Brother Dave - Dave Burkhart mentored a young Tony Baxter in the WED model shop in 1969. By 1971 he was the field art director for the *Haunted Mansion*, meaning he supervised the on-site assembly of the ride, which is why he gets a tombstone here. He also was the project lead on Universal Studios Japan.

Master Gracey - as everyone knows, Yale Gracey. Unless X was intending to complement Yale on his mastery of special effects, "Master" here is likely used in its obsolete 19th century form, meaning a young man. Yale was no younger than any of the other guys at WED at the time, but X probably just liked the sound of it.

Good Friend Gordon - Gordon Williams of the WED sound department.

Wathel R. Bender - Wathel Rogers, who wins the award for the most laboriously phrased of the tombstones. Rogers was a mechanical and animation supervisor at MAPO along with Bill Justice. Wathel was also one of the studio's railroad enthusiasts, the "fender" in this case is almost certainly not the kind we have on cars, but the large scoop on the front of locomotives.

Good Old Fred - Fred Joerger, from the WED model department, was by 1971 primarily involved in show quality assurance of field art direction, meaning it was his job to ensure that the rides ended up looking like the concept art and models. Fred was also famous for his rockwork. Maybe his masterpiece is *Big Thunder Mountain*

Railroad, but just as impressive was the rocky sea bottom in *20,000 Leagues Under the Sea* and the original rockwork atrium at the Polynesian Village hotel.

Mister Sewell - Bob Sewell accompanies Fred Joerger in representing the WED model shop. Although I can't speak for Bob's leisure activities, perhaps X was thinking ahead to the Ballroom scene when he wrote of "a dirty duel".

Cousin Huet - Cliff Huet worked as a lead interior designer.

Frances Xavier - X Atencio's tombstone gives himself "no time off for good behavior", which is either a comical put down of his work ethic or an acknowledgment that putting your co-workers names on tombstones is kind of a dickish thing to do. No matter; his comedy epitaphs have immortalized men about whom very little other information is available.

  The original twelve tombstones were joined by an aesthetically dissimilar thirteenth in 2001 paying tribute to the Madame Leota character, but we'll get to that later. Leota was not intended to be the original thirteenth, but we'll have to wait awhile before that story can be told.
  The original set of twelve tombstones were made of hollow fiberglass, which I never suspected until early one morning as a Cast Member I was traipsing around up inside the Family Plot and accidentally tipped over Good Friend Gordon as if it were made of foam. I nearly fainted.
  When the *Haunted Mansion* was new in 1971, the gravestones were painted flat white with grey flecks; the inscriptions were re-lined in black, making them very legible and also very obviously fake. At some point in the 80s, the graves were given a more realistic stone finish and allowed to slowly accumulate mold and lichen to the point that they were indeed nearly impossible to tell apart from authentic stones. When the graveyard queue was

1. A Cold Welcome

redone in 2011, the fiberglass models were thrown out and replaced with actual cement versions from the original molds.

The graves shifted about over the years. Good Friend Gordon began life up on the hill behind everyone, but erosion and runoff meant that his gravestone did a very slow faceplant all through the late 80s and early 90s. In 2003, his tombstone was extracted from the hill and moved up next to Yale's. At this point, several others were moved around so that Grandpa Marc was nearest the queue area and first visible on the left, followed by Frances Xavier.

2001 brought the addition of the Madame Leota animated tombstone, which pays tribute to Leota Toombs Thomas, one of many women employed by the WED model shop. She painted and prepared attraction models and props for show installation, and also oversaw field installation and attraction quality on-site at Magic Kingdom until 1979.

As a tribute it's all well and good, but from a design perspective it has little in common with the other gravestones, and uses a typeface commonly circulated in the late 90s as the "Haunted Mansion Font".[3]

The main feature of the Leota tombstone is a large bas relief face above the inscription, which bears very little resemblance to the Leota encountered inside the attraction. The animated face can move in and out, as well as open her eyes and look around.[4]

When the figure was first installed in 2001, the animation was extremely subtle - so subtle, in fact, that most guests never saw it move! By 2003, the basic animation program was running twice as fast as it originally was designed to, meaning each group of tourists waiting to enter the house got to see at least two iterations of her face move/eye blink animation. Originally, it was subtle enough and new enough that usually the only guests to notice her moving were children - and more often than not, they'd be shushed by their parents!

By the mid-naughts, the entire Family Plot scene had become nothing but a giant amphitheater where a hundred people at each time would wait for Leota to open her eyes and roar with approval when this happened.

One fascinating thing about the Porte Cochere area of the *Haunted Mansion*, is that we enter an impossible door at an unlikely location... and nobody seems to notice. Now, to be clear, there's only one *Haunted Mansion* where we enter in through the front door, and that's *Phantom Manor* at Disneyland Paris. At Disneyland, we walk *past* the front door and enter through... a door next to it. Most are so taken with the *Mansion*'s porch and their proximity to the house that they don't even notice that they actually enter through an oddly asymmetrical door off to the side.

In Florida, we see the house up on a hill, then slowly wind our way alongside it until the Family Plot comes into view. At this point, the house is now directly above us, over us, and mostly blocked from our vision by a permanent shelter structure and tall hedges. We *sense* that we're getting nearer and nearer the actual house, but we lose our sense of how it is situated in the last few moments before we enter. This is crucial.

Actually our entrance is through a historically justifiable architectural feature, one which has essentially been made less and less obvious by decades of redevelopment of the basic queue area.

Before the entire entrance area of the *Haunted Mansion* was consumed by a ridiculous canopy, we approached the *Mansion* via a green canopy which led directly into a stone structure resembling a crypt. This is a porte cochere, or a sort of horse and buggy loading and unload area. Porte cocheres, in history, were always situated on the side of the house, and never opened into a formal foyer but rather a sort of out of the way reception room. In other words, we enter the Florida *Haunted Mansion* not into a formal foyer, but through the visitor's entrance which would lead to the social areas of the house.

This is a distinction worth contemplating. At Disneyland, upon passing the threshold of the house, visitors fill a small foyer area with an elaborate chandelier, wall sconces, a mirror and wainscoting - in other words, a room explicitly designed to welcome guests. There are two large doors and two doors only, which we understand lead deeper into the house. Since we aren't supposed to know that there are two Stretch Rooms, we imagine that the door we do not go through will lead to more formal areas - the ballroom, perhaps, or a study. The room is brightly lit, shaped like a rectangle, and immediately visually understandable.

Upon entering the Florida *Haunted Mansion*, however, we're presented with a bewildering assortment of visual cues. We step directly not into a welcome area, but a sort of alcove off a larger room where, we imagine, hats and coats may be taken and stowed. Then we walk into a very dark room of no understandable shape - walls jut left and right and doors are randomly placed. There's a central fireplace with dying embers, presumably to warm our feet on a cold winter's night, but no other visible signs of habitation. And,

most crucially of all, we are not supposed to notice the two doors to the Stretch Rooms.

This is a key and radical re-conception of our entry to the house. We're thrown into a room which is mostly wood paneling,

1. A Cold Welcome

and instead of being visually delineated with two doors leading deeper into the house, an entire wall unexpectedly opens up into yet another, even less inviting looking room. Disneyland's *Haunted Mansion* plays it cool until we go into the next room and it starts to stretch, but everything about the Florida foyer is meant to keep you on guard. Until the floor starts to drop in the portrait gallery everything about the Disneyland *Haunted Mansion* looks as it should - neat, clean, even inviting. Magic Kingdom, where there's a bat on the top of the belfry and a distant wolf howling, begins to mislead you immediately. The chandeliers are already covered in spiderwebs and the portrait over the fireplace is decaying. And is that a face in the fireplace grate?

And the Foyer *does* confuse people. This is definitely some sort of formal reception room - and there's enough doors and potential alternate ways to proceed deeper into the house that it's not too strange that a ballroom or great hall could be behind any door, but our only reception is a disembodied voice and a man who decays into a skeleton. Even the embers in the fire are dying. It's an evil sign.

But in another sense, at this point in the experience the Florida *Haunted Mansion* has ticked off an amazing number of boxes which constitute elements from the classic ghost story - the isolated spooky old house out on the edge of nothing, the creepy cemetery with a fresh grave, a howling wolf, a spooky servant who greets you at the door, the dying embers in the fireplace, a sliding panel, a secret room, and a scream. At the equivalent moment in the Disneyland show we're still watching the old house unfold its tricks to us, whereas at Magic Kingdom we're already entrenched deep, deep into fantasy.

And so we hang back at the entrance, quite naturally. Things are escalating quickly. But at the same time, it would almost be a crime not to stride into possible doom. After all, that's what they do in the movies.

2. THE STRETCH ROOM

At Disneyland, the stretching gallery is one of the great, fascinating highpoints of the attraction, an illusion comparable in scale and imagination to the Ballroom scene. At Walt Disney World, it... isn't. Not only is the effect superior at Disneyland, but it's a bigger, taller room. But our Magic Kingdom version of the illusion has some unique qualities, qualities which open the door to resonances perhaps unintended.

The Disneyland model is, as will be a shock to nobody, an elevator.

Specifically it's a piston-based Otis Elevator identical in operation to the one that carries performers up to ground level at the Tomorrowland Terrace. This is why you are asked to "gather your bodies towards the dead center of the room"; moving towards the middle more evenly and safely distributes weight onto the central piston. The original illusion is a holdover from the mid-sixties Rolly Crump and Yale Gracey version of the *Haunted Mansion* and was built into the attraction in 1964 along with the facade and Foyer - this part of the house was around in Walt Disney's era and has never changed.

The key to the whole illusion is the part nobody talks about, and that's the ledge that surrounds the guest viewing area. Because the viewing area is dark and the upper area where the stretching illusion takes place is bright, to the eye the upper area is as large or larger than the viewing area. It isn't. The striped wallpaper area actually nests *inside* the dark paneled area.

At Disneyland, the "expanding" section of the room is hidden above a stationary ceiling and pulled down into view by the descending elevator, simultaneously unrolling the portraits hidden behind the wall. Further complicating the illusion, at a certain point the portraits appear to stop stretching but the room *continues* to do so.

2. THE STRETCH ROOM

The additional space between the ceiling and the top of the portrait that grows is actually still part of the same piece of material that the portrait is painted on, only painted to look like it's part of the wall. This is why the Stretch Room is lit with hard light from below; it casts a shadow up onto the wall above each portrait to hide the fact that the striped wall panels and what appear to be part of the wall are actually moving at different speeds.

The grace of this version of the illusion is that there is no reference point for how it's done because the floor, the ledge, and the walls all move at different speeds. As a result not only does the room seem to grow bigger but every part of the room grows bigger in uneven, confusing ways. It's similar to a collapsing telescope, if you can imagine the wider end of the telescope being where guests stand and look up.

There is some evidence that this version of the illusion was intended for Magic Kingdom until the front part of the attraction was redesigned in early 1970. The new version of the Stretch Room operates on the same principle, but is functionally extremely different. When the room is parked in its "unstretched" mode, it's very similar to the Disneyland version: the dark paneled viewing area is nested outside the brightly wallpapered area, with additional wall space hidden above the false ceiling. The action of the stretching portraits is reversed in terms of the direction they travel; instead of being pulled down by a descending elevator to unroll they are being pulled up by a rising ceiling.

Behind the dark paneled walls of the Orlando Stretch Rooms are motors, two for each room. They're several feet tall, painted blue, and look very much like crude single-cylinder turbines. These are the new models; the originals would fire up loudly and a distinct "hum" could be heard through the walls. The motors start cranking airplane cables that run up into pulley rigs in the ceiling to hoist the Stretch Rooms up. If one motor turns slower than the other, the Stretch Room can stretch unevenly, and sharp eyed viewers can sometimes see this in action. Stretch One - to the left while facing the "Aging Man" portrait - often seems to stretch and reset unevenly.

What makes the hoisting possible is that the scrim ceiling is a kind of false front. At Disneyland the ceiling, molding, and attic set with hanging body behind it is one solid piece that stays firmly in place for the entire stretching sequence. At Magic Kingdom, the ceiling *rises* to meet a stationary attic set and hanging body.

In fact, close observers may note that there remains a gap between the bottom of the Attic set and the top of the Stretch Room. Stretch Two, and to a much higher degree Stretch One, don't rise as high as they're supposed to; I have no idea if it's always been this way or if this was instituted due to wear and tear.[5]

So it's in many ways a much cruder effect. Yet, in other ways, it's a little more complex as a *theatrical frisson*.

To be sure, there is no mistaking the fact that the floor is moving at Disneyland - it's more of an intellectual exercise of "ah, but maybe the floor is not moving!" But the entrance and exit doors to the room open and close exactly like elevator doors, and we are obligated to step over two metal plates with a gap between them while entering and exiting, a task which often results, even if subconsciously, in a look down so we don't fall. It requires no effort to discern that the room is an elevator.

In comparison, Walt Disney World doesn't use double doors that slide left and right, but a single wall that slides open, which removes one visual cue about what you're entering. And the entire expanse of floor from the Foyer to the Stretch Room to the Load Area is evenly carpeted, removing another subtle cue.

And then there's the fact that the floor *doesn't* move, but *appears* to. Disneyland's Stretch Room gives you a sinking feeling because you're literally sinking, and the walls reflect this change. Walt Disney World gives you a sinking feeling but doesn't move you anywhere, and many people are genuinely fooled. They think the illusion is so good you can't feel the floor move!

And while Disneyland's Stretch Room may be a superior illusion, there's something to be said for the fact that Walt Disney World's is not required to stretch quite so far. At Disneyland, the reveal of the full version of the four portraits, the most visually striking part of the entire show, is completed 2/3 of the way through the sequence; from there on it's all walls moving. Close examination of the stretching portraits themselves shows that Marc Davis drew them in equal thirds, most obvious in the Quicksand portrait: a normal-looking upper third, a middle third where something is revealed to be amiss, and a lower third where mortal danger (or at least serious consequences) are apparent.

Similarly, the Ghost Host's narration can also be broken into thirds, an opening narration of a normal room (*"Our tour begins here..."*), a middle section where intimations of danger are alluded to (*"Your cadaverous pallor..."*), and a final section where a direct threat is manifest (*"...this chamber has no windows and no doors."*). By slowing down the stretching process at Magic Kingdom, the visual of the room stretching directly matches the narration; the Ghost Host launches into his final observations at the exact moment the four portraits reveal grim surprises of their own. All four people in the portraits "die" at the exact moment the Ghost Host alludes to his own suicide.

Thus the Stretch Room becomes much more sinister at Magic Kingdom. The suicide image presented behind the ceiling (and subsequent blackout) is the strongest content in any Disney attraction; as a Cast Member I once led a guest out in tears because a family member had hung themselves just a few months before her visit. Disneyland's Stretch Room somehow comes off as more fascinating than scary; but Magic Kingdom's is a real suspense piece with a nasty sting in the tail.

And let's consider those doors into and out of the room. At Disneyland, inside the Foyer we are presented with what are obviously doors set into the walls; though they lack doorknobs they are framed and presented as such. Disneyland's Foyer has wainscoting to waist height and wallpaper above; the doors are properly decorated with bevels and cornices to appear to lead deeper into the house.

Walt Disney World's Foyer is much more severe; there's just a short strip of wallpaper near the ceiling. The lower section of the room is dark paneling, and the doors are hidden inside this paneling. If you didn't know any better, you'd assume the door into the Stretch Room is just a wall, and in fact dozens per day do make this mistake and lean on the door, preventing it from opening. At Magic Kingdom, the entrance to the Stretch Room isn't a door, but a *secret panel*.

Disneyland - Entrance Doors

Magic Kingdom - Sliding Panel

The difference in the way they open is functional; Walt Disney World can't have doors that open at the center because the panel behind the wall would interrupt the rear-projected Aging Man effect. But the idea that one could very easily pass by this room, the same room that maybe just opened for *you* and *you only*, the same room that looks normal but is a trap and the same room where a corpse is hidden maximizes the creepiness of the experience.

At *Phantom Manor*, the portrait gallery is actually straight up called "The Secret Room", and it holds a secret that's the linchpin of the whole story. Because visitors don't expect there to be a door where there is one, there's a genuine trepidation in entering the room at all; often when working I'd come around the corner and see the whole group just staring at it in silence without entering it.

There's a fascinating bit of weirdness about the Stretch Room exit door, too. Before the 2007 refurb in which timing of all of the spiels and door opening was rethought (and much improved), Maids and Butlers were instructed to open the exit door *during the blackout.*

To aid them in this, the antechamber outside the exit door was painted and lit in such a way as to be just nearly dark - dark carpets, a single dim light fixture, and the ceiling was painted flat black so as to bounce nearly no light. Even stranger, the sound effects during the blackout - the scream, crash, and subsequent Ghost Host lines were not played in the Stretch Room, but out in this darkened hallway!

The intended effect was that the exit would simply appear out of nowhere, during the time audiences were distracted by the hanging body. When the lights would be relit, what was previously a wall would now be a door!

Sometimes this came across. However, frequent riders caught onto the trick quickly and so would position themselves by the exit door and dash out of the Stretch Room during the blackout, hoping to beat the crowd to a Doombuggy. This often simply resulted in the Stretch Room crowd walking out of the room while the show was still running. The current version of the Stretch Room show relocates these sounds back into the room and does not open the exit door until the lights have been relit, resulting in a much more complete experience.

Inside the Stretch Room is the first example of one of the *Haunted Mansion*'s key leitmotifs, appearing here as the portrait of the sweet old lady who, as it turns out, put an axe in her husband's noggin. There is, in fact, a rather persistent theme of wives murdering their unsuspecting husbands, and it does not come directly out of the mainspring of Marc Davis's imagination. Audiences in 1969 would have recognized this as a playful riff on an idea which was very current in popular culture through the 50s and 60s and the memory of which has largely been obfuscated by subsequent developments in horror cinema - developments which, unlike the murdering spouses motif, actually stuck around. Let's rewind the clock so we have the appropriate cultural context.

The ur-text of the whole cycle is David O. Selznick's 1940 film version of *Rebecca*, directed by Alfred Hitchcock in his first American movie job. *Rebecca* is not a horror film, but it is something like one - a glossy, romantic take on the haunted house genre where the ghost of a former wife hangs palpably over the lives of a newlywed couple. Indeed, Maxim de Winter did murder Rebecca - intentionally in Daphne DuMaruier's novel, and "accidentally" in the film version, and her vengeful spirit does cause the ruin and eventual destruction of the de Winter family mansion, Manderley. An Academy Award winner and insanely popular film amongst young women of the 40s, *Rebecca* launched an entire cycle of gothic romantic melodramas in the early 40s, and it was these films, not the later hard-edged thrillers of the 50s, which established Hitchcock's career in America.

The next watershed in the genre is *Gaslight* in 1944, based on Patrick Hamilton's 1938 play. This is the origin of the modern term gaslighting, as a Victorian husband manipulates his wife into believing she's going insane as cover for his jewel smuggling operation. *Rebecca* and *Gaslight* really kicked the genre of "suspecting wives" into high gear, resulting in such deliriously strange melodramas as Hitchcock's *Suspicion* (1941) and *Spellbound* (1945), *Hangover Square* (1945), and *The Spiral Staircase* (1946). By the late 40s, with Fritz Lang's *Secret Beyond the Door* and Anatole Litvak's *Sorry, Wrong Number* (1948) the whole genre was pushing in an increasingly morbid, fantastical direction, less Agatha Christie than Edgar Wallace.

But the true film that finally pushes the genre out of the feminine thriller and into the realm of the horror film is Henri-George Clouzout's *Les Diaboliques* in 1955. A frail wife and her (potentially lesbian!) conspirator murder her satanic, abusive husband and sink his body in a wicker trunk at the bottom of a muddy swimming pool, but the body keeps showing up.... The relentless bleakness and nasty narrative twists put *Les Diaboliques* firmly in the terror film category, and it was a massive, worldwide success - not insignificant for a film made in France! In the United States, Alfred Hitchcock began to feel the heat of competition and struck back, first by adapting another of the novels by the writing team behind the story of Les Diaboliques into *Vertigo*, in 1958. Hitchcock then produced his own, Diaboliques-inspired shocker *Psycho* in 1960, which itself established its own horror-film lineage through the 60s.

And while today we think back on *Psycho* as the key terror film of its era, it took a long time for the influence of *Les Diaboliques* to fade - it lingers in William Castle's *The House on Haunted Hill* (1959) and *The Tingler* (1960), in Robert Aldrich's *Hush, Hush Sweet Charlotte* (1964), Hammer Films' *Scream of Fear* (1961)... and now we are getting very close indeed to the development cycle of the *Haunted Mansion* as we have it today. Indeed, anybody going out to see a terror film in the mid-60s would probably have ended up sitting through a spin on *Psycho* or *Les Diaboliques*.

1964 also saw the release of William Castle's *The Night Walker*, a near identical replay of the plot of *Les Diaboliques*, which begins with a spoken prologue by.... Paul Frees, getting an early workout on the voice he would later perfect as the Ghost Host. It seems we've come full circle now, and without even touching on a legacy of murdering spouses in EC Comics, in radio and television on programs like *Thriller, Alfred Hitchcock Presents*, and more. Let's just listen to Paul Frees' sonorous narration and watch the old lady perched on her tombstone stretch and reflect on three decades of popular thriller tradition bringing us to this moment.

Why is the Stretch Room so perfect?

Make no mistake, it's perfect. It's so perfect that not only did it invent its special effect, but it did it so well that it outlawed its use forever more. Other attractions, of course, have gone ahead and done it anyway, but these efforts are always met with a loud poo-poohing: "That's from the *Haunted Mansion*!".[6]

I think it's because the Stretch Room is so key to building us up for the experience to come. I'd actually argue it may be the key to the success of the whole venture. The *Haunted Mansion* is the ultimate cult attraction, the ultimate deep-dish aesthetic experience, leading to poor souls like myself who are doomed to write books like this one. It inspires not just love, not devotion, but obsession, and obsession across cultures and generations.

The Stretch Room is really a clever magic trick, and it's one of those rare moments where everything synthesizes. It's the Disney equivalent of the ending of *Casablanca*, or the song montage that ends *Abbey Road*. Everything clicks into its perfect form. You have Yale Gracey's brilliant stretching optical illusion, Marc Davis's iconic portraits, and X. Atencio's perfectly gauged script, all joining together to tell us... what exactly?

What does the Stretch Room do? At Disneyland it gets us downstairs. Why did it need to be repeated at Magic Kingdom?

Because it perfectly sets our expectations, and does so by presenting us with an optical illusion, a result of ghosts, we are told. Yet even as it's doing this, Atencio's script presents us with what in magic is known as misdirection. We are being asked to choose between two false values: is the room actually stretching, or is it only your imagination? It's actually neither, nor is it ghosts: it's a bunch of lumber sliding up and down.

But in doing so, the *Mansion* prompts us to look closer, to stay on our toes. We - meaning you and me, dear reader - and generations before, and hence, have been doing just that.

Far, far above the Stretch Room floor, seen so briefly many guests are not even sure if they saw it, is the hanging skeleton of the Ghost Host. Indeed, despite a good eight foot height difference between the viewing altitudes for the two skeletons, the Disneyland hanging body is often much easier to see - not because of the height so much as the scrim which makes up the ceiling. At Disneyland, the scrim stays put at the bottom of the belfry set inside the *Haunted Mansion* facade, and so collects dust only slowly. At Walt Disney World, the scrim is moving up and down constantly all day and so acts as something of a charcoal air filter for the entire front part of the attraction. It should be vacuumed about once a month but seems as if it's only done three or four times a year.

There's differences in the hanging bodies, too. Disneyland's is a standard anatomical skeleton with a custom skull, hair, and shredded costume. I think Walt Disney World's started off that way, but by the time I saw the figure while working in the attraction he was less like a laboratory skeleton and more like a prop; his ribcage was a hollow cylinder painted with ribs and a skull made of styrofoam to which standard skeleton arms and legs were added.

This was necessary because the way the two figures are animated is different. Disneyland's Hanging Body uses a knocker mechanism; this is an air pressure valve hidden up above the set which opens and closes rapidly. Attached to the valve is a long wire that snakes through a hole in the set and over to the rope from which the skeleton is hung; when the set is illuminated the solenoid pulls on the wire to swing the Hanging Man. Magic Kingdom's knocker tugs on the top of the rope hidden above the set, which consequently sways gently and requires a lighter skeleton.

Years ago, Walt Disney World sold a Kermit the Frog statue on Main Street; this was a "Big Fig" statue of Kermit with his banjo seated on a log as seen at the start of *The Muppet Movie*.

Now, one feature Cast Members have access to is a backstage merchandise shop called Property Control. If you ever lost a pair of sunglasses at Walt Disney World and never returned to pick them up? They were sold at Property Control, probably for about ten cents. Property Control also handles strollers, jewelry, and broken merchandise, and one day a Kermit the Frog, with one broken arm, appeared inside the *Haunted Mansion* break room courtesy $15 and Property Control.

We kept him atop a cabinet for a few months until the novelty wore off and discussions began of slipping him into the junk amongst the Attic, or perhaps perched on a gravestone in the Graveyard, or on the Ballroom balcony looking down at the dancing ghosts.

One day I was waiting for the end of the Stretch One show cycle and, during the reveal of the hanging body, looked up to see Kermit perched in one of the windows that surround the Hanging body up in its attic set. I began laughing so hard guests assumed it was part of the show. And there Kermit stayed for about a month until Maintenance found him up there and threw him away.

Regardless: fifteen dollars well spent.

After the Ghost Host says "of course, there's always my way" we see his hanging body, there's a blackout, and we hear spooky sounds.

Since 1969, these spooky sounds have been a scream, and a crash. What has always interested me is what *type* of crash is heard; it's bizarrely specific and yet seemingly irrelevant. It's not a kind of car crash or a body-falling-over crash... in fact it sounds exactly like the kind of crash that would result from precisely the method used to record it: a big pile of crates, maybe some furniture, and maybe some dowels or blocks being knocked over in a recording studio.

There's something perfect yet weirdly inappropriate about those sounds because it's long been my contention that those spooky sounds do not represent any particular event, they're simply the spooky sounds that were chosen.

Which is to say they could indeed have been any spooky sounds: chains rattling, bats flying overhead, a train coming through, etc. If anything, the idea of a blackout in which a scream and a crash are heard from places unknown is the single spot in which the *Haunted Mansion* most obviously owes a debt to traditional "old dark house" stories like *The Bat* or *The Cat and the Canary*. It's the sort of moment where we half expect the lights to return and see the Duchess fainted in a heap on the floor.[7]

In 1995, Disneyland's *Haunted Mansion* received a significant sound upgrade in their Stretch Rooms, and as far as I know this remix was the first time that the Stretch Room scream was made to pan from the upper part of the Stretch Room and end with a crash at the bottom.

Ignoring for a moment the fact that the scream is totally inappropriate for the Ghost Host, this seems to be where the idea that the scream and crash represents the Hanging Body "falling" and breaking apart on the floor comes from. The 2009 Magic Kingdom

Stretch Room show repeats this absurdity. Some have even begun to speculate that they can see the Hanging Body start to fall just before the blackout. I encourage everyone to resist this concept.

The scream is a mysterious, ghostly scream, possibly from another visitor, and the crash is simply an unidentifiable creepy sound. They are no more particular or freighted with significance than the later "spooky sounds" heard upstairs in the Corridor of Doors.

One final tidbit regarding the Magic Kingdom iteration of the Stretch Room show is the handling of the Ghost Host narration itself. Paul Frees was a wild improviser; some of the recording session extracts usually presented as alternate *Haunted Mansion* narrations are actually Paul hamming it up at the expense of Disney. As a result, his perfect reading of the script is not always word perfect, and at one point he included an extra "here":

> "Our tour begins here, in this gallery, *here* where
> you see paintings..."

In 1969, WED snipped out the second "here", resulting in a bit of a cleaner read on the line but which has a very obvious cut if you listen carefully:

> "Our tour begins here, in this gallery, [cut] where
> you see paintings..."

For whatever reason, Paul's original read on the line with the duplicate "here" was restored for the Florida show in 1971. But even stranger was the shuffling of two lines. At Disneyland, the Stretch Room entry spiel plays:

> "Welcome, foolish mortals, to the Haunted
> Mansion. I am your host, your ghost host!"

2. THE STRETCH ROOM

"Kindly step all the way in, please, and make room for everyone. There's no turning back now."

"Our tour begins here, in this gallery, where you see paintings of some of our guests as they appeared in their corruptible, mortal state."

There's then a very strange pause as everyone enters the room and then the maid or butler activates the elevator and the next line begins.

In Florida, the second and third lines were switched, meaning that the line "There's no turning back now" is allowed to both end his opening narration on a much more definite note of warning as well as provide a cue for the Stretch Room door to ominously close:

"Welcome, foolish mortals, to the Haunted Mansion. I am your host, your ghost host!"

"Our tour begins here, in this gallery, here where you see paintings of some of our guests as they appeared in their corruptible, mortal state."

"Kindly step all the way in, please, and make room for everyone. There's no turning back now."

That may not be a gigantic difference in the larger scheme of things, but not only does it contribute to the greater sense of suspense experienced in the Magic Kingdom Stretch Room, but it shows just how exacting WED Enterprises was when it came time to polish up their latest effort for a new theme park and audience.

3. THE GREAT HALL

Both Stretch Rooms exit into a short, dark hallway lined with doors. Few take the time to notice one door placed between the two exit doors, mysteriously positioned on a 45 degree angle. Don't bother trying to open it, it's always locked. But... if you *could* go through this door, you would find yourself looking at the "Aging Man" portrait in the Foyer - from the reverse side.

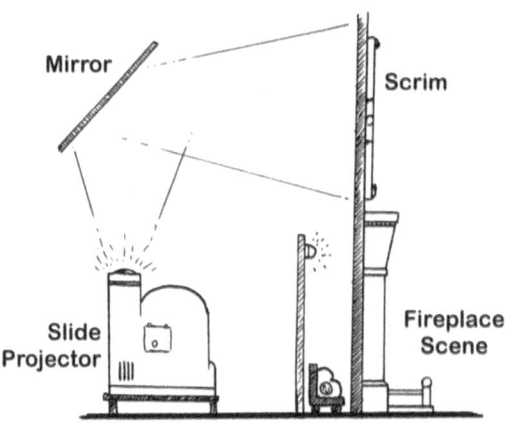

The "Aging Man" is projected onto a stretched theatrical gauze from this small room. In 1971, a large proprietary box built especially by MAPO[8] for the attraction was positioned here, which contained what amounted to an elaborate slide projector. Inside were eight glass slides on two rotating carousels to create the changing portrait effect - the first stage, the Aging Man in his youth, was repeated twice, and the eighth slide was blank.

Originally, the effect was achieved by alternating the lamps inside the projector on dimmers. After the slide being projected by one carousel would fade out, the carousel would advance to the next slide, then fade up. In this way a seamless fade from one slide to the next could be accomplished without creating "the slide show effect".

Disneyland used to have a rash of these in their Hallway to Load show scene. Disneyland's portraits began life in 1969 flashing back and forth in time with lightning strikes; later on they were changed to fade in and out like the Aging Man.

The second version of the Disneyland portraits were a more sophisticated effect than Magic Kingdom's Aging Man; the beams of the projector was interrupted by a pivoting mirror, allowing the portraits to "wipe" from left to right or top to bottom as they changed.

It wasn't until fairly recently it was discovered that the five portraits at Disneyland were intended to go through six-stage transformations. Since glass slides of the six-stage versions were produced, WED intended to install this effect, until the idea was abandoned in early 1969. My guess is that the slide projector used at Magic Kingdom until 2007 was built in 1968 by MAPO for Disneyland's *Haunted Mansion*, and was brought out east when the six-stage portrait effect was eliminated.

The Aging Man rarely looked as good as he was intended to. Depending on the way the slides were mounted in the carousel, the projection would usually be *slightly* off-alignment, resulting in an image that would "dance" around the frame as the eight slide sequence unfolded.

Adding to the difficulty of lining up the slide sequence, the slide projector and the box that housed them was not sitting upright, but *on its back* - the slides were projected straight up, towards the ceiling, as there is not adequate space inside the room to project from straight on. The projection then bounced off a mirror mounted at a 45 degree angle to line it up with the frame seen in the Foyer.

My favorite thing to do in the tiny projection room was to duck underneath the projector beam and look down into the little fireplace space below the changing portrait. The blacklight which illuminates the painted bricks can be seen, and far below the tiny "fireplace log" tableau, with the dying embers in the fireplace, may be observed at length. This simple gag is nothing but a sculpted stack of firewood with a clear window in the front looking down inside, where a cylinder covered in aluminum foil slowly rotates. Sometimes the cheapest effects are the best ones.

In 2007, the original slide carousel was replaced with a digital projector which "morphs" the six images together. Jumping around inside the frame is no longer an issue, however, the more recent Imagineers failed to take the angled mirror into account, meaning that their projection was not being flipped once, but twice, and as a result the man in the portrait now faces the wrong way.

The name of the fellow in the portrait, by the way, is "Aging Man", not Master Gracey, nor the Ghost Host. He's just any old Aging Man.

Over the years, guests and Cast Members have assumed that "Master Gracey", seen on a tombstone outside, means "master of the house" instead of its appropriate eighteenth century meaning of "young man".

This is also how Master Gracey and the Ghost Host became conflated, especially since the only outright skeleton seen in the house, except for the last stages of decay of the Aging Man, is the skeleton seen hanging in the Stretch Room. Therefore, Master Gracey = skeleton = hanging body = Ghost Host.

In 1971 blueprints, one tombstone may be seen for the Family Plot outside the Front Doors which did not survive to park opening but which places the term "Master" in its intended context. It's an elaborately carved stone which reads:

Phineas Pock
Lord and Master of the Haunted Mansion

Imagine how different fan theory would be had *that* made it to opening day!

And if the Aging Man portrait has *already* given rise to fantasy and fiction surrounding it, imagine how easy it would be to completely unbalance the attraction simply by changing this one effect. Imagine if the portrait were Marc Davis' concept for a young bride who rots into cobweb-covered bones; we would expect the attraction that follows to tell the story of a doomed romance. Or if it showed the outside of the *Haunted Mansion* slowly decaying to its present state, we would naturally expect this to be a set-up about the story of the house itself.

The "Aging Man" is really economical because it points towards themes we will see explored inside: illusion vs. reality (the portrait maintains the illusion of youth while its subject is long ago dust), youth vs. antiquity (a beautiful house reduced to a crumbling wreck). Pretty much the only way to maintain the thematic value of the Aging Man while being *less* specific and suggestive would be to have the portrait show an object rot, like one of Marc's concepts for a vase of flowers that blackens, which is a much less effective variation. For such a simple touch it's nearly perfectly chosen, and demonstrates how easily one can send the delicate house of cards down by meddling with even minor elements of the ride.

Accessible from the exit hallway for the two Stretch Rooms is a panel which opens to reveal a control switch for the Stretch Room exit doors, blended into the wainscoting. It's there to control the doors in case of an emergency evacuation, and please don't go poking around looking for it like I did in high school.

Magic Kingdom used to have an especially prankish Maintenance worker who especially enjoyed working at *Mansion*. Ginger Honetor tells a story of giving a *Mansion* tour to the future head of Maintenance at *Phantom Manor*; she was showing him how the Ballroom effect worked.

As she tells it, after explaining the effect she left him alone down there to head back to the Load Area and turn on the show lighting so he could see the reflection effect working. All the way from the Load Area, she could hear the Frenchman screaming! In the darkness, our prankish Maintenance Man had silently snuck up behind him...

This same maintenance worker was one day inside the projection room working on the Stretch Room door control switch. He had it unscrewed from its mount behind the hidden panel just when he heard a trainer approaching with a new hire. Improvising a new prank, our Maintenance man fitted the control switch into place just in time for the trainer to open the wall panel.

The trainer explained how to open the Stretch Room doors, closed the wall panel, told the trainee to try it themselves a few times, and walked away to talk to a co-worker. The trainee opened the wall panel and reached for the switch — but instead saw a man's face behind the wall!

"*Don't make a sound!*" he hissed.

The girl slammed the panel shut and went to get the trainer. When she opened the panel again, the control switch was firmly in place behind the wall.

The girl quit.

The Load Area of the *Haunted Mansion* is officially known as the Great Hall. Many old houses of the early eighteenth century had great halls, a large social space that runs across the entire lower floor of the house. The White House has one that's very well known.

One of the interesting things about the *Haunted Mansion* is how logically organized our experience of moving through it is. We begin in foyers and galleries and proceed through rooms designed for social events - libraries, sitting rooms with pianos. It isn't until we get upstairs, where the *private* rooms are, that things begin to turn really menacing, and reach a head as we enter the Attic - a room of secrets, a room we are not supposed to see - at which point we flee the house through an open window. The increasing privacy of the rooms as we proceed through the house mirrors the peril of the journey.

The *Haunted Mansion*'s Great Hall is done up in flocked wallpaper, baroque wainscoting which suggests skulls, and giant marble urns, suggestive of a funereal atmosphere. At the end of the Hall, a carving above an arch suggests a swooping bat. At the south end of the Hall, an endless chain of Omnimover cars emerge out of a dark turnaround space and proceed through the Hall, vanishing under the bat-arch on the north side.

This is, arguably, one of the first significant departures the Florida house interior takes. At Disneyland, the hallway to load is a *true* hallway to load instead of a dark gathering place with some doors. It's a long, tapering hallway with changing portraits on one side and windows looking out on a storm-battered landscape on the other, and it's one of the most richly evocative things in the whole ride.

After a quick trip past a turning bust illusion, the line proceeds into a darkened space which is neither inside or outside. The Omnimover cars descend a staircase draped in spiderwebs, scoot alongside a moving belt to pick up passengers, then turn and ascend a giant staircase to the second floor. In the distance, blue clouds - or perhaps fog - rolls along the back wall.

At least, that's how it's *supposed* to be. In the early days of the Disneyland *Haunted Mansion*, the "limbo" load area was a weird mass of giant spiderwebs, chandeliers hanging from no visible source, and eerie quiet, but those days left with the rise of the lawsuit. Now a room filled with some webs and some candles, it's too bright and the walls don't fade away - they're plain as the flat black paint they're painted with. Instead of a boundless realm of nothing, it looks like a dusty room with no decorations.

On a straight conceptual level, the Florida Great Hall is a bore. But, while it's suffered no less of a brightening than Disneyland's load area has, because it was from the start intended to be just another room, the Great Hall has improved instead of declined as stuff has been added to it. It's a functional room that gets you into the ride without much fuss, not the sort of place to stop and rubberneck.

3. THE GREAT HALL

Along the right side of the Great Hall, cordoning off where the Doombuggies emerge from the dark, is a chain of stanchions with brass toppers which resemble bats with upturned faces.

These don't take much damage at Disneyland where the queue space is wide enough for everyone to stand with no need to paw all over the bat stanchions, but in Florida they see a lot of abuse. As a result, the bat heads, especially those nearer the pinch point along the load belt, get rubbed quite a lot. But for many years, the very *last* bat, at the point where the queue makes a 180 degree turn to head back towards the cars, had been touched by so many uncountable millions of hands that all of its features had been rubbed smooth!

This fascinating artifact was replaced with the current version in 2003, to my disappointment - the tactile evidence of so many generations passing through the *Haunted Mansion* was beautiful. It should have been put on display somewhere.

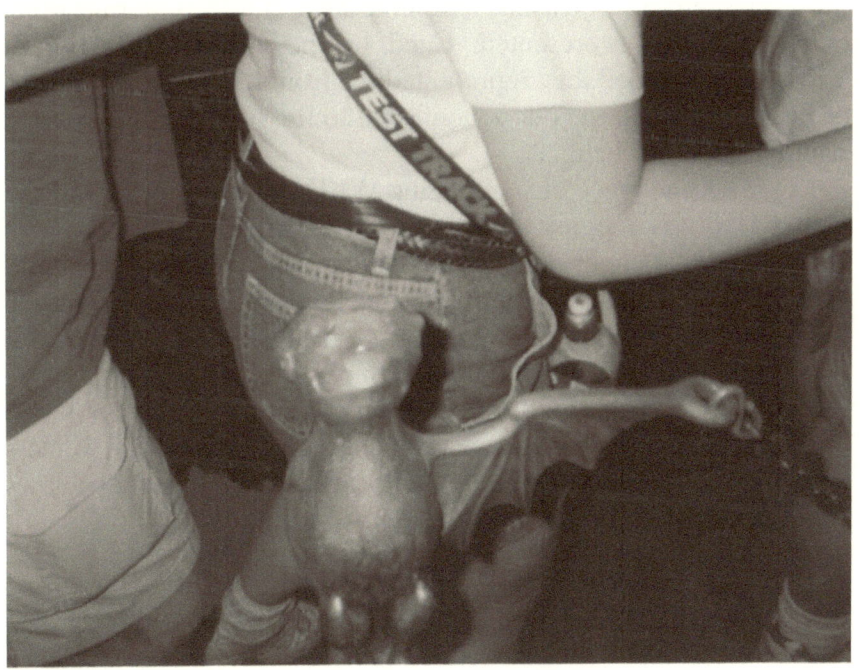

Since the current bat stanchion has only been in there for a little over a decade now, please join me in rubbing your hand on it every time you walk past it. It should only take another twenty years to return it to its perfectly smooth state!

Today it's too bright in the Great Hall to fully enjoy the effect, but originally the dark room the Doombuggies emerged from was tantalizing and scary. What could be back there? Why did a normal looking arch in the house open into nothing?

This, arguably, is Claude Coats' attempt to realize his "boundless void" concept in a more manageable form. The walls in that dark room really did melt away and the Doombuggies swinging out of the pitch black into the semi-gloom did look exactly like shadows were somehow being given form.

I spent an unusually long time as a child wondering what, exactly, the cars represented. Cued by the Ghost Host's use of "carriages", I decided they represented the front of a horse-drawn cart or hearse. A friend in college confessed to me he thought they were giant Darth Vader helmets!

The one piece of set dressing WED saw fit to include in the Grand Hall was a simple tableau on the other side of the chain of Omnimover cars, in a dark corner of the room. It was a small end table with a red tablecloth and a dusty old chair pulled up alongside it. On the table, a *Gone With the Wind*-style lamp flickered as if it were a gas lamp, and an open book sat near the chair.

It was a simple but effective little scene, and the book was one volume of a multi-book encyclopedia, which Maids and Butlers kept open to the entry on "Ghosts". The other encyclopedia volumes could be found in the Library, Ballroom and Attic.

3. THE GREAT HALL

Don't go rushing to an interpretation of this loaded image, it was there for a very practical purpose. The table and tablecloth hid a simple speaker pointed in the direction of guests. The speaker played a safety boarding announcement by the Ghost Host:

> *"And, now, a carriage approaches, to take you into the boundless realm of the supernatural. Take your loved one by the hand, please, and kindly watch your step."*

The placement of the speaker and the props which concealed it had the doubly positive attributes not only of drawing viewer's attention towards the corner, and thus towards the cars, but suggesting that the invisible Ghost Host was seated in the chair, reading a book!

In the old days, the Great Hall was dim and quiet; nearly all of the light was cast by fluorescent tubes set into the half-wall along the load belt, a harsh blue light which fell on the cars and cast tall shadows. In 2003 the blue lights became yellow lights and were toned down significantly thanks to new wall sconces added to the Load Area. The sconces added some visual interest and helped light up the room in a more theme-appropriate way. These joined a row of speakers playing a new English and Spanish safety spiel, housed in indifferently executed new wainscoting and vases above the queue.

In 2007, the Load Area was repapered in a new flocked pattern which is purple under normal light but which has gold paint blotched over it; the gold cleverly catches, reflects, and models the dim light in the room. At this time a new ledge was added about ¾ of the way up the walls of the room and the space above the ledge painted black. This was an effort to create the illusion of a lowered ceiling, making the room a little more attractive. With the moving of many of the thirteen original "moving eye" portraits into this room, the Haunted Mansion's Great Hall is currently more interesting and attractive than it's ever been.

The least popular feature of the Great Hall is a pinch point near the top of the Load Belt which always forces a backup of guests before they get on the ride. The pinch point is not popular, but it serves a purpose.

Following the pinch point, the single-person line proceeds down the west wall of the Great Hall, turns around, then proceeds along the side of the loading belt to the top, where guests board.

This is intended solely to allow guests to first observe the Omnimover cars themselves, then to proceed along the moving walkway and observe the boarding process. It does not invariably help, but it does give a full tour of what guests will be expected to do to continue through the *Haunted Mansion* successfully, and was presumably instituted after experience at Disneyland, where the loading belt is hidden from view until the last moment.

3. THE GREAT HALL

I understand Imagineering's concern, because despite multiple recorded warnings, a substantial number of guests pay no attention to any of this whatever, step onto the moving belt, and promptly fall flat on their faces.

At the top of the belt is the most hated position for employees working in the *Haunted Mansion*: Load 1. The job of the Load 1 Cast Member is to announce the moving walkway and attempt to direct guests into cars.

I have no idea why, but for many guests this simple action is a monumental challenge. Some days, one can simply walk forward and announce repeatedly: "two or three per car, watch your step." Other days, this same tactic will result in guests performing a circus tumbling act.

You hope the guests have bothered to see the moving floor, because if you're saying "watch your step" and turning to gesture to a moving car every few seconds, you don't have time to stop and point directly at the moving floor for each guest. There are several ways to manage this.

The most popular is to stop the first person who comes out of the Stretch Room and reaches the front of the belt, then wait a few seconds before starting the loading procedure. What this accomplishes is it causes a backup of people at the turn towards the belt, which forces people to move onto the belt more slowly and pay attention.

The other alternative is to scream loudly. The Great Hall's tapering walls bounce a shouted command marvelously well, and some Butlers like to constantly bellow "FLOOR IS MOVING, TWO OR THREE PER CAR" until the first guest reaches them. Most often all this accomplishes is creating a lot of unneeded noise pollution.

I must confess that more often than not I did not actually walk on the moving belt. At Load 1, you walk all the way up at the front of the belt, where the rubber tread slips out of a toothed plate. All I needed to do was step forward a few inches and stand on the plate, and shuffle around just enough to create the illusion I was walking. If a manager or co-worker appeared I simply took one, unnoticeable step backwards onto the belt and resumed walking.

This was lazy. But then I saw that this is the way that Maids and Butlers are directed to do it - at Tokyo Disneyland! So you can think of my laziness as a subtle tribute to the hard working Cast Members of Tokyo.

Despite the incredible effort exerted in getting people onto the belt, one could not ensure they *actually got into the damn cars*. Sometimes, guests would get on the belt and simply stare at the empty car, dumbfounded. Other times, they'd step onto the space **between** the cars, which is a thin metal plate that rides along the floor just above heavy machinery and a live wire. Because of this, a third position was sometimes added to the rotation - Load 3 - simply to direct guests into cars.

At the end of the belt, just before the ride proper begins, is the most highly coveted position at the *Haunted Mansion* - the heavenly Load 2. Load 2's job largely involves walking on the belt in comparative peace and ensuring the lap bars close automatically. The bar is lowered by a simple hook-and-latch mechanism under the floor.

Every so often, a guest will go wandering down the belt and try to walk into the ride. Other times, a family will try to rearrange their seats at the last moment and will invariably scowl at the Load 2 Maid as the bar lowers and thwarts their attempt.

Every so often, a mom will get out of the car near Load 2 to shout instructions to the car behind her and the bar will close, locking her out of the car. Almost immediately a torrent of shrieks will result and the ride will have to be stopped, the Cast Member will have to cross the ride path, use the emergency release pedal under the car, open up the car, allow her back in, then close the car.

I have very little sympathy for these guests. Ladies: stop leaving the Doombuggy! In contrast, dads invariably like to stand up inside the car, facing backwards and shouting instructions, inevitably resulting in the bar closing on their butt. This is very entertaining instead of annoying.

Far and away my favorite kind of person whom you meet at Load 2 are the dudebros. You invariably see them from far away, sauntering down the Grand Hall with their arms swinging like monkeys and their backwards "NY" or "LA" hats wobbling back and forth on their gaunt, vaguely featureless heads. These fine specimens of manhood will then fling themselves into a car and slump down in the seat, their long legs splayed out to the left and right.

Here they will come, riding down the belt towards you! They spot you walking along the control console. Their grey eyes will flicker with life! Their mouths will pucker. The endless swaying of their heads will cease as you approach.

Then, the buggy clamshell will close, slamming their splayed knees, and you'll only hear their screamed profanities as they travel off into the house. I once saw it happen to two dudebros at the same time, resulting in a torrent of swearing and, I can only assume, angry punching at each other.

The dudebros always made coming into work worthwhile.

Load 1 and Load 2 are feast or famine. On busy days it can be madness for fourteen hours. On quiet nights it turns into social hour.

Both positions are given small remote controls called "handpacs", which can either slow or stop the ride. Games of toss with these handpacs late at night are not at all uncommon, nor are games of tic-tac-toe between Load and Unload played on the back of Doombuggies with masking tape.

One night, two Butlers who shall remain nameless were playing toss with a handpac which bounced off the top of one of the frosted glass lamp shades in the chandeliers, whereupon the glass fell and exploded on the floor.

Airborne handpacs and guests attempting suicide-via-omnimover aren't the only hazards in the Load Area; guests simply wreck the attraction. Despite two trash barrels inside the ride and many more in the queue, many guests enjoy sitting down in their Omnimover and promptly throwing an empty bottle of water or soda out of the car to their right.

Ride *Haunted Mansion* at the end of a very busy day, such as New Year's Eve, and right after you sit down lean out of the car to your right and you'll see them all on the floor. What evolutionary compulsion causes humans to throw trash to the right after sitting down in a moving vehicle is beyond my ken to know.

Cast Members leave junk lying around the Mansion too; we were simply sneakier about it. It is a longstanding tradition observed by departing Cast Members since time immemorial to leave their shoes behind. The rafters of the *Jungle Cruise* were once draped with shoes, belts, hats, and other souvenirs of bygone employees.

Apparently at *Haunted Mansion* this ritual was originally observed by riding the attraction and tossing your black work shoes in with the junk among the Attic. Every few years Imagineering would remove dozens and dozens of shoes from the set dressing. The ritual died out at *Mansion*, partially because of the rise of the college program - finding new places for 20-30 pairs of shoes every six months would create such a volume of shoes to actually disrupt the show.

Still, longtime Maids and Butlers found a place for their shoes after retirement: in the tall urns that line the back wall of the Great Hall. I never looked myself, but I've spoken to someone who did once climb up the urn and look down. He told me that the shoes nearly filled it.

4. THE WATCHFUL EYES

As it existed from October 1971 to August 2007, the first two rooms encountered once seated on the *Haunted Mansion* established an atmosphere of trepidation as the buggies moved down into the depths of the house.

First passing through a tall room where a stairwell wraps three walls, at the top of the stairway an old candelabrum hovers in midair. This is only briefly glimpsed as the cars then head down a long, sloping hallway lined with evil-looking portraits whose eyes glowed and seemed to follow the cars. The overall effect was that the *Haunted Mansion* was curiously observing *us* as much as we were curiously observing *it*, watching and waiting.

The Stairwell scene has long fascinated me. The ride blueprints give no hint if the scene ever had an official name, and many riders no doubt miss it entirely. As cars move through the Great Hall, attention is directed forward and to the left, where the Cast Members walk on the ride belt. Immediately following the move under the bat-faced arch into the ride proper, the foot of a balustrade with a bizarre, gothic light fixture comes into view.

This is one of the most interesting props in the house, and only after inspection under work lights did I realize that it had been soldered together from a number of unrelated objects. The bottom is a decorative, recoiling griffin which strongly suggests it was liberated from a larger decorative metal piece. All by himself, the griffin is subtly sinister, his clawed hands extended towards the passing cars as if to slash at riders. Atop this, a five-pronged candelabrum has been added, perhaps once part of an outdoor gate lantern. It's passed by so quickly and covered in so many cobwebs that most never think twice about the tone set by this simple assembly of cast-off items.

Eyes drawn towards the left by this bizarre light fixture are then intended to travel up the stairwell and see the floating candelabrum on the balcony above, perhaps for just a second. The

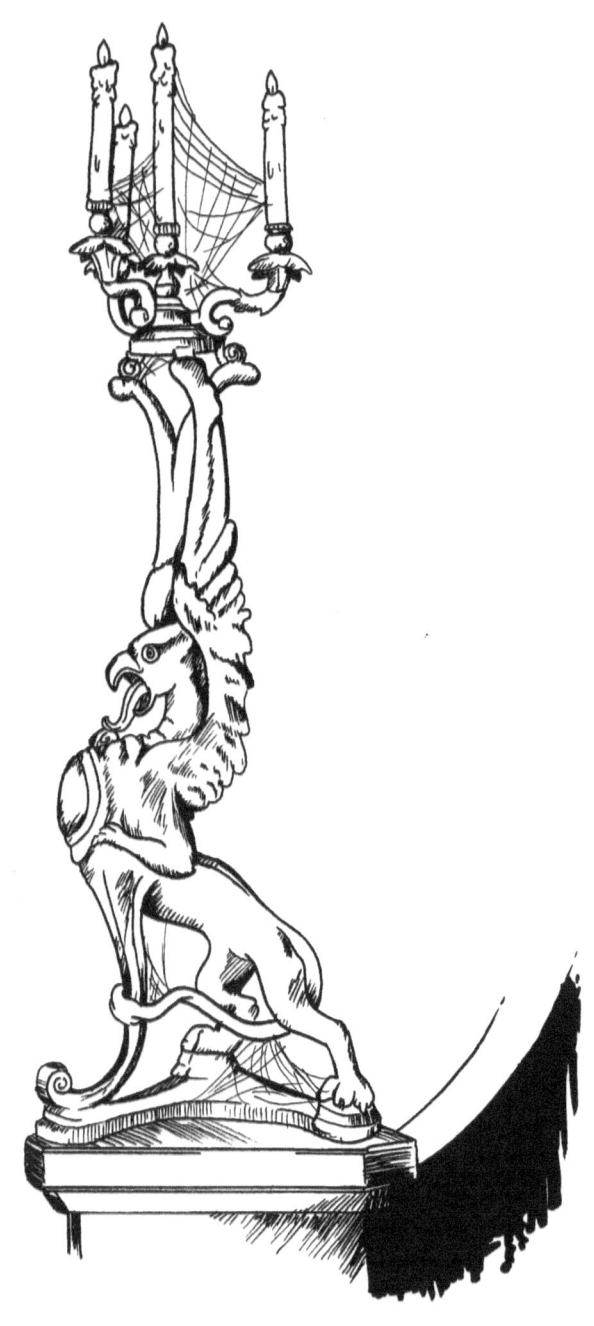

stairwell has more than a decorative purpose; it foreshadows what will be seen once cars ascend to the second floor of the *Mansion.* Just what awaits upstairs?

The design of the balusters strongly echoes those seen later in the attraction's Ballroom scene, as well as subtly reminding us of the balustrade which surrounds the stone terrace on the facade.

What's perhaps most interesting about the stairwell scene, besides the fleeting sense of unease it effortlessly conveys, is why it was included at all.

The floating candelabrum is, of course, the exact same one which is later seen restlessly pacing the Endless Hallway. When I realized this as a child, the very idea frightened me badly. Most visitors, I think, are subtly but deeply unnerved by the Endless Hallway and those dancing candles, and the idea that this same unseen ghost was watching you enter the house, unseen by most, was simply too creepy for my gothic imagination.

But this story becomes more interesting when we learn that those dancing candles upstairs were actually not intended for the Endless Hall scene at all; in all blueprints for the Disneyland *Haunted Mansion* they are actually inside the Seance Room. They were only relocated because the big special effect for the Endless Hallway didn't work out in that space.[9]

There are two clues for what was originally intended: the *Haunted Mansion*'s model as seen in the television episode *Disneyland Showtime,* and the *Story and Song from the Haunted Mansion* 1969 LP.

In *Disneyland Showtime* we see the Endless Hall as it was intended to appear: empty, long, and dark. On the 1969 LP, at the point where the teenagers "Karen and Mike" would be looking down the Endless Hallway, the record describes a ghost rushing towards then down a hallway accompanied by footsteps and screams. And this is more or less what the original scene was intended to convey.

As planned, the view down the Endless Hallway was to be accompanied by thunderous echoing footsteps, which would seem to move towards the cars, then pass over your head, accompanied by a blast of ice cold air. With each footstep, a nearby suit of armor would bounce and shake.

The effect was actually installed during construction, and the Disneyland ride scene still has unused speakers lining it, and more hidden above the cars. It isn't hard to figure out why this didn't work; with cars moving 2-3 feet a second, there was no time to enjoy the full effect from a moving vehicle. Instead, possibly very late in the game, that dancing candelabrum was relocated out of the Seance Room and moved into the hallway to give the scene a focus.

I'd give a lot to know who moved the candles. Drawing distinctions between "jobs" in a collaborative enterprise like the *Haunted Mansion* may be a fool's errand, but it's one of the most inspired accidents in Disney history.

Moving those candles was a master stroke, but they apparently bothered Claude Coats enough that he felt the scene needed a setup. I think most people would agree that the Endless Hallway as it appears now is eerily, hypnotically perfect, but from a creator's perspective it's a quick salvage of a lot of failed effort.

Like a lot of failed *Haunted Mansion* effects, the original idea for the Endless Hallway was revisited by Claude in his *Cinderella Castle Mystery Tour* attraction at Tokyo Disneyland. Our very same thunderous footsteps could be heard - and seen, as glowing footprints - passing by a suit of armor, which would jiggle as the ghost brushed it. They would then proceed towards a stone tomb and an unseen hand would raise the lid, revealing wailing faces and clutching hands. Appropriately, those faces and hands were originally sculpted by WED for the Haunted Mansion - as the faces of the banshees ascending from the pipe organ. It seems that neither Marc Davis nor Claude Coats could quite escape from their original plan for the Mansion as a walk-through attraction.

What's interesting, actually, is that for all its massive import as a theme park classic, nobody in 1969 or 1971 seems to have been totally happy with the *Mansion*. Marc Davis spoke more often about *America Sings*, and Claude Coats would've more likely pointed to *Pirates of the Caribbean* as a truly successful attraction. At

4. THE WATCHFUL EYES 121

Disneyland, *Haunted Mansion* opened in late summer of 1969 to gigantic crowds but fairly tepid reviews, and it's always been more of a cult item there, sitting between *Pirates of the Caribbean* and *Splash Mountain*.

At Magic Kingdom, *Haunted Mansion* occupies the "Prestige Attraction" spot occupied by *Pirates of the Caribbean* at Disneyland. With Magic Kingdom's reduced *Pirates* and less opulent *small world*, the 1971 version of *Mansion* - longer in duration and more complete in conception - is *the* classic of classics, the widely recognized best thing in the park. It has a demand and a queue which lasts all day and sometimes all night, times when its sister at Disneyland is a walk-on ride.

Which is one way to say that, as a "second draft" attraction and one overseen by the principal movers behind its first version, the Florida *Haunted Mansion*'s differences are *very telling*.

WED Enterprises had just opened an elaborate, long gestating attraction that was nobody's favorite, and then was given the chance to immediately turn around and try it again. This is one of the reasons why I'm comfortable saying that the *Haunted Mansion* as it appeared in 1971 is the "Claude Coats Approved" version, and I'll be digging more deeply into the places where the two versions depart meaningfully and how this could reflect its designers' feelings about the ride as we go on.

Following our brief but memorable trip along the stairwell and under the balcony, the Doombuggies slide down the Portrait Hallway.

Originally this was a tall room covered in dark, red and black stripes. Three chandeliers hang from above, each with pale red glass shades. On the left and right walls were hung five portraits each, with one above the exit at the end of the hall. These portraits were collectively referred to as the "Sinister Eleven" by fans until 2007, when the reconstruction of the scene scattered them throughout the

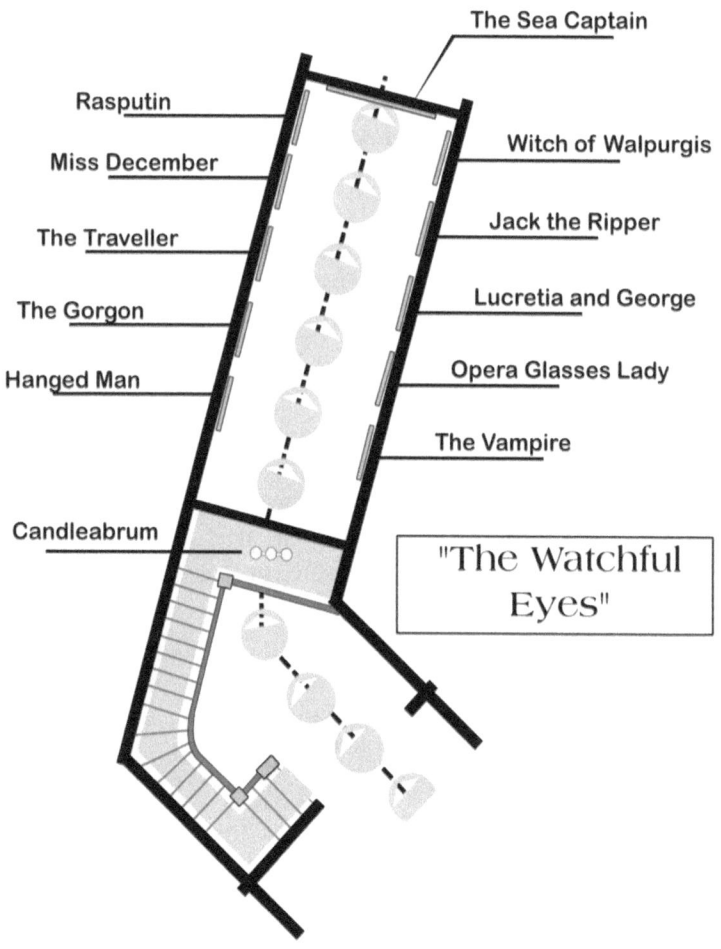

attraction. Each of them was based on a piece of Marc Davis concept art.

There is some disagreement as to whether Marc Davis executed the original Sinister Eleven portraits, as he had done the original set of eight stretching portraits seen at Disneyland in 1969. The Sinister Eleven certainly reflect Marc's bold, unusual color choices and strong, rough brush strokes, quite unlike the refined style reflected in, say, the art executed for the "Aging Man" special effect slides.

I've examined photographs made of the portraits in the 1980s, as well as my own photographs from the late 1990s, and a set prepared for the Tokyo Disneyland Mansion in 1983.

I personally believe that the portraits were done without Marc's involvement. In this case we actually do have a precedent to draw on - Ed Kohn's changing portraits for Disneyland in 1968. Marc directly oversaw Kohn's interpretations, and in places where Kohn's changing portraits hew closely to Marc's concept art, the "Sinister Eleven" portraits diverge. For a full discussion of these portraits, readers should refer to Appendix D.

In 2007, the Portrait Hall was essentially removed entirely and replaced with a new scene. The original black and red striped wallpaper in the Stairwell and Gallery all came down, and was replaced with an orange-colored floral print wallpaper, which here and there has been painted to suggest water-damaged silk. All eleven portraits were relocated, and a new scene was created.

Along the left wall, three windows have been cut into the space between the show wall and outer wall, and narrow little dioramas of bushes, branches, and clouds have been placed behind the new windows, with elaborate ornamental window hangings placed over the scenes. Across the way, four new portraits imported from Disneyland - the Tiger Girl, the Flying Dutchman, the Black Prince, and the Gorgon - have been installed, timed to transform with the flashes of lightning outside the windows. In lieu of a fifth portrait, a small table with a peacock statue, dead flower arrangement, and mirror hanging above has been placed.

The new effect is well done, and in fact it's even better than the similar but slightly older effect at Disneyland, where the portraits look a bit too much like digital images blinking on and off. They aren't; it's actually a light-up image that can be seen through the top layer, which resembles a real painting instead of a projection on silk.

And now we should grapple with an irony. When the *Haunted Mansion* at Disneyland opened in 1969, the portraits in its Portrait Gallery - the scene that our new Portrait Gallery in Florida is modeled on - flashed back and forth with strikes of lightning outside the windows. Then, at some point in time, they did not anymore. The portraits now faded back and forth between images, and did so until 2005. Nobody really knew why. There were whispers that the effect had to be changed due to guests having seizures. So when the new version of the "portrait hall" effect was introduced, it was hailed as a return to the originally intended version.

But what we didn't know until 2015 was that we were wrong. Out of nowhere, slides for six-panel versions of the Disneyland changing portraits appeared at auction[17] and rewrote history.

This wasn't concept art; these were intended to be used as glass slides in the attraction. So, for the first time, it was understood that the original version of the effect in Disneyland was to have all five portraits fading through multiple-panel shows, which was then *changed* to the flicker effect for opening day, before being *changed back* to a fading version later. By changing the portraits back to a fading version, the ride designers were *restoring* an effect they had been required to change.

In other words, the new "lightning flash" version of the portraits does not restore a discarded effect, but discards a restored effect.

After a great deal of research and discussion, Dan Olson believes that the intention was to have the crowd at Disneyland head down the hallway, stop, and then watch all five portraits go through their show, before heading off to the Load Area. In other words, Claude Coats intended the Portrait Gallery to work exactly how the Magic Kingdom Foyer has since 1971, and this is *why* they moved the changing portrait effect out to the Foyer. Supporting this hypothesis, Claude Coats's final Disney attraction, the *Cinderella Castle Mystery Tour* at Tokyo Disneyland, began with a number of changing portraits in a foyer, again replicating the effect that never made it to Disneyland.

So in other words, not only did the new "lightning flash" scene displace the *intended* version of the effect out in California, but by being introduced to Florida it made redundant the whole reason the "changing portrait" was moved out into the Foyer.

The small table at the top of the hall provides a few interesting items to look at as the ride begins. There's a vase of dead flowers placed beside a peacock statue. The peacock is symbolically associated with renewal and vigor, making perhaps an ironic juxtaposition with an image of decay and death.

But even more close to home is the fact that the peacock has been used to represent resurrection; this is why peacock feathers make their way into altar arrangements in many churches at Easter. Thus, on the same table we have two contrasting images: an animal representing vitality and resurrection and a plant representing wilting and death.

The real item of interest, however, is the mirror above this table. Several years ago, I was working at Unload when a guest disembarked the ride with a strange question: when was the special effect in the mirror at the start of the ride added? I responded that I was not aware of any special effect in the mirror, or at least if there was one, I had not seen it yet, and apologized. He walked away looking rather annoyed.

I should point out that this was not a dark and stormy night in Orlando, it was the middle of the day, if not early evening. I didn't give it any more thought until months later, when I overheard somebody asking a similar question to a friend outside the ride. This time her question was very specific: when was *the face of the boy* added to the mirror at the start of the ride?

Now, this mirror does *indeed* reflect in such a way that a portion of the window across the way is reflected in it when the lightning effect goes off, and since guests are in a moving car slipping past this effect, it could easily be misinterpreted to be an image of a face or something. Eyes play strange tricks in the dark. But I've heard of other guests asking the same question, and usually describe it as specifically and exactly as a boy's face.

It wasn't until I was doing research for this book that I came across a purported ghost photograph taken in the Portrait Hallway. It's a nightvision photo taken from a Doombuggy at the top of the Portrait Hall showing the cars descending on the left and the original lineup of portraits on the right. In the photo, a young boy is leaning out of his buggy and looking back up the gallery at the photographer. The photographer swears that nobody was in any of the cars ahead of him.

On one hand, besides early digital camera grain, there's nothing unusual or ghostly about the appearance of the boy in the photograph, and the same image could easily be accomplished today. On the other hand, the boy is leaning out and looking back in a way that's very uncomfortable to actually perform, and what's weirder, he's looking *dead into the camera*.

A photo taken with nightvision has no flash so how anybody could quickly lean out of a car, look all the way backwards to a darkened Doombuggy and look directly into a camera in time to be photographed but not be seen by the photographer is an open question.

But what *is* in that general area where the boy appeared now is our mirror, which some people sometimes say they see faces in. And just a few feet away, for over thirty years, hung the Witch of Walpurgis portrait. And in the upper right hand corner of that portrait is a pentacle for summoning spirits copied pretty much verbatim out of a book on witchcraft.

I don't believe that just having a pentacle posted means much - you have to use it for it to mean anything - but maybe just having that around, in a ride where thousands of people a day are expecting ghosts to arrive, in the same building where an incantation summoning spirits plays hundreds of times a day over the course of nearly a half century, maybe, *just maybe*, that was enough.

Or maybe everyone is just seeing things.[18]

5. PRICELESS FLAT EDITIONS

The Library is the first real scene on the ride, and it's the first scene which begins to hint at the opulence of the experience ahead. It's visually intricate but not overwhelmingly large; the Library is where we first begin to wonder just how large this dusty old house is.

Which isn't bad for a scene motivated by a desire to revisit a special effect. The effect being those eight *"marble busts of the greatest ghost writers the literary world has ever known"*, and the reason they motivated a complete redesign of their original presentation is interesting to consider.

At Disneyland, the busts are situated alongside the queue near the Load Area. This means that as the line passes, riders are allowed to interact with the effect, but this also introduces a problem. From a certain point, riders can also turn around to see the negative bust image from the side, which makes it very evident that the busts are actually a concave surface.

The Library scene is *expressly designed* to minimize your chance to decode this effect. Because the busts are situated about six feet away from the cars, perspective of the busts is limited by the forward movement of the cars. If the ride stops in the Library, the busts appear to stop moving. Because they're arrayed in three walls which recede away from the cars, there is no opportunity to observe the busts from an extreme side angle. The illusion is so perfect it took me years to realize that the busts cannot be controlled by motors because the effect must work for every car passing simultaneously!

The Library has eight busts in four designs, each repeated twice. Since the scene is over and out of sight before each bust can be examined in detail, this is less problematic than one may suspect: hardly anyone has time to look at more than one or two busts while the scene is in view.

The effect is, of course, done by directing the interior of a hollow mold of a sculpted bust at the riders. The busts are made of plastic and back-lit with a dim light, which is the key to the whole illusion and what makes the *Haunted Mansion* version of the effect so convincing.

Generally, the "hollow face" illusion must be lit exactly right to work properly, because the eye's tendency to recognize the human face as a convex surface cannot be contracted by shadows falling around it. By lighting an apparently convex, but actually concave surface from the *rear* means all opportunities for the eye to recognize how the illusion is achieved are removed. It's a very sneaky variation on a classic trick.

There's an even sneakier trick in the Library, but it's one that most riders don't notice. The entire scene is tilted. While the Portrait Corridor sequence was designed to encourage us to notice the downward slope of the floor, the Library hides it by having the central chandelier in the room anchored to a wire attached to the wall so it hangs at an angle appropriate to the sideways pitch of the scenery.

Explanations for this extraordinary bit of set design differ. Some think that this was intended to make the scene "feel creepy", but I don't think that's true. Just a few feet away from the Library, the Music Room reaches the lowest interior point in the attraction's elevation and then proceeds directly up the Grand Staircase. Why design an attraction with a ride track which begins elevated, goes all the way down near the foundation for a few feet, then rises back up? And if you did this just to make the Library "feel weird", why bother to disguise it by anchoring the central chandelier to the wall?

I have established that the Florida *Haunted Mansion* was originally intended to have an elevated facade with two elevators inside it. Although we can't be certain about these things, *could* it be that the entire "Ground Floor" sequence of the attraction - the Great Hall, Stairwell, Portrait Corridor, Library, and Music Room - was intended to rest on the same flat elevation - the same way the scenes upstairs do? Is the Library tilt coincidence or stylization?

And then there's all of those hundreds of books themselves, no more than painted flats. The theatrical flats were painted by R. L. Grosh & Sons, who built most of Disney's sets in the 1960s. Grosh was established in 1913 to provide scenic paint for Hollywood studios throughout the golden era of film and the same company operates today as Grosh Backdrops and Drapery. According to Bruce Stark,[19] WDI executed the Library backdrop for Tokyo Disneyland on site and filled the book spines with classic rock acts. Most of the spines in Florida are blank, although they have attracted the odd embellishment by Mansion Maids and Butlers with paint and markers.[20]

The Library scene is reinforced with a few simple prop gags which begin to more forcefully suggest the "home life" of ghosts. A library ladder is bolted to the floor with a hinge and moved side to side by a moving bar hidden inside one of the shelves, a tactful recycled mechanism from the Carousel of Progress.

At the top of the library ladder are nine shelves of dimensional books, just enough to sell the idea that all of the books are real in the single spot where the eye is likely to be drawn.

There are two animated books which slide in and out of the shelves as if being examined by an invisible bibliophile. One nice touch is that that books don't simply push in and out as they would in a less imaginative haunted attraction; they actually tilt up or down as if somebody is trying to read the spines. Another nice touch, usually unnoticed, is a pile of a few books on the floor by the ladder which have already been selected.

Nearby, the so-called "Donald Duck Chair" rocks by itself, a simple custom rocker mechanism run by a rotary motor attached to a gear shaft. It appears that only the base was manufactured by WED Enterprises, suggesting that, at least at first, this chair was a standard wing back armchair given a distinctive re-upholstering job.

Just past the Library, the Music Room is, I think, one of the *Haunted Mansion*'s most evocative sidebars. The Library is a social space; it's where men would drink and smoke while women went off to a room of more feminine decor and entertainment. As a tiny glimpse of a real social life the *Mansion* would have enjoyed in its heyday, the feminine charms of the Music Room are too easy to glide past unappreciated. The Library is full of dark wood and large, comfortable chairs, while the Music Room has dainty, beautifully crafted furniture and a commanding view.

What really makes this scene work is the window. It's the visual and conceptual centerpiece of the entire scene, and the most interesting visual flourish of the front half of the *Haunted Mansion*. There's the design of the window itself - a giant half-round creation flanked with casketlike carvings, with a top checked in green and yellow stained glass. Just beyond the window, the stone railing that surrounds the facade may be seen, with three dead trees draped in moss and distant clouds moving through a dark sky. It's one of the moments where the *Haunted Mansion* seems to be a believably real place situated in a credible landscape, and it's one of the most basic illusions in the entire house.

The trees, no surprise, are real tree limbs. They're cut down from somewhere on Disney property and painted with clear-coat, the same resin material that keeps the *Jungle Cruise* hippos and crocodiles looking fresh. Three small "muffin" fans keep the moss glued to the branches moving gently, and the clear-coated branches have the extra benefit of better catching and modeling the dim light.[21] The black backdrop is nothing more than a sheet. Since the Music Room scene is situated parallel to - but at a lower elevation than - the Endless Hallway upstairs, the black backing which stands in for the sky is literally hanging off the backside of the Endless Hall set.

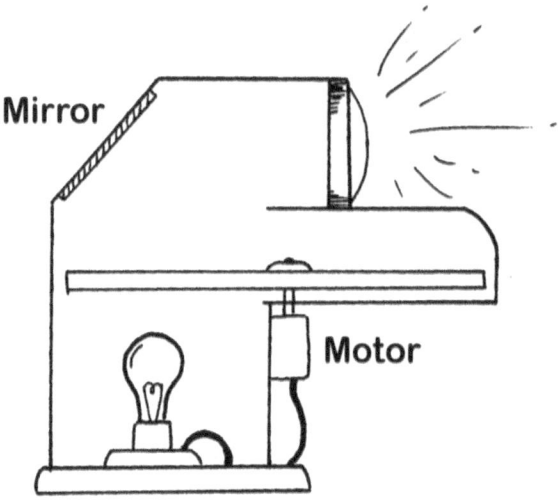

WED Enterprises 10 x 10 Effect Projector

The cloud projection is a genuine Yale Gracey original, and one of the cleverest, most enchanting special effects ever devised. Originally created for *Pirates of the Caribbean*, the versions found at Magic Kingdom are more complex in the sense that they're built into actual custom boxes instead of just perched on top of buildings, as those found within Disneyland's *Pirates* are.

Contained inside a box with a diffusion lens, Yale's ingenious cloud effect boxes are called "10 by 10 projectors", meaning they can cover an area ten feet by ten feet, and are the workhorses of classic Imagineering illusions.

The cloud effect is basically a gobo, or a die cut shape placed in front of a light to create a patterned projection. Gobos are used in the *Mansion* to create descending shadowy demon claws and

5. PRICELESS FLAT EDITIONS

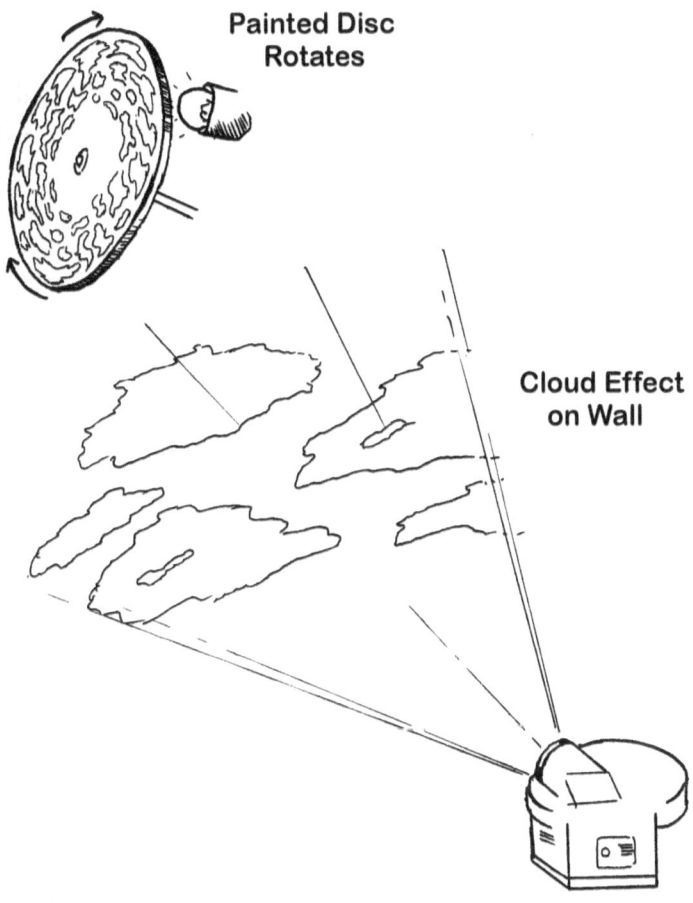

invisible piano players, and the crisp lines resulting from a gobo projection effect would likely be inappropriate for the haze of clouds rolling through the sky.

Gracey's inspired variation is a thick circular pane of glass with wavy black lines painted in an erratic spiral. A light is placed near the rim of the pane of glass underneath a blue diffusion glass while the circular glass is slowly rotated. The projection is then bounced off an angled mirror and through a wide angle lens. The distortion of the edges of the lens corrects the angle of the spiral, and the "clouds" appear to gracefully float by. The blue light shines through and appears to be the "sky".

These clouds are the basis for the fog which drifts lazily through the *Haunted Mansion* graveyard, the rising ghosts as seen from the *Mansion*'s balcony, and - greatly sped up to mimic hurricane-force winds - the ominous storm clouds zipping by the ballroom windows.

Just a few feet to the left of the Music Room window is a detail even less likely to be noticed: an enormous, double door.

At the top of this double door is a half round window, the panes forming an elaborately sinister face. The model of this door may be seen in the *Wonderful World of Disney* television episode *Disneyland Showtime*, being busily "painted" by a scenic shop lady late in the episode. Prior to the 2007 refurbishment, there was a blue light directed onto the rear of the window, making it somewhat possible to see while ascending the stairs.

In 2007, the Music Room was augmented with more instruments - an upright double bass, music stand, and a violin resting on a nearby settee. What at first may seem to be a prop director on a rampage is actually a very clever reference back to the *Mansion*'s long development period.

The great grand granddaddy of the Music Room scene seems to be Ken Anderson, who drew phantom footsteps leading to a pump-action organ, apparently playing itself. Allowing for the different instrument, Ken's piece seemed to be the nearest in tone to the final scene in the *Haunted Mansion*, but his art inspired a deluge of development art in the 1960s. Marc Davis drew white-sheet ghosts sawing away at violins, and Claude Coats drew a formal string quartet of ghosts playing for an invisible dancing couple whose shadows were thrown on the wall.

X. Atencio also produced art for the *Haunted Mansion*, but few of his ideas seem to have made it into the final show. X.'s crack at the ghostly musician concept shows a shadow playing an upright piano - cast on the piano itself, not the floor, by a spotlight. Yet in appearance and design, this matches the final scene in the *Haunted Mansion* nearly exactly. To the left and right of the piano in X.'s art sit ghosts playing - well, an upright double bass and violin. Some attentive Imagineer snuck that one in, and it's a nice nod to a man who contributed more to the *Mansion* than just an excellent script.[22]

There is a lot of romance about the props and details throughout the *Haunted Mansion*, a romance that the house itself carries with it. And yes, it's true that the *Mansion* is furnished with a lot of period appropriate antiques, but it's just as true that a lot of the stuff inside can be more accurately categorized as "old junk". A lot of the chairs, tables, and incidental props came direct from the Disney Studio prop department.

In the studio system of Hollywood, a prop warehouse was a huge on-site building filled with miscellaneous items of use to any production - chairs, tables, clothes, carriages, wagon wheels, and so on. If a film was being made and a dining room needed to be furnished, then the art director could go down to the prop department, choose the furniture he wanted to use, and haul it all over to the soundstage. Major studios bought furniture in vast lots as restaurants and hotels refurbished their interiors, making them vast depositories of the out-of-date. Since Disney already owned this stuff, a lot of it ended up being used here and there around Disneyland.

If you look carefully, a set of chairs identical to the one that used to sit alongside the table and lamp in the Great Hall may be spotted in use on the set of Disney's 1967 film *The Happiest Millionaire*. Other props in the *Mansion* are less glamorous. Most of the flickering table lamps in the house may have been no more than a few years old at the time the ride was new. The release of the film *Gone with the Wind* in 1939 created in the 1940s a craze for gaslight-style lamps appropriately called "Gone with the Wind Lamps". The craze lasted well into the 1960s; Imagineers would have needed to do nothing more than buy a number of these and wire them into a flicker junction box.[23]

Similarly, there's nothing fancy, special, or Victorian about the numerous books that litter the various *Mansion* show scenes; the bulk of them are things like encyclopedias and law books, which is to say they're the sort of books likely to go out of date and need to be replaced every few years.

Speaking of customized props, some of the most extensive customized props in any classic WED attraction were actually found in the 1973 *Pirates of the Caribbean*, especially the final scene at the treasury. Originally this depicted the pirates, having raided the town's valuables, cavorting drunkenly with their loot - and, through an arch behind them, two Spanish soldiers tied to two chairs on top of a table.

At the feet of the soldiers was a large, open book with a sword run through it. Only as a Cast Member could you go up to the table and read the book - the top two pages were a long dissertation on hallucinating faeries! But, if you pulled up the top pages a little, you could read a bit of what seemed to be some kind of large religious tract - I could just barely read the word "hell" on one page and "salvation" on another!

What of the Music Room's central piano? It is a real piano, manufactured very late in the ninetieth century. It's a "Square Grand" in rosewood made by Schomacker and Company, of Philadelphia. Identical pianos may be found on the secondary market today, and the *Haunted Mansion* example is in excellent condition and outwardly quite complete.

Urban legend once persisted that the piano was removed from the *RMS Queen Mary*, itself a very haunted boat. The *Queen Mary* was decommissioned in 1969 and was actually owned by Disney until 1994, no doubt lending apparent credence to the rumor.

Disney owned the *Queen Mary* because it was part of the holdings of Wrather Corporation, which they bought entirely in 1989. Disney bought the Wrather Corporation to gain ownership of the Disneyland Hotel, which Walt Disney had persuaded his friend Jack Wrather to build in 1954 because Disneyland had sapped all of Disney's monetary resources.

In the early 90s, Disney had taunted Long Beach with promises of a "second Disneyland" built up around the *RMS Queen Mary*... provided that Long Beach could make the tax breaks work!

Imagineering designed a resort called Port Disney, complete with a theme park, a cruise ship docking terminal, and an entertainment district based around the vessel. They then proceeded to dangle a similar offer in front of Orange County, promising to build a second theme park across from Disneyland. In the end, Orange County offered more tax breaks and infrastructure upgrades, and Disney sold off the *Queen Mary* and began to move ahead with Disney's California Adventure.

The theme park designed for Port Disney, called DisneySea, ended up getting built across from Tokyo Disneyland. One of the areas of Tokyo DisneySea is American Waterfront, depicting New York City at the end of the Industrial Age, and that land is anchored by a gigantic vintage ocean liner. It's not the *Queen Mary*, which is still permanently moored at Long Beach, but a complete vessel constructed expressly for the park called the *S. S. Columbia*. And that's how the *Queen Mary* ended up traveling into and out of Disney's orbit.

I personally don't think our Schomacker square grand came from the *Queen Mary*, I think it came from the Disney prop warehouse. In 1967, Disney released a fantasy western starring Roddy McDowell called *The Adventures of Bullwhip Griffin*, and the film climaxes in a saloon. Up there on the stage is a piano awfully similar to our Schomacker. At the end of the film it's picked up by a villain and thrown, and later we see it on fire.

It's possible the piano was treated in some way to allow it to be set on fire, or that the Schomacker that ended up in the *Haunted Mansion* was a spare. Regardless, by 1967 this piano was gutted of its internal mechanism, given the way it's tossed around in *Bullwhip Griffin*.

Disney may have ended up using the *Bullwhip Griffin* piano as a second-best choice; a surviving photograph of the model for the Music Room shows a very different piano, with a raised lid painted with gothic details of flying serpents and elaborate, custom carved legs. Perhaps the money ran out to build another custom prop, or perhaps the shadow effect could never quite work right with the grand piano, but it's a tantalizing look at what could have been.

The piano still has its keys intact but Disney replaced the strings with a simple mechanism that pushes two different clusters of keys down with pegs attached to pneumatic solenoids; the weight of the keys brings them back to their normal position once the air is released. I'm told that the fingering is correct.

The Music Room scene ends on a grace note.

Just as our attention is drawn to the piano, suddenly a large metal griffin fills our view, emerging suddenly from the left and heralding the start of the Grand Staircase scene.

Flat painted stone baluster outside music room window – Courtesy Dave Ensign

The idea of drawing your attention to a deeply-set scene - and the Music Room has the most depth of any scene yet seen on the ride at this point - then suddenly and unexpectedly introducing an element in the extreme foreground is pure Claude Coats. It's how he achieved such a rich texture in *20,000 Leagues Under the Sea*, especially in the Graveyard of Lost Ships, where distant ruined hulls were interspersed with destroyed mainstays or crow's nests popping up in the extreme foreground to create a sense of unpredictability. The griffin statue announces the arrival of the part of the ride where the creepy atmosphere is about to ramp up, and there's something distinctly unreassuring around its extended, grasping claws - is it attacking us? Or protecting something up beyond it in the dark?

The griffin is a hand-me-down from Disneyland, and Disneyland actually has two of them - one on each side of the staircase that cars ascend after leaving the Loading Area. However, at Disneyland the effect of the gryphons is somewhat diluted, despite having been doubled. They sit low to the ground, and since the cars are oriented to face them directly - and there's nothing else to look at this moment - they register more as decor, passed on our way to something more, instead of an unexpected and somewhat unnerving addition to the scene.

This is because Claude Coats stages the griffin in Florida so it appears not at the base of the Grand Staircase, but a few feet up it. This means it pops into your line of vision higher than you'd expect a stairway post to appear, seeming to momentarily dwarf the buggies, and it's only after a few seconds that we realize that we're ascending up past it. It's not the first or the last time that the architecture of the *Haunted Mansion* momentarily seems capable of attacking us.

In fact, before 2007, there wasn't even a light on the griffin - it was a dark looming shape in the foreground, claws poised to attack.[24] In 2007 he got his very own blue spotlight and consequently the overall effect was a bit diluted. But it's still a brilliant little bit of staging business typical of Coats, and so effective it hides what would, in any other attraction, qualify as a gaffe. In what other haunted house on earth can one find a staircase with a balustrade that only exists on one side of the staircase?

6. ENTR'ACTE: THE GRAND STAIRS

And so we float up into the darkness. And before the big 2007 refurbishment, there was a *lot* of darkness. The walls seemed to drop away until only the slightest hint of the staircase remained, and at the top of the steps, two enormous spider webs could be seen.

One, on our left, was empty, while a large web on the right housed a super-sized spider. Around a corner past them, hidden behind a half wall, another spider and web lurked alongside the ride path.

For some of us who grew up on *Haunted Mansion* "Mark 1", the Grand Staircase scene was one of the essential moments in the ride, because it's where the ride began to feel dangerously unpredictable. So far we've seen haunted house stuff based mostly on traditional gothic literature and spooky house movies of the collective unconscious past; portraits decay, busts turn to follow you, objects seem to float, and are those eyes peering out from behind that portrait? With the exception of the truly bizarre Stretching Room, it's been fairly rote, although beautifully realized, Ghost Stories 101. But now suddenly the *Haunted Mansion* makes the extraordinary leap of *removing the Mansion*.

There are no longer any walls; the buggies gently float up a staircase attached to nothing and floating up towards nothing. And at the top are irrationally large, glowing spiders. The effect was surreal.

Large spiders are the domain of traditional fairground spook houses, which were often "catch-as-catch can" in terms of content. The idea of juxtaposing large spiders and rickety old staircases isn't even unique to Disney: Bill Tracy, head designer of Outdoor Amusement Displays, had a "stunt" in his catalogue where dark ride cars approach an old staircase with two large skull-spiders spinning erratically alongside it.[25] Of course, there's no real evidence that either Tracy or WED were influenced by each other, so perhaps there's something inherent about big spiders and old staircases buried in the collective unconscious. The idea perhaps stretches back to Universal's 1931 *Dracula*, where Bela Lugosi walks through a huge spiderweb stretched across a staircase without seeming to disturb it.

Disney's giant spider actually came from the *Jungle Cruise*. As part of the 1963 reboot of the "Sunken City" show scene which kicks off the ride, Marc Davis devised a tableau of an ancient shrine protected by a giant spider and three crocodiles. The spider was sent off to the MAPO model shop, and my best guess is that the arachnid was sculpted by Adolfo Procopio, WED's resident wildlife expert sculptor who did a lot of the *Jungle Cruise* animals over the years. And so, in 1963, Disneyland's genuine first giant spider appeared in the *Jungle Cruise*.

In 1969, his twin joined the Disneyland *Haunted Mansion* Load Area which, as originally conceived, saw the Doombuggies appear on a dusty staircase far above the line, turn, then descend through the center of a huge spider web. But WED was just getting started on spiders.

The spider in the Disneyland Load Area was a prop in the truest sense of the term, while the *Jungle Cruise* and Magic Kingdom *Haunted Mansion* spiders were what were known to be "animated figures". Each spider was attached to a thin wire that ran to a small solenoid valve in the floor. The solenoid would open and close, thus gently "jerking" the spider and making it appear to subtly twitch. The solenoid produced a distinct "*click-click, click-click*" sound which most people attributed to the spiders.

Since Disneyland upgraded their *Jungle Cruise* in 2005 and Magic Kingdom ditched the arachnids in 2007, the last place to enjoy this simple tableau is in the Florida *Jungle Cruise*, where two glowing spiders lurk deep inside the Cambodian Ruins. The *Jungle River Cruise* in Hong Kong Disneyland uses about a dozen spiders in their "sunken city" sequence, but none of them move.

Since the Stretch Room the two *Haunted Mansions* have been treading divergent paths; the Grand Staircase scene was, until 2007, where they once again begin to mesh together. In intent it was basically a ride-through version of the Disneyland Load Area: a lot of

6. Entr'acte: The Grand Stairs

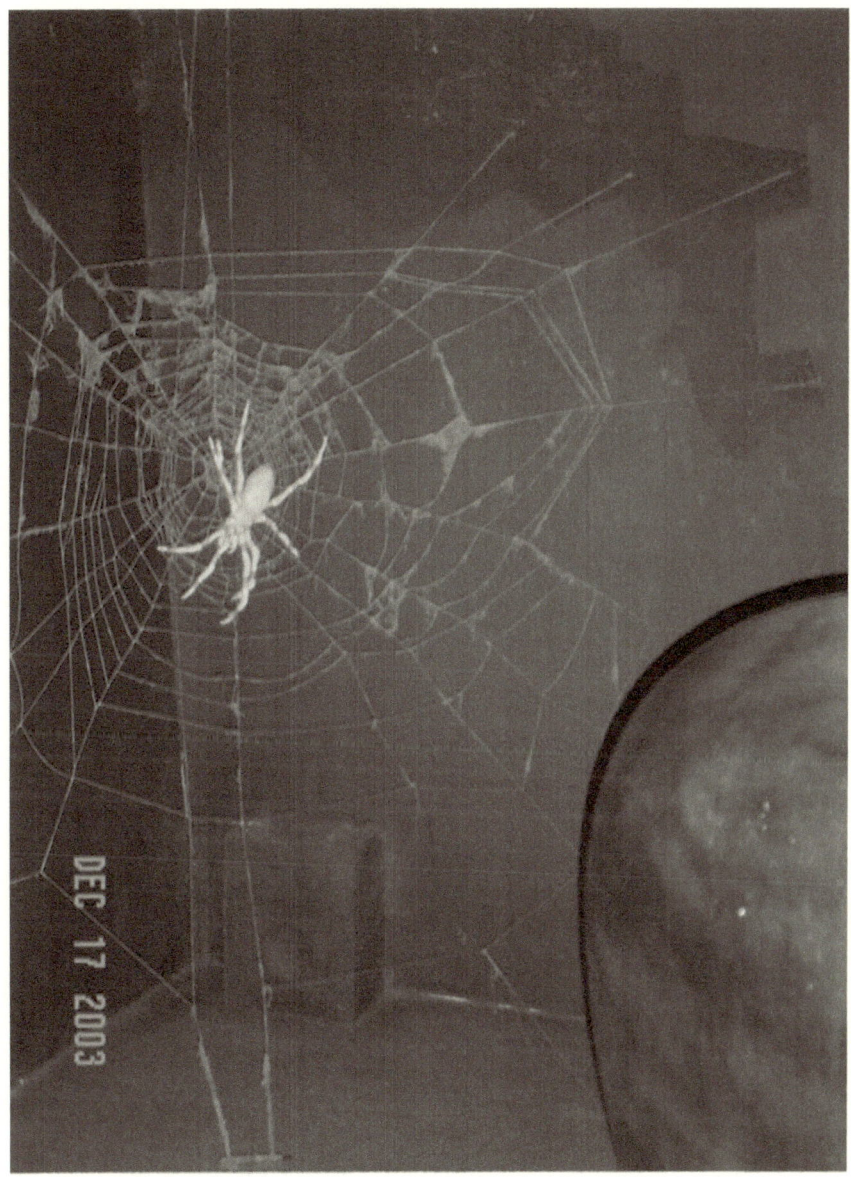

darkness, a lot of webs, and maybe a big spider or two. The effect, however, is quite different in that the Grand Staircase scene - for this is what this was called - is the end of "Act 1" of the attraction.

Where the acts begin and end is an interesting point, in that the *Haunted Mansion* has an abnormally long Act 1 and Act 3, with a short, highly eventful Act 2. I'd carve the experience up slightly differently for Disneyland, but at Magic Kingdom, Act 1 begins upon seeing the *Haunted Mansion* in the distance - perhaps from Frontierland - and deciding to go inside, and it ends here, on the Grand Staircase.

There is a visual break, for one. Perched up on her hill overlooking the River, the *Haunted Mansion* dares you to come inside and discover what's in those old stone walls, and, at this point, you have discovered a genuine haunted house. The "Ground Floor" sequence represents "business as usual" in the day to day of being a ghost - portraits are creepy, there may be some large scale hallucinations, but ghosts also must do things like read books or play the piano and stay active. A hint that you, yourself, could very well be in danger has only just started to brew, and now the cars are silently floating up an impossible staircase with no possible end point towards an unknown destination as the Ghost Host whispers in your ear:

> *We have 999 happy haunts here, but there's room for 1000 - any volunteers, hrm? If you should decide to join us, final arrangements may be made at the end of the tour!*

What was going on here, originally?

When the *Mansion* was in the testing phase in August and September 1971, the scene played out a bit differently.

For one, it is relatively certain that the empty spider web on the left was home to a skeleton, possibly wearing a tattered garment of some kind. Supposedly this "Man in the Web" figure was removed either before or shortly after opening.

And although the traditional tellings of this story do not include this detail, I'm fairly certain that the large web on the right did not yet have a spider in it. My guess is that the right-hand web was intended to be lit very dimly, because it's placed only a foot or so away from a flat painted wall. This is one of the reasons the Grand Staircase looked pretty shoddy for years: because the ultraviolet spotlight required to make the rubber spider glow also dimly illuminated the rear wall, and I cannot believe that WED would have placed the web so close to this wall without considering its show illumination. The triangular web, to the right, actually had a bit of space around it and so could be illuminated more brilliantly without giving away the flat black walls around it.

"The Man in the Web"

If my estimation is right, then this is how the Grand Staircase scene would have originally played out: after the cars slip up past the threatening gryphon statue, they'd ride up into the darkness as the Ghost Host recited his famous "999 happy haunts" narration. The walls would appear to drop away as, up ahead, the only visible thing would be a huge, dimly lit web that the buggies appear to be heading straight towards - again, this strongly brings to mind Universal's *Dracula*. This effect could still be seen until 2007; the spider and web were fully visible from the bottom of the Staircase.

While ascending the staircase, the skeleton and web on the left would not be immediately apparent from inside the cars due to the way the cars themselves go up the Grand Stairs at an angle - the skeleton would come into view only about when the Ghost Host would be saying "Any volunteers, hrmm?".

Then, instead of proceeding directly into the large web on the right as riders initially feared, the buggies would pivot in the near darkness and the giant spider hiding in that perfect "reveal space" behind the wall would come into view.

In other words, the scene as originally presented would have been the first time in the *Haunted Manson* that the *Mansion* itself presented an imminent physical threat to you, the viewer - making it a suitable Act 1 climax. This will happen twice more in the ride, each time at an appropriate moment.

The idea that the spider in the large web on the right was only added after the skeleton was removed is pure conjecture, but is supported by evidence in the ride. For one, to only have one spider in the scene - and hiding behind the wall - immediately solves three problems the Grand Staircase scene always had in its modified state:

Problem One: The right-side giant spider was visible for the entire climb up the Grand Stairs. You could see him very clearly from the Music Room, in fact, then slowly watch him wiggle in his web as you climbed up to him.

Problem Two: The scene had no dramatic thrust. You simply moved up a big staircase and saw some big spiders.

Problem Three: The scene had no resolution. You saw big spiders at the foot of the stairs, then moved past them. It was the only scene in the whole house with this problem.

By presenting an immediate threat to rider safety - you can get eaten by a giant spider and join the *Haunted Mansion* - the reveal of the one and only spider lurking in the dark just as you escape adds immediate value to an unimpressive figure.

Also, this reading aligns the scene with its nearest antecedent - the Load Area of the Disneyland *Haunted Mansion*, where the (vacant) buggies descended a large staircase through a huge spiderweb spun by a glowing spider. Connecting the two scenes thus becomes more logical: Claude Coats decided to shift the "glowing webs in endless darkness" scene to later in the ride and make that spider more of a threat.

In the years following the removal of the "Man in the Web", he became something of a legendary figure. Supposedly the skeleton was stashed somewhere in the house for a few years, meaning anyone wandering the dark, unfinished, rather spooky behind-the-scenes crawlspaces and hallways of the *Haunted Mansion* could come across a skeleton in tattered clothes at any time. Cast Members used him to scare each other until eventually the body went missing, thrown out or recycled elsewhere in the Magic Kingdom.

By far the single person most responsible for keeping the story of the Man in the Web alive was Ginger Honetor, who worked at the *Mansion* from 1980 to 2012. Ginger mentioned the Man in the Web in nearly every walking tour[26] of the Mansion for over twenty years, setting the stage for later discoveries by Brandon Champlain and others.

The common rumor is that the Man in the Web was removed for being "too scary", tellingly the same misguided tall tale told about the Hatbox Ghost for thirty years at Disneyland. Some people even gleefully reported that the "figure" would wiggle in the web while emitting bloodcurdling screams to give credence to the story.

This detail seems to be descended from Lee Nesler, who worked in the artist prep department for Magic Kingdom prior to opening. Nesler spoke to Mike Lee and Dave Ensign in the 90s and told the story of how he mocked up the scene "complete with bloodcurdling screams", but nobody seemed to really like it. He says it may have been in place for only a day or two.[27]

The Man in the Web may never have been seen by riders, but he was included on early maintenance diagrams. These papers indicate no motion or sound; the skeleton really was just a prop. In fact, the only sound in this area, besides the evocative echo from the Music Room piano, was the sound of creaking floorboards as the buggies climbed the stairs.

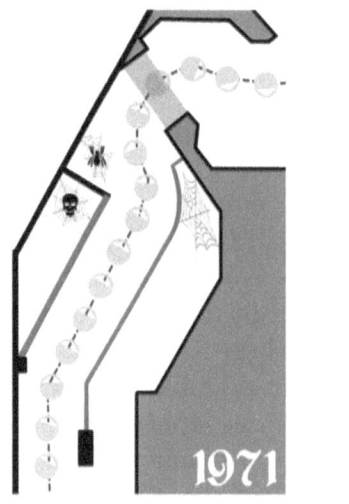
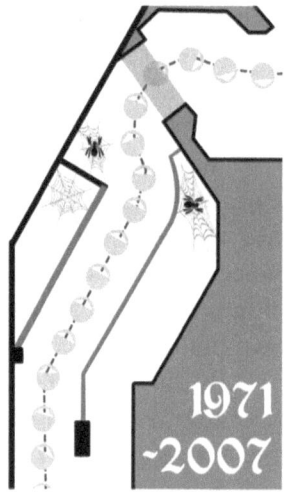

Layout Comparison of Grand Stairs (Theoretical)

Even had the Man in the Web stuck around long enough to be seen by all, I'm not sure it would have made much of a difference to the scene. As it existed until 2007, the Grand Staircase[28] was, amongst fans, the least popular element in the ride. When I began first interacting online, the *Haunted Mansion* fan community was limited to a single mailing list. In the late 90s, the internet was limited to a dial up connection and photos from inside the ride were rare, precious things. Video was totally unheard of, yet we dissected the *Mansion* in what amounted to, for the 1990s, exacting detail. And even in this specialist community, the Grand Staircase was widely derided as cheap and unimaginative.

Which is kind of a shame, because it's got one of the most interesting ideas in the *Mansion* at its core: the idea that ghosts could affect the corporality of the house. The Stretching Room is only the most obvious version of this, because the Ghost Host actually brings it up - is this a manifestation or hallucination? And where did that door go? But in a larger sense, it's carried through the entire show in many ways - from the twisting, labyrinthine interior where doors and windows never appear where logic dictates they should be, to the fact that the house is somehow huge on the inside but small on the outside.

And so we have a section of the house which simply *ceases to exist*, becomes an impenetrable darkness. At Disneyland this was visualized through rolling blue clouds and cobwebs, but at Walt Disney World, it's simply no longer there. The darkened section of the scene architecturally widens to create a subliminal sense of having lost bearings, as if one could simply turn the wrong corner here and be lost forever in boundless black space.

It's a creepy, almost Lovecraftian idea, and as far as I know has only been used in one other horror effort: the goofy but agreeable *House* (1986). There, William Katt's child has vanished inside a haunted house; the child turns out to be hidden in a black space behind his bathroom which he discovers by smashing a mirror. Personally, I've always wondered if the idea suggested itself to Claude through a viewing of *2001: A Space Odyssey*, where the inscrutable darkness of outer space and the "alien monolith" stand in for something unknowable and terrifying.

Which is not to say that Coats hadn't tackled material like this before. He would've been coming straight off the 1967

Tomorrowland attraction *Adventure Thru Inner Space*, which simulated a shrinking voyage into the core of an atom in the name of science. In reality, the attraction was nearly entirely black walls, light effects, and sounds, a totally abstract light-show "trip" appropriate for the Summer of Love.

In 1972, he would design *If You Had Wings*, ostensibly a ride-through ad for Eastern Airlines but in reality more of an extended travel-themed freak-out of polyester, mariachis, and white birds flying though negative space. The *Haunted Mansion*'s "boundless void of the supernatural", as Atencio's script puts it, is the middle panel of this high-concept triptych.

Indeed, as Dan Olson has pointed out,[29] it seems likely now that shrinking was intended to be one of the features of the *Haunted Mansion*, where oversize portraits, doors, and fireplaces were to loom over spectators and make them feel like children. One of the great scary Disneyland moments of all time was in *Adventure Thru Inner Space*, where a gigantic blinking eyeball stared down at riders through a tremendous microscope. Oversize architecture was used very effectively by Dario Argento in his film *Suspiria*, where door knobs at shoulder height suggest that the girls in a bewitched dance academy are actually children.

And this is one valid way to interpret these scenes in the *Haunted Mansion*, where cobwebs are 30 feet tall and spiders are the size of house cats. Reality is warping, things are not as they should be.

Which is not the same as saying that these ideas were a *success* — after all, ideas and ambition don't always collide with execution, and depending on how you looked at it, the "boundless void" was either a creepy abstraction or a big, dusty, empty room.

I said my goodbyes to the original Grand Staircase on Easter 2007. When the *Haunted Mansion* returned in October, the Grand Staircase had become the Endless Stairs, an acceptably eye-boggling take on the famous Escher engraving. And while I may wish that the scene was accomplished with something other than painted metal flats, it's hard to argue against such a visually interesting scene replacing a room with almost nothing to see.

The new Endless Stairs are home to several sets of Claude Coats-inspired glowing footsteps, which climb "up" (really down) staircases, stop at carpeted landings, and blow out candles where they stop. It's a pretty creepy thing for ghosts to be doing, especially ghosts which walk upside down on impossible staircases. And, it must be said, the scene is much shorter than many design teams would have wanted to make it - it takes several seconds for the eye to resolve, visually, what's happening with the architecture of the room, resulting in a total overload of stimulation, by which time the scene is half over. A barely understandable glimpse of something crazily impossible that's over before you know it isn't a bad way to improve a scene.

And, I would argue, it's actually accomplishing the same thing as the "supernatural void" in a more visually compelling way; it offers the possibility that at any moment the *Mansion* itself could break out into an irrational hive of frightening abstraction. In this sense, at least conceptually, this is an upgrade of the scene's original purpose.

Where our second giant spider once threatened, now a short, very effective scene is situated where eyes blinking in the darkness slowly transform into the eyes in the famous "Corridor of Doors" wallpaper,[30] providing something of a "visual overture" to the Second Act. It's a great effect, and it builds on an existing WED tradition, derived from, weirdly enough, *Pirates of the Caribbean.*

At the very end of the Disneyland version of *Pirates*, glowing green eyes peer out of the darkness as boats ascend back to the "present day". It's a vintage Yale Gracey effect, accomplished with nothing but a black tin can with holes in it and a blinking light. The new version is an upgrade, with a terrific "blink" animation, and absolutely nothing about it is a projection effect.

The new scene makes literal a motif which has always existed in the *Haunted Mansion*, where walls and wallpapers may conceal faces and eyes. Ultimately descended from Charlote Gilman's *The Yellow Wallpaper*, there is a reason why the ride designers hold off on that iconic wallpaper until you have moved deep into the darkness of the *Haunted Mansion*. Those subtly unnerving repeating faces may really be ghosts, or again your mind may just be playing tricks on you. No matter, the *Mansion* now has its claws in you - or perhaps more appropriately, has you caught in its web - and there's no turning back.

7. DOWN THE DARK HALL

So far we've luxuriated in hundreds of differences between the *Haunted Mansions*, but have you ever stopped to look up at the ceiling?

Around the corner from the Grand Stairs lurks the Endless Hallway, and the start of the *Haunted Mansion*'s most blissfully brilliant stretch. This is also where Disneyland's *Haunted Mansion* begins, and the location of the ride's first major abandoned effect.

As already discussed in Chapter 4, the original plan was to have thunderous footsteps rushing down the hall towards riders, which would then pass over the Doombuggy with a blast of cold air. In order to accomplish this, WED created a false ceiling. It's a black scrim nailed to some boards, and hiding above it is a catwalk installed to maintain the speakers they intended to stash above the Doombuggies.

In 1969 the idea of panning audio across multiple speakers was not yet as musty as it is now; in those days, most movie theaters and home music systems would've been single-speaker affairs. It wasn't until practically concurrent with the opening of the *Haunted Mansion* that most pop groups would have begun processing and mixing their records with stereo listening in mind.[31]

In the Stretching Gallery the Ghost Host's narration would bounce around from wall to wall - there was no real attempt to "pan" the sound to create a true "traveling sound". So it is intriguing that WED was prepared to attempt a true sonic audio pan as the major special effect component of a scene - with *fifteen* speakers!

This idea had long been germinating inside the walls of the Disney studio. During the production of *Fantasia* in 1939, Walt was unsatisfied that the available sound systems could not fully recreate the experience of attending a concert. As a result he commissioned the creation of Fantasound, a directional multi-channel sound system which ran with the original version of *Fantasia* in 1940.

But *Fantasia* didn't really do much business outside New York, and played in most of the country in an 80 minute, mono version. Only audiences in major cities could actually experience the chorus of voices in *Ave Maria* seeming to progress into the theater from a distance, invisibly pace the theater aisles and then gather at the front of the room below the movie screen.[32]

But twenty-five years later, New York audiences experienced a similar effect in a very different Walt Disney extravaganza - *Great Moments with Mr. Lincoln*.

At the climax of *Mr. Lincoln*, as the dawn sky alights behind the Capitol building, a chorus of voices singing *The Battle Hymn of the Republic* grows and grows in volume. The voices begin at the back of the theater and "progress" down the aisles, growing in intensity as the two channels meet at the central stage. This effect was restored to the *Lincoln* show in 2009 and something close to the original intended effect can be enjoyed today.

A simpler form of "surround sound" was used for the 1967 version of Circle-Vision which premiered in Tomorrowland, with voices and effects played from speakers located above one of each of the nine screens. This system, effective as it remains, was itself modeled on the unique seven-speaker system introduced with Cinerama in 1952.

Maybe the most impressive Disney attraction sound system remains the *Hall of Presidents*, which uses dozens of individual speakers built into the walls and ceiling of its 850 seat auditorium. Besides replicating the "invisible procession" of singers to the front of the theater at its climax, *Hall of Presidents* used five widescreen screens and numerous multi-directional speakers to bring to life historical debates, civil liberty struggles, and the Civil War. It was the first surround sound theater built in Florida and remains one of the best.

So the loss of an ambitious panning sound effect just when the technology was starting to become really exciting is unfortunate. Although dropping the "dancing candles" into the Endless Hallway solved the problem of giving the scene a purpose, it still means that the Ghost Host's instruction "sh- listen!" has no real payoff.

His previous line about "hot and cold running chills" has no payoff either, becoming just another a bit of wordplay. Originally, vents located to the left and right of the Endless Hallway were intended to blow cold air over the buggies as they faced the hall; you can hear this effect described on the *Story and Song* LP and see it on some early maintenance diagrams.

For whatever reason this was either never realized or removed almost immediately. That cold gust of air, by the way, is supposed to be what's motivating those curtained doorways to flutter menacingly in the breeze; that's why you enter the room, see a fluttering curtain, then turn to look down the Endless Hall.

Basically, the scene as envisioned was not realized in any way at Disneyland in 1969, but Claude Coats tried again!

1971 Maintenance Diagrams for the Mansion show that the traveling sound was planned for the Florida show as well, although in a different arrangement. The 1969 version traveled down the length of the hallway and over the heads of riders, whereas the 1971 version began at the entrance to the hallway and turned the corner, traveling past the coffin, in effect "chasing" the Doombuggy track. The speaker arrangement was either going to be different or the catwalk and scrim ceiling was deemed to be unnecessary, because the ceiling in Florida is solid. This allowed two fans to be embedded in the ceiling pointed at the ride cars; although the air is not always reliably "deathly cold", there's a definite blast of air as you look down that hallway.

The traveling sound was either cut before installation or removed at some later date, because by the time I knew the Mansion well the various Jimmie MacDonald screams, groans, and shrieks were played from two pretty well undisguised hi-fi speakers flanking the entrance to the corridor - good and loud, loud enough to startle you as you passed by. In 2007, the original "travelling sound" was brought back to this scene, rushing down the corridor, past the coffin, and ending near the start of the Corridor of Doors, just as originally planned. Details like this are why, until the 2018 Phantom Manor refurbishment, this was considered to be among the best efforts ever undertaken to spruce up one of the classic Disney ghost attractions.

Claude revisited the ideas he abandoned in the Endless Hallway once more - in the 1986 *Cinderella Castle Mystery Tour* at Tokyo Disneyland. This time, a ghostly face would appear in a endlessly mirrored corridor, and in another room, glowing footsteps would brush past a suit of armor, making it shake. The Mystery Tour also included a glowing black-lit spider and projected shadows, making these as certain trademarks of Claude's work as drunk humor was trademark of Marc's designs.

In 2007, new, smaller speakers allowed for the return of the "traveling sound" effect. Upon the reopening of the restored *Haunted Mansion*, the screams and shrieks now seemed to race down the Endless Hall past the Doombuggies before turning and proceeding down the Corridor of Doors. This lasted about two months before the shrieks were confined to just the Corridor of Doors and a new, ominous rumble could be heard rushing towards the cars out of the Endless Hall.

Interestingly enough, during Cast previews the unused 1969 "booming footsteps and chains" sound effect was used - not here, but for the footprints going up and down the Endless Stairs in the new Grand Staircase scene.[33]

The Endless Hall overall may be a slice of perfection, but one problem is that it never looks as long as it really is. The Hall runs alongside the Ballroom and has a mirror at the far end, meaning that it should look twice as long as the Ballroom - but it doesn't.

Phantom Manor actually uses a one-way mirror at the end of their Endless Hall, meaning that their version of the effect really does appear to go off into infinity. One reason the *Mansion* hallways look shorter than they really are is because the dancing candelabrum is so huge. It's wider than the shoulders of an adult, and a couple of feet tall, but seen from a distance it looks maybe a foot wide.

You can get a slightly clearer view of it at the start of the ride, but for a really good look you need to ride *Phantom Manor*, where it's used as a prop in the Phantom Canyon scene. There, directly juxtaposed with a human animatronic figure, you can appreciate how unreasonably large it is.

Looking down the hall is the main dramatic thrust of the scene, but WED still delivers two memorable secondary tableaux to the left and right: the suit of armor and the "Donald Duck chair". Of course the "Donald Chair" is no such thing - it's a Rolly Crump-style grotesque, and it is designed by Marc Davis.

The Donald Chair is fabricated by WED expressly for the attraction, although I have no idea why. At Disneyland, the armchair is weirdly boxy, with a distinct glossy finish.[34] It's subtly pitched forward and the face is unnervingly asymmetrical. For the Florida iteration, a much less artificial-looking chair was created. The job is convincing enough that it's almost possible to mistake it for a stock chair with some new upholstering - that is, of course, until you get close to it and realize just how close together those arm rests pinch towards the back. It's a comfortable looking seat that's impossible to sit in.

I've always wondered if the weird shape and somewhat unfinished look of the Disneyland "Donald Chair" was the result of it being manufactured fairly quickly. The attraction model shows a standard pink armchair in that spot, not a grotesque custom prop. We also know that certain decorative embellishments were in and out of the attraction throughout 1969, and things like the stairway gryphons were only finished by hiring more sculptors at WED. Perhaps the "Donald Chair" fell between two poles - between "must have" and "nice to have" - and this explains the very different appearance of the two models.

I wasn't there to see this story firsthand, so you and I will just have to believe it. For about a year in 2005, the "Donald Chair" went missing in Florida, and a chair in the Music Room[35] was moved up to its place. Supposedly, during a show quality walkthrough, an Imagineer approached the chair and touched it. To everyone's surprise his finger went right through the front, then slowly the whole front of the thing began to crumble and deflate! It had sat there gathering dust since 1971, and was by 2005 entirely covered in - dried spit. The saliva was the only thing holding it together.

Spitting to ward off evil spirits is practiced in India, parts of Europe, and South America, and many Walt Disney World guests like to do it. If you're ever riding through the graveyard and notice a weird glowing blob on one of the scrims? It's spit.

If I seem unusually casual about this, it's because spit in the *Haunted Mansion* is nothing compared to literally anything else at Walt Disney World below waist height. There probably isn't a single square inch left on the outdoor pathways that hasn't hosted spit, vomit, blood, or other less sanitary guest explosions at some point.

Besides, as later-day Pumpkin Kings have proven, there's still less respectful ways to contribute to the *Haunted Mansion*.

Which leaves the jiggling suit of armor. Any suit of armor in any haunted house, of course, is a prime location to conceal a maniac - or a corpse. The one in the *Haunted Mansion* holds a large axe, the sort that has fallen in "Old Dark House" movies since time immemorial - even in *The Berenstain Bears and the Spooky Old Tree*. The axe doesn't fall in the *Mansion*, although the moment we see a menacing suit of armor, everyone is immediately on notice for it to move.

Disneyland's armor was designed to move in a way which accented the "thundering footfalls" sound effect intended for the Endless Hall. It's more of a twitch... the shield lowers slightly and the battle axe tips forward, almost as if it's about to fall. The effect is actually rather nice - it has a subtle "did I actually just see that move?" quality to it.

In Florida, the Suit of Armor was entirely redesigned. It held a spear instead of an axe and had no shield, and an entirely different way of moving. The Florida knight would slowly shift its weight from side to side and move its arm up and down, almost as though it were starting to come to life. The effect, instead of being a kind of "did that just move?" moment, was seriously creepy - you expected him to bolt off the platform and attack you at any moment. In its way this was more appropriate for the escalating tension of the start of the ride's second act instead of the more leisurely version of Disneyland's Endless Corridor, where the ride has just begun.

As part of an irksome effort to bring everything at Walt Disney World closer in line with the Disneyland originals on the part of Imagineering, the Florida armor was given an axe and shield in 2007, and worse, the mechanism was altered to make the armor continuously jiggle instead of slowly shift its weight. In 2014 the armor went under refurbishment and returned - still with the axe and shield, but with its original motion restored.

And so thank goodness for small things.

7. Down the Dark Hall

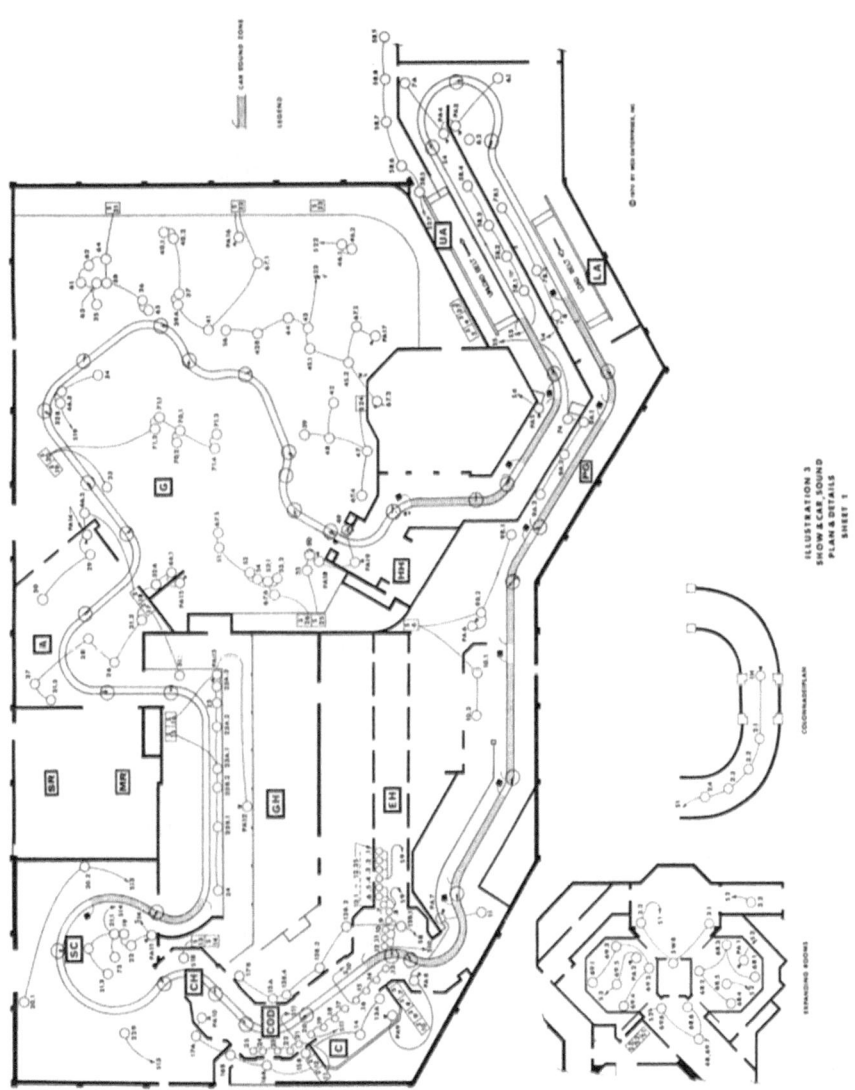

8. TIME VORTEX

If I had to choose a single spot in the *Haunted Mansion* where I feel most at home and at peace, it's right here. As the Doombuggies turn backwards and slip underneath the curtained arch leading to the Corridor of Doors,[36] a deep, blissful sense of zen overcomes me. Life turns on outside the gates of the house and the berm of Magic Kingdom but right here, at this spot, everything is right in the world. It's just one of those spots in Disney - like the long, dark lead up to the first drop in *Pirates of the Caribbean* at Disneyland or sitting at the bottom of the lift hill on the *Matterhorn* where nothing could be more soothing.

Generally, the *Haunted Mansion* operates on instantly visually comprehendible concepts. Our emotional reaction to these visuals act as the tone setting of the scene. We know, innately, that things are getting scarier once we approach the Endless Hallway because it's dark, dim, and unfriendly looking. The Grand Ballroom is grander than we could ever imagine in the seconds before we see it - grander than is rational for the house to contain. Its awesome size corresponds to our amazed emotions.

Clear, concise visuals orient us geographically inside the house. There is no question that we have found the Attic, for example, because we see unfinished wooden beams, dormer windows, and forgotten objects.

How unlike real life this is. In real life, with its messy adjuncts and uncinematic transitions, we generally take longer to orient ourselves in a new environment than microseconds. But there's two spots in the *Haunted Mansion* where the designer's unerring eye for the instantly visual comprehensible failed them totally. We'll come to the second one later, but the first is the Conservatory sequence.

Conservatories became popular in eighteenth century Europe as a way for the nobility to grow valuable but delicate tropical fruits in northern climes. They weren't really an American thing at

8. TIME VORTEX 163

first - the colonies got their citrus directly from the Caribbean - but as always anything popular with the continental wealthy was eventually copied here in the states.

Given the Victorian preoccupation with gardening, a conservatory full of creepy old plants entered into the lexicon of the haunted house. There is something romantic and powerful in the notion of a glass room filled with dead plants, their collector long turned to dust. It's a powerful image of wealth and status turned to neglect and decay, and it implies a little story.

Hill House in *The Haunting* (1963) has a big old glass conservatory, with a creepy statue which may or may not sometimes be watching. That's not what I call a "smoking gun" source, but it is a possible source. Or perhaps the *Haunted Mansion*'s Conservatory tableau is an update of one of those classic spook house "stunts" where the little cars barrel towards an open casket, only to have a body shriek as it sits up; the Pretzel Amusement Company manufactured these gags under the name "Dead Dan".[37]

In truth there always seems to have been a plan for a room in the house with a large window. Ken Anderson's earliest plans for the *Haunted Mansion* included a large room with a picture window and a moonlit landscape beyond. Anderson had the Headless Horseman ride past in this scene, and ghosts were to begin rising up from a distant graveyard.

A 1964 script treatment for the *Mansion* written by Marc Davis - back when the show was still a walking tour - describes a crucial scene taking place in "a room that has a garden view". The Ghost Host reveals that a bride and her fiancée were murdered in this room, before materializing out of a rainstorm outside the windows and revealing that he was the murderer, at which point guests were expected to flee the room![38] The notion of large windows, gloomy weather, and death may have evolved into the Conservatory we know today, a scene which synthesizes these suggestive elements while dispatching with the plot elements.

Why is a funeral still laid out upstairs? Dan Olson[39] thinks this suggests rapid abandonment. A family member passed[40] but *something* so horrible happened that everyone fled the house, never to return again. Or perhaps we could be seeing the last of the family line - the last family member passed on, there were no heirs, but enough money for the house staff to continue to attend to the place, so they left him stretched out upstairs in the Conservatory. Nobody lives up there anymore, but sometimes they hear sounds...

But perhaps thinking about this literally is beating around the wrong bush. I think the meaning of the scene has to do with clashing visual concepts, an approach generally seen in the *Mansion*'s changing portraits - those unused ones where a vase of roses wilts and dies or a young bride instantly rots into bones.

In this case, we see a conservatory - a place of life - that's become home to a funeral, an image of death. The scene hinges on this imagistic power. It's a dreamlike image, irrational and scary, but that's what the *Haunted Mansion* has been driving towards for these past few minutes. The twist is that the corpse is alive and kicking.

So maybe it is just another checkmark on the list of "stuff you expect to see in the haunted house", and this is a twofer: rotted old conservatory and a funeral. What kind of haunted house doesn't have a coffin laid out somewhere?

Disney's done stuff like that before. In constructing Walt Disney World, Walt Disney Productions did polls on things folks would like to see when they visit Florida, and white sand beaches and palm trees were on the list. So Disney planted palm trees and put down white sand beaches and placed them to be clearly seen from the monorail - just one more thing visitors would not feel compelled to leave Walt Disney World to seek out.

The Conservatory is the starting pistol for the rising action of the attraction's second act. The scene was designed for the Disneyland house, where it serves a much more definitive purpose. At Disneyland, we've only *just* seen pretty undeniable evidence of a ghost: an object floating in midair. The Stretch Room and Portrait Gallery could, possibly, just be a hallucination - especially following the Ghost Host's suggestion of such, pointedly the same thing many people who are seeing real-for-real ghosts in real life say to themselves. As such, the Endless Hallway represents daily life in the *Haunted Mansion* - and now, suddenly, something changes.

In Florida, we've already had a lot of "day to day life" material already - ghosts reading books, playing piano, yet it's all been pretty laid back so far. And thus when we get upstairs and it's super creepy, and there's screams echoing everywhere, it feels like the fire is turning up on us although we don't know why. Both Conservatory scenes, therefore, serve the same function but have different meanings. They both set up the séance, but each feels like a different dramatic beat depending on what has come before it.

Why does all hell break loose at this point in the *Haunted Mansion*? Taken as is, exactly the way the show presents it, one could believe that we see the coffin being pried open because the séance down the hall has already begun, and I admit that this is the interpretation I tend to side with. However, there is another way of thinking about it. An even creepier suggestion is that the ghosts are responding to *you*.

In classic ghost cases, especially poltergeist cases, often a rash of supernatural activity is set off by the presence of a teenager in the house - suggesting that pubescent sexual and anxiety energies can literally feed otherwise dormant supernatural entities that exist anywhere, everywhere.

Indeed, people who live with especially scary ghosts can become trapped in cycles of anxiety, leading to ever greater and greater supernatural manifestations as the ghost "feeds" off their fright.[41] Some even believe that ghosts can be willed into existence by belief in them, and these entities are sometimes called "thought forms" and are said to very quickly turn nasty.

The standard narrative ploy of the theme park attraction is "something goes horribly wrong". In this interpretive scheme, the thing that went horribly wrong was *you walking in the door.*

Lending possible credence to the theory is some narration which was apparently cut from the *Haunted Mansion* either shortly before or shortly after opening. It was restored at Disneyland in 1995, then removed in 2004 or thereabouts.

Mansionologists can have endless debates about whether or not these lines can be considered "canon". I feel that they were removed for a reason and not repeated at Magic Kingdom or Tokyo Disneyland, so I view their status as questionable. They read:

> **At the Coffin:** *All of our guests have been dying to meet you. This one can hardly contain himself!*
>
> **At the Corridor:** *Unfortunately, they all seem to have trouble getting through.*
>
> **At the Clock:** *Perhaps Madame Leota can establish contact. She has a remarkable head for materializing the disembodied!*

Except for actually naming Madame Leota, I think this is obviously second rate Atencio. Still, if you believe that the ghosts start raising hell in reaction to your "sympathetic vibrations", and that the séance lasts only so long as you are in the room, then this bit of narration is a clincher, and supported by the subsequent comment about the spirits "having received your sympathetic vibrations".

But really, if we want to be strictly practical, the coffin scene is there to set up the subsequent sequence as we head down the Corridor of Doors. Edgar Allen Poe, J. Sheridan Le Fanu and H. P. Lovecraft wrote stories based on the expressive power of escaping from a tomb, and this loaded image of the return to life presages the part of the *Haunted Mansion* I think is truly scary.

The ride isn't generally considered to be scary; most reviews, and indeed most young boys under the age of twelve blurt this out at the exit. And yes, it isn't scary in the *contemporary* sense of the term; there's very few cheap scares and no creepy long haired children flickering in and out. It belongs firmly to a much older fashioned form of scary. Its suspense is largely child-friendly.

But the *Mansion* does have plenty of things in it that can get under your skin. The idea is banished too soon for it to sink in, but the suggestion of being trapped in a room with no windows and no doors, and having to hang yourself to escape, is not a pleasant thought. Neither is the idea that there's some moldering old corpses stashed up in the Attic. And, although I've touched on this before in this text, that floating candelabrum is not the sort of thing you'd want to glimpse floating past your bedroom door late one night.[42]

This sort of horror is called "Icebox Horror" because it creeps up on you late one night as you're standing there in front of your fridge trying to find something to eat. Everything from the tiny, shrunken woman who begs you to "hurry back" to the notion that you could turn a corner - any old corner - in an old house and stumble into a gigantic black void never to return, the attraction is rife with seriously upsetting ideas. The epicenter of this is the Corridor of Doors scene.

The tone is set immediately by the fact that the buggies turn and head down the scene *backwards*, something they do not do anywhere else in the ride. In the *Mansion*, our view is already restricted by the set design and direction of the car, but inside the Corridor of Doors, the sinister edge of the visuals threaten to boil over. We can't see what we're coming up on next, and the visual tension this generates is palpable. There's nothing quite so unnerving as a blind corner - think of Danny on his tricycle turning that corner in *The Shining* - and the *Mansion* generates one for us entirely through blocking.

What are the Doombuggies? They aren't actually really themed to anything - in fact, in the strictest sense of the term, they're out of place, but who actually looks at how dumb that chain of pods looks once you're actually inside the ride? Nobody, that's who. Just as nobody questions what a conveyer belt is doing in a Victorian mansion. This is the "white noise" that the genre of the theme park has taught us to mentally screen out - like the edges of the movie screen.

The Doombuggy represents **us**, on foot. Although we are seated on the ride, notice that the cars are elevated so that the height loss is minimal - walking through the *Mansion* isn't grossly different than riding through it.[43]

Largely, the buggies represent your perspective as you move through the house, turning to face points of interest in the same way your head would turn. And yet, when they flip around and move backwards down the hall, the disturbing effect is that the ride is no longer obeying the rules it had established. It feels as if you're being drawn involuntarily into a vortex, while all around you reality goes haywire. Door knockers knock - as possible allusion to the "gentle knocking" of Poe's *The Raven* - handles turn, ghostly voices are heard taunting you from behind every locked door, and just when it seems like it's too much, the doors begin to warp and weft in impossible ways.

There are two dark hearts of the ride - this scene and the Attic - and they're bisected with the key visual sequences of the ride, the Ballroom and Séance. The fact that the ride is being actively frightening whenever it's not being visually eye-popping is what contributes to the sense of escalating chaos in its second half.

In Florida, the Corridor of Doors takes the extra step of dispensing with theatrical lighting. Disneyland's scene had three flower-style gas lamp chandeliers lighting the way down the hallway, entirely for show - the scene is lit with pale blue and white spotlights. Florida's version replaces the downward-facing flower gas jets with New England-appropriate hurricane lamp chandeliers. The flickering, shifting light created by these became the scene's primary source of lighting, lending the hallway a credibly dangerous atmosphere.

Each individual door effect is supplemented with small pocket spotlights drawing attention to moving door knockers, or a twisting handle. Accentuating the effect, each hurricane glass lamp was fitted with a red glass shade, turning the trek down the Corridor of Doors into a shifting world of dull red light. What feels wide and safe under white and blue light at Disneyland feels narrow and suffocating under dim red light at Magic Kingdom. The doors were given a subtle green wash to make them visually 'read' as brown under the red light.

Disneyland's upstairs corridor was lined with ghoulish photographs - literally dressed up versions of the pop-up ghouls from the Attic and Graveyard, outfitted with various hats and wigs and printed as sepia-toned cameos. Magic Kingdom dispensed with these props - the only wall hanging was the "Tomb Sweet Tomb" sampler near the end of the hall, hung at a jaunty angle. This meant that the movement on each individual door was much more apparent to riders as they passed. The only prop in the scene was a dusty-dead plant in a corner and, at the end of the hall, a small table with a flicking lamp atop it.

One detail that was **not** changed in Florida is what I think is the most inexplicably popular detail from the ride, which is the famous custom wallpaper. I say "inexplicable" not because it's bad, but because the wallpaper never played as large a role in the ride as it does in the fan iconography of it.[44]

How did a big purple wall of faces end up in the *Haunted Mansion*? Like other effects in this scene, it is said to come from *The Haunting*. Late at night, the main character in that film hears a voice emanating from an empty room while the camera tracks into a detail on the wall which increasingly resembles a face.

Almost everyone agrees that the "demon wallpaper" seems to be descended from this scene. But the face in *The Haunting* and the demon faces covering the walls of the *Haunted Mansion* just aren't that similar at all; for one thing *Haunting* director Robert Wise's camera finds an eyes and mouth in the *negative* space of a textured wall, and the *Mansion* faces are just plain old *part* of the wallpaper pattern.

The piece of art which inspired the pattern isn't shown much, which is a shame because seeing it makes the connection obvious. It's Rolly Crump's idea for a man eating plant.

This version of the chain of influence is the only one that makes any sense to me because it's the only version that explains how those faces ended up on that wall. It's because they're scary plants, and plants are what you usually see on wallpaper.

In this context, the "demon wallpaper" snaps into focus as a very creative twist on the idea seen in *The Haunting*. Thanks to Tom Morris, we now know that the design was created by Tania McKnight under the supervision of Claude Coats as part of the Mansion's interior design team led by Dorothea Redmond. As Dan Olson has pointed out, all of the other (stock) wallpapers in the attraction seem to be chosen for their resemblance to this pattern. We can pick out faces in nearly any Victorian floral pattern, but as the ride becomes scarier the faces become real!

At the end of the Disneyland Corridor of Doors, there occurs one of the few definitive links between the *Haunted Mansion* and *The Haunting*. We now know that *The Haunting* was in fact screened for the Mansion team in 1967. There's a lot of things they

could have been inspired by, but here in the Corridor of Doors is the single "smoking gun" - a door that bulges outward.[45]

In *The Haunting*, a scary high point of the film occurs when all of the characters are gathered behind a sealed door, on the other side of which a ghost lurks. The ghost wants to get into the room where they are but can't, and the door begins to heave forward in a menacing way. The effect is quite subtle but, designed to appear as it did on a screen 60 feet wide, pretty frightening. It rides the borderline between plausible and outright impossible.

MAPO replicated what's seen in *The Haunting* as well as they could. The two final doors bulge outward surrealistically while, from behind each door, unnatural and frightening sounds may be heard - another scary moment lifted from *The Haunting*.

But somehow the lighting of the scene makes these two final effects appear to move less than they do. I've brought many first time riders through the Disneyland *Haunted Mansion* who simply didn't see it at all.

The breathing door *would* be seen at Magic Kingdom. The dimmer lighting of the corridor, besides setting a stronger key note of danger, was intended to help highlight the new breathing door effect. At Disneyland, just as in *The Haunting*, the edges of the door remain firmly sealed and only the center bulges outward. The Magic Kingdom door is held into its frame only at the corners and the entire door heaves forward. From behind the door, a ghoulish green light shines. The effect is almost cartoonish, but barely glimpsed at the end of a dark hallway, it's also pretty scary. The payoff to these green lights is when we turn the corner into the séance room and see a green point of light dancing along the rear wall.

Many riders at Disneyland fail to notice that the final door in the Corridor bulges outward as well. If a rider is looking left at this exact spot in the *Haunted Mansion*, her attention will be directed upward by the Tomb Sweet Tomb motto. The car then pivots left and past the final door, directing attention up and away from the last effect.

I suspect that Coats noticed this and that the bare walls in the Magic Kingdom Corridor were a deliberate strategy to draw attention to the Tomb Sweet Tomb motto, which is why it was twice as large and hung at a crazy angle. From there, anybody looking left would already be positioned to see the new topper gag in the Corridor: a pair of dead-looking hands prying off the top of the final door from within. Green light shone around the cracks.

All of these door gags originate from Marc Davis. Marc's doors were more whimsical, networked with chains and multiple locks. Several Davis gags had long, dead looking arms burst through the door, grasping for the handle.

Another, extremely chilling piece shows one of the upper carved panels in the door sliding open to reveal evil-looking eyes. It's next to impossible to imagine any of these working in the *Haunted Mansion* as we have it; Marc and Claude wisely withheld the single "arm-sticking-out-of-a-door" gag for the very end of the *Haunted Mansion*, where it feels earned.

Some commentators object to visible hands and arms at this point in the ride. I agree that Marc's drawings were overkill, but the hands on the door felt essential to me. It was *just enough* of a visual cue: ten fingertips, just barely glimpsed. They not only provided a topper to the scene, but felt as if the riders were now in more peril than ever before - now there's a ghost mere inches away, just on the other side of that door, and not a friendly one.

Are the hands on the door, and on the coffin as well, corporeal? Dan Olson thinks that the hands on the coffin represent a ghost still trapped inside his decayed mortal body,[46] but given the fact that I grew up seeing *two* pairs of hands at this point in the ride, I'm not quite convinced. Despite the apparent corporeality of both sets of hands, they both struck me as totally plausible ghost hands, or at least monster hands. The hands represented the idea of ghosts trying to tear past barriers to get at me.

This portion of the ride seems fascinated with hands! It only made poetic sense to turn the corner to face the grandfather clock only to see the shadow of another hand crawling across the wall.

At Disneyland, the shadow hand descends down and to the right, as if to grab riders, but at Magic Kingdom it swept across and to the left. At Magic Kingdom, my assumption always was that the ghost behind the door we had just seen had burst through, and now was stalking behind the Doombuggy, out of sight in the shadows. I'm not sure which version is scarier: a shadow hand that drops out of nowhere to grab you, or a monstrous ghost lurking just out of sight behind your car. At no other point does any attraction so strongly resemble the logic of a nightmare.

The emblem of the second floor of the *Haunted Mansion*, and indeed to me of the entire ride, is the short scene officially known as the Clock Hall. You sweep past the clock, its hands madly spinning out of control as you press on, shadows of hands wiping across the clock face, hands carved into its sides, and reality seems to be undone.

As John Hench points out,[47] Magic Kingdom and Disneyland are reassurance machines. Everywhere we look, decisions have been made for us; trash is swept up, things are freshly painted. These things, we understand, have been done *for us*, for our pleasure. Buildings are charming and quaint, and we are not presented with too many choices at once. These parks don't cheat on us or mislead us. We trust them.

Clocks stand throughout as reminders of civility and order. At Magic Kingdom a huge clock is positioned above City Hall; another helpfully on Main Street,[48] and a third beams down from the Train Station. Everything is on time, these clocks say to us, nothing is out of sorts.

A huge clock fills the front of Cinderella Castle, and another atop the *Hall of Presidents* deepens the associations. Even Fantasyland's Village Haus has a working glockenspiel that chimes at 15 minute increments. Riverboats and presidents perform on time; the rafts to Tom Sawyer Island never stop running, and the logs at *Splash Mountain* drop regularly. A theme park in full operation is like the clock itself, with millions of tiny little pieces all ticking away in harmony.

Remember the famous image of the fellow who hangs off the minute hand of a clock? He wears horn rim glasses and a boater hat. His name has largely been forgotten by posterity but his name is Harold Lloyd and he was once the highest-grossing comedian in the world. Harold hanging off the clock comes from his 1923 hit comedy *Safety Last!*, but the image has outlived both the man and his fame.

That image is eternal because it's both precise and general; it represents both us and all of modernity. It's open ended; nobody questions how Harold got in that situation because we've been there ourselves. The key to the image is that he can fall off the clock; how much more common and typical the image would be if the clock could fall on him. We're used to seeing giant clocks bearing down on people, like the villain in *Castle of Cagliostro* who's crushed between the minute and second hand of Big Ben.

8. TIME VORTEX

The *Haunted Mansion*'s grandfather clock is an image of a similar power. Consider how *right* it is, and how easily it could have gone wrong; the minute hand sweeps forward wildly, so there's no misapprehension that we're time traveling or any such nonsense. The hour hand remains fixed on the number "13", which has replaced the number 12 on a typical clock face. It's the only number on the clock face, so we aren't distracted thinking about 3, or 6, or 9. The clock chimes continuously, alerting us to the notion that it's chiming an hour, and so we understand that it's chiming 13, yet any attempt to analyze it further is defeated by the wildly spinning minute hand. The clock itself is the face of a snarling beast, its forked tail the clock's pendulum. It's an image of total conceptual anarchy, madness. Yet it's perfectly clear; we see it for less than 5 seconds but everyone understands it clearly.

This is what pulled us backwards down the Corridor of Doors, this pure slice of madness waiting at the end. We were swept down the hall against our will and the clock is like the eye of the maelstrom, where none of the signifiers of our reality are valid. The secret at the heart of the *Haunted Mansion* is that all those reassuring clocks we walked past on our way into the park are no longer reliable.

2007 saw a number of changes to the Corridor of Doors undoing some of the work that Claude Coats put into the Florida-specific revisions.

The ghoul photographs belatedly arrived and, although they're very creepy, do have the effect of unfocusing our laser-like attention on the doors. There's also an excessive number of them; Disneyland's *Mansion* has a mere sixteen compared to the absurd twenty-seven in Florida. Less acceptable was the downgrading of the original, supersize "Tomb Sweet Tomb" sampler to a small one.

Even less acceptable, the red globes on the hurricane lamps were removed and discarded, spoiling the carefully planned lighting in the scene. Worst of all, however, the hands on the final door were removed. They came and went for a few weeks; maintenance kept putting them back on the door and WDI kept removing them. Eventually a show designer from WDI came and confiscated the props.

The sad reality is that they were removed because the hands aren't at Disneyland. Disneyland is, of course, a brilliant theme park, but the same designers which created it also created Magic Kingdom, and on the whole avoided the temptation to repeat themselves.

The mere fact that the hands on the door appear in a subsequent version of the same ride designed by the same folks gives them, to me, what's called in literary circles "textual authority". Claude Coats put them there for a reason, and without them the scene is missing a little extra punch in the tail it once had. Hopefully some enterprising future Imagineer will see fit to correct the oversight.

One last moment to contemplate the grandfather clock, if you will. Time is a human invention; it measures our planet's cycles around the sun and provides us with a countdown to our own deaths. This is why clocks and timepieces often are used in films to reflect mortality. But as scary as the *Haunted Mansion*'s grandfather clock is, I don't think the mortality interpretive scheme is responsible for the power of this image in the attraction. I think it works because a berserk clock reflects how it actually feels to be inside the ride.

At the point we see the crazily spinning clock, we're still less than halfway through the ride. We've only been seated in our car for about three minutes and 45 seconds on an eight minute ride.

It seems strange to think that the whole experience is only eight minutes long; add a few minutes in the Foyer and Stretch Room, a few to wander out, and say five while waiting to board the cars, and it's still only about twenty minutes of your life, but you live richer, see brighter, and think faster in those eight minutes than in practically any other. The *Haunted Mansion* produces a remarkable natural high. Sit outside the exit of the ride sometime and look and listen to people leaving; they float off it like it was a roller coaster.

How do we allow for our time inside the *Haunted Mansion*? How long were we "really" in there? Almost nobody thinks it was eight minutes; not when you've packed so many unique experiences into one ride.

There's a common lame joke that Disney uses often; in an index of popular theme park tropes, I called it the "Three Hour Tour".[49] These are leisurely, often scenic rides which conclude by telling us that we've experienced days or months of adventures in the few minutes we've been on board.

This is used on both the Disneyland and Walt Disney World Railroads, the *Mark Twain* steamboat, the *Columbia*, and more. It derives from the *Jungle Cruise*, which has always claimed to offer weeks of adventure in a single trip. As that ride became increasingly rooted in comedy, this concept stuck around as a kind of phantom idea, a weird punchline divorced of reality.

In Shakespeare, scholars have debated the existence of a "double time" scheme. Double time doesn't mean twice as fast; it refers to the tendency of Shakespeare to present a rapidly moving, propulsive plot which also seems to take place over months, years, or decades. Indeed, one of his great accomplishments may be "turning the accomplishment of many years into an hour-glass".

The problem is heightened in *Othello* because the entire tragedy depends on a tissue of lies which is not unraveled in time to save many lives. The plot in *Othello* must move quickly or it will falter. Simultaneously, characters in *Othello* continually refer to great passages of time which are only implied, so that the plot appears to be moving in two different time frames at once.[50]

Isn't this how it feels when we are on a great attraction? Time somehow moves simultaneously faster and slower than it does elsewhere in life. Therefore, I think it's fair to speak of the great WED attractions as inhabiting not double time, but *compressed* timeframes.

In the same way that the *Jungle Cruise* is weeks of safari with the boring bits left out, the *Haunted Mansion* is a twirling, whirling impression of a night in a haunted house played at manic fast forward.

This is what the clock is doing. It doesn't spin backwards, but wildly forwards, perpetually pointed to a time which is impossible.

9. INTERMEZZO: RESCUE CIRCLE

Like a scene in a play, the eloquent richness of her drawing room could be on view whenever she chose to show it; and not, as in the houses of so many of her friends, be kept shrouded in eternal gloom to exclude the dread sunlight - for there was nothing more feared by all Victorian housekeepers. - Frances Lichten, Decorative Art of Victoria's Era [51]

Now we need to take a detour. Let's leap out of our imaginary dusty old house and move across the county, to a tiny rural hamlet outside of Rochester, New York in 1848.

The location was an insignificant village then known as Hydesville which, like many small New England villages, no longer exists - having been swallowed up by the nearby town of Arcadia. The nearest cities - Rochester in one direction, or Syracuse in another - are both over a day's travel by horse. Hydesville was out there, not far from Lake Ontario. The winters were bitterly cold and even today few highways cross the area. The story begins with a family known as Fox.

The family was not settled in the area. They had recently moved into a house which had a reputation for being haunted. It was a standard austere saltbox cottage with two floors, two windows on the north and south sides, and four on the east and west sides. With four women in the house and one man, it's not hard to imagine the tedium of waiting out the long, cold, dark winters in the drafty, ugly, isolated cottage.

And so on March 31st, 1848, the three Fox sisters began to play an elaborate prank on their mother. Using an apple tied to a string, and later by popping their toes and joints, the girls began to "manifest" various thumps and pops to frighten and annoy their parents, leading up to the big show on April Fools' Day, when they

appeared to "communicate" with the spirit by asking it to respond to various commands. Despite their immediate efforts to apologize, this display terrified their mother, who insisted on bringing over a neighbor to witness the phenomena.

Caught in their lie, the sisters would not reveal how they had staged their trick for another fifty years. In the interim they became a sensation. The notion of communicating with the dead swept the countryside - in time becoming a new religion called Spiritualism. It isn't hard to see why the Fox sisters moved to capitalize on the craze they had started - a way out of that cramped cabin in the middle of nowhere would have been impossible to pass up.

Spiritualism was a strange mania. The Fox sisters set the standard, by producing raps and knocks with their joints. At least, that's what they confessed to doing much later. Nobody could ever account for how they achieved this exactly; can you pop the joint of your big toe loudly enough to sound like a knock coming from the surface of a table?

What's more likely is that the girls eventually became adept at wielding sticks or vibrating the legs with their toes. In later years, Kate Fox described how she would "rap" on the chair of a seated customer, who would exclaim that the ghost had touched them!

For those of us who are genuine believers in ghost phenomena, it's difficult and embarrassing to account for this period of frenzied "ghost" activities in parlors and drawing rooms across the world. Participants would often sit around a central table and join hands; supposedly this prevented chicanery but anybody with an ability to slip their foot out of a loose shoe and manipulate a concealed bell with their toe could be a medium. Many employed a second who could "float" trumpets, tambourines, or bells, or poke their heads through the heavy curtains found in many a Victorian drawing room to produce a manifestation. Tipping tables could be achieved through nothing but magnets. In the dim lighting of a séance, to a crowd receptive to the idea, such parlor tricks could be very effective.

Spiritualism was exactly the right thing at exactly the right time. The Industrial Revolution was underway, displacing workers and spreading misery in city centers. Revolutions and wars overseas undermined a sense of stability, amplified by the fact that in the

1840s the spread of newspapers and telegraphy meant this generation was the first to be made aware of happening in far-off lands relatively quickly.

The South, meanwhile, was increasing and amplifying its threats to secede from the Union, and war seemed inevitable. Reforms in church and social institutions saw a move away from Puritanism and Calvinism, a social move which the event of apparent *direct contact from the other side* seemed to legitimize. The world was ready for a new belief structure.

Spiritualism employed these changing social mores. The Fox sisters' rapping table method was modeled on the telegraph, introduced by Samuel Morse in 1840. For citizens in that earlier time, the idea of sending information over wires was tantamount to magic.

Also new was the burgeoning technology of commercial photography. Cashing in on this new trend, photographers would use a double exposure technique to produce "spirit photographs". If all of these techniques seem embarrassingly crude today, it may be well to think back to the early days of internet chain letters or prank websites - the unfamiliarity of a new technology legitimizes even the most dire efforts.

And yet Spiritualism was also an important social force for emerging trends that would birth feminism. For the first time since the days of herbalists and potion healers, women had a way to earn their own way in the world, and the bulk of Spiritualist seers were women. It would not be until the 1880s and the temperance movement that women would have an ally as powerful as the supernatural to affect change in the world.

Even stranger, amidst all of this apparent fakery, some genuinely baffling things did occur. Folklorist Joseph A. Citro relates an 1874 investigation in rural Vermont[52] at a farm run by two illiterate brothers, William and Horatio Eddy, which defy all logic.

But as investigated by lawyer Henry Steel Olcott over ten weeks one summer, the Eddy boys were, by his account, able to manifest hundreds of spirits from a "spirit cabinet" - as many as thirty at a time, of all shapes, sizes, eras, and colors.

9. INTERMEZZO: RESCUE CIRCLE 183

During the day, Olcott relentlessly poked around the Eddy farmhouse looking for trap doors and secret passages, and traipsed the area looking for places to hide actors and costumes. Somehow he never turned up anything. Olcott would subsequently convert to Theosophy and write a book about his investigation, *The People From The Other World.*[53]

On one hand, Olcott, like other men, was capable of convincing himself of anything he wanted to believe badly enough - and in later years the Eddy brothers would be exposed by magician Chung Ling Soo for using extremely cheap parlor tricks involving, believe it or not, a fake lead hand. Still, I find Olcott's testimonial hard to shake. If it's true, the brothers' charade would have required dozens of actors, hundreds of costumes, and a method to get them in and out of a small farmhouse which somehow fooled carpenters and investigators for ten entire weeks. And who would mount such a production in the middle of nowhere in Vermont?

Magicians exposed a lot of Spiritualists. By far the most famous of these was Harry Houdini, who revealed hundreds of frauds in his lifetime. But when we consider that the bulk of these were lower class women trying to achieve a measure of independence, our admiration here may weaken.

Spiritualists, magicians and scientists all occupy a very strange Venn diagram in this era, all overlapping at a crucial point. Scientists attempt to explain phenomena using theories and investigations to produce new technology and spur the forward progress of mankind. Magicians used these emerging technologies - not to advance science, but to fool people into believing that they had frightening and extraordinary powers. Spiritualists used these magic tricks to profit from a willing population - except they claimed their powers came from the "Other Side". At what point does fooling people for money stop being showbiz and become a sham? Professional magicians still maintain that there is a distinction - but is there?

And then we come to Yale Gracey, who was a magician, and not the glossy, candy-coated Disney style of magician either, but a genuine professional magician, who hung out at the Magic Castle in

Los Angeles. You can still go there to this day and see a model he was working on in the early 60s that was the basis of the Ballroom illusion.

The *Haunted Mansion* is a magic show. And now the circuitous path we've been taking to get here begins to fold in on itself. It's a magic show about ghosts, but in the era of the *Haunted Mansion* - the Victorian era - ghosts *were themselves* a magic show. *The Haunted Mansion* collapses all of those eras into one, bringing with it urban legends, supernatural lore, theater, magic lanterns, cinema, fairgrounds, and everything else into one concise experience centered on this room - an American Phantasmagoria. The echoes of previous eras of terror shows thunder down these halls.

And so here we go into the *Haunted Mansion*'s séance room. It's pitch black all around, just as the Victorian parlor would have been under the same circumstances. Yes, as a hardcore Mansionoloist you know those walls are just hung with black curtains, but pretend they're hiding wainscoted walls or something. In the center of the room is a circular table. As the Doombuggies enter, they form a circle around the table. At Disneyland, a spirit cabinet stands at the back wall. This is exactly the scenario which played out in thousands of sitting rooms between 1850 and 1915.

Around the room, glowing instruments hang from strings. A tambourine shakes. Knocks are heard coming from a table. Moaning fills the air. Ectoplasm is produced. Does any of this sound familiar?

The Séance Room is the eye at the center of the maelstrom. There's something calming about the room; it's the only point in the *Haunted Mansion* you can look across a room and see another rider. When the *Haunted Mansion* was in testing in Summer 1969, Tony Baxter was a test rider; he and his friends would shout details they had noticed at each other across the Séance Room during employee test rides. So as you can see, this business of fanatically obsessing over this ride began long before it was even actually open.[54]

And it's here where the ironies of the *Haunted Mansion* seem to duplicate themselves on and on. The Séance Room presents us with what, in the *diegesis* of the ride, is a *real* séance, which will

9. INTERMEZZO: RESCUE CIRCLE   185

summon *real* spirits. And yet, the style, method, and era of the séance alerts us to the fact that that Madame Leota was a sham Spiritualist - which is, of course, why she is ironically trapped inside her crystal ball. And yet, having passed over, Madame Leota has now become a *genuine* medium, whose sham séance produces *actual* results.

And yet the scene itself is a recreation of a genuine fake Victorian séance in nearly every detail. Never mind that the instruments are moved by motors instead of hidden assistants; a horn on a string is a horn on a string. The rapping sound is a mechanical knocker screwed to the underside of a floating table which produces the desired sound live, in the room. And the projections are film, laserdisc, or digital video instead of a magic lantern, but we're still not outside the fuzzy realm of honest fakes vs. dishonest fakes.

Take, for example, the crystal ball itself. Concepts for a séance in the *Haunted Mansion* date back to Ken Anderson in the 1950s, but the crystal ball idea seems to come from Marc Davis. It's not clear who decided the medium would be inside the crystal ball instead of outside it - Marc's sketches show various old women or gypsy fortune tellers hovering over the crystal summoning spirits. My guess here would be Yale Gracey placed the medium *inside* the crystal, an image that seems linked to Universal's *Inner Sanctum* mystery films. *Inner Sanctum* was a series of paperback thrillers, then a radio serial, and finally a series of B pictures produced between 1943 and 1945. Each begins with a baleful warning spoken by a face floating in a crystal ball in an empty room. Although the *Inner Sanctum* films are psychological thrillers, not ghost stories, the uncanny weirdness of the face in the crystal and its doom laden pronouncements have lingered in the memory of many a viewer. The *Inner Sanctum* head is the only such face in a crystal ball that I've encountered that seems to resemble Leota in any meaningful way.

But a crystal ball is a loaded image. The tarot cards sitting on the table in front of Madame Leota still carry some authority, but few professional psychics use crystal balls today. The crystal ball is a symbol of illegitimacy, and although the notion of doing a full-scale honest fake séance in the *Haunted Mansion* probably descends from Yale Gracey and Rolly Crump, the funhouse mirror-like reflections of real and fake in this scene probably come to us from Marc Davis.

Which is not to say that the honest fakes are not beautifully engineered. The Séance Room is the only scene in the attraction which has no aesthetic indulgences; it's nothing but special effects in a dark room. Yale's effects have nothing to compete with, here.

Riders may notice that smaller instruments basically just spin in circles while the large ones bob up and down; the larger floating objects are moved by a MAPO device known as a "Balloon Hoist". This is because it was invented for *it's a small world* back in 1964 and used to bob the various flying contraptions which appear in that show.

The glass lamp which once hung above Leota - and the smaller lamp which floats above the "rap on a table" table today - is a slight anachronism, as the style was introduced by Louis C. Tiffany in 1895, and most of his lamps were electric, not gas, contraptions. It hardly matters, because the cut glass lamp above Leota, much like the candle which sat to her left for 35 years, served the sole purpose of adding additional specks of light reflected in the glass to distract from the inevitable reflection of the projector lamp.

Most riders, I'm afraid, don't have enough time to enjoy the intended full effect of the surprise that Madame Leota is in fact *inside* her crystal ball. Before she started flying, the staging of the scene was slightly clearer. The intent is made more obvious by the Ghost Host's deleted narration which sets us up for a medium with "has a remarkable head for materializing the disembodied."

At Disneyland, the ride designers went through the effort of designing a special chair in which a speaker could be hidden so that Leota's incantations seem at first to *come from the chair*; as we enter the Séance Room, we see the back of a chair pulled up to a table and are primed by the Ghost Host to expect to see Leota seated in the chair.

The second reveal, as the cars pivoted, was that the chair was empty, but for a few moments it was also not yet evident that Leota was inside the ball. The rear of Leota's head used to have a very simple lighting effect, much like a color wheel used to illuminate those midcentury tinsel Christmas trees, so that her hair appeared at first glance to be a swirling pattern of light inside the crystal ball. It was only about a third of the way through the scene that riders realized that she was a head inside the gazing ball.

Maybe the most beautifully simple but astonishingly complex effect inside the *Haunted Mansion* can only be seen briefly from near the exit of the room; it's a glowing green ball that leaves a faint trail behind it. This is not a projection effect.[55] It's a gigantic mechanism hidden behind a scrim, the front painted flat black to match the walls, leaving an oval shaped "screen" unpainted. The rear of the scrim is painted in glow in the dark paint.

Behind the scrim is a huge device with two crossbars - one horizontal, one vertical. Cams move the arms up and down and left and right randomly. Where the bars cross is a standard light bulb. As the light bulb moves across the rear of the scrim painted in the light sensitive paint, a dim glow may be seen from the opposite side. The green trail behind it fades slowly thanks to the light-sensitive paint.

It isn't easy to describe this mechanism, but it operates on the same principle as the humble Etch-A-Sketch, another product of the 1960s.

If you ride the *Haunted Mansion* immediately after opening for the day, there will be only a faint trail where the light bulb has traced its path only a few times. As the day wears on and the arms move over and over the surface of the scrim, the "path" will become more like a fat green blob.

It's a good reason to keep coming back.

10. FURIOSO: DANCE MACABRE

Act Two of the *Haunted Mansion* ends as the cars climb up into the darkness out of the Séance Room and move out onto the balcony of the *Haunted Mansion*'s Ballroom - figuratively and literally the capstone of the entire attraction. It's the room that the attraction is designed around - literally, the rooms and show scenes orbit this central room like planets around a sun. The shape of this room determines every other shape and angle of the attraction.

The Ballroom astounds with its scale - not only its physical size, but the scale of its ambition. Every surface is covered with detail, in a room wider than the human eye can take in at once, and taller than can be seen. There's a floor, but no ceiling. There are windows taller than is possible in this house.

One reason the Ballroom impresses is because it totally throws our sense of space into haywire mode. So far everything we've seen can be, with some possible liberty taken with atmospheric illusion, plausibly contained within an old, dark house. But the Ballroom is a physical impossibly, an impossible sight.

The only real precedent for attempting something of this scale at Disneyland was the Bombardment Bay scene in *Pirates of the Caribbean*, where what appears to be a full sized pirate ship firing upon a fort appears out of nowhere halfway through the ride. And yet *Pirates of the Caribbean*, especially at Disneyland, has pulled this trick before - it's already turned day into night, indoors into outdoors, pirates into skeletons, today into the past, so it almost perversely isn't too shocking to see an indoor pirate ship and ocean at that moment.

Furthermore, the visual comes about halfway through the attraction, at the start of Act Two, to signify that the boats have now travelled back in time. The *Haunted Mansion* pulls its impossible visual when the ghosts finally become visible and the party begins, placing it nearer the emotional climax of the attraction. The result is a knockout. It's amazing that the ride even recovers from it.

10. FURIOSO: DANCE MACABRE

And yet, in another sense, there isn't as much here to discuss as being the visual highlight of the attraction implies. Everything about the room is designed to support the astonishing scale of its special effect - its single special effect. It seems almost silly to try to draw attention to little details tucked away in the corners of a room when everybody's only looking at the brilliant disappearing ghosts, but there *are* details worthy of consideration here.

Who is the very first ghost to materialize in the *Haunted Manson*? Up until 2003 it was actually a wisp of a phantom that appeared in the Séance Room. He was immediately behind the buggies as they entered the room, which means guests couldn't see him until they were leaving - a nice little trick to use the interior space of a room to imply a dramatic progression. He looked like a hooded, wraith-style ghost with raised arms, somewhat like the "flying ghosts" in the Graveyard. The effect was achieved by painting him on black silk, illuminating the silk with an ultraviolet light, and blowing the silk with a fan. He disappeared in 2003 and has not returned.

Once the ghost on silk flew the coop, then the first proper ghost we get a look at became the "Mantle Ghost" in the Ballroom. Our eyes are drawn to him immediately because he's the only ghost in the ballroom to appear nearly at eye height, and he cues us immediately to look down and see the action.

As simple as that seems, given the fact that none of the illusions are located on the same eye level as the Doombuggies, without this guy sitting there right off the bat it's possible some viewers may not realize to look down in this scene.

Mantle Ghost is an appropriate first ghost to see, because he's doing something pretty silly: he's got his legs crossed and looks quite pleased sitting next to that stern bust of Aunt Lucretia, whom last we saw in the Library. His goofy expression and jaunty crossed legs immediately establishes that these ghosts will be silly, not scary.

Interestingly, this ghost was put in only very late in the game. Dan Olson has established[56] that the "Mantle Ghost" may not have been added to the *Haunted Mansion* show until the summer of

1969, just a few months before opening. Furthermore, he probably displaced the Duelists, who were relocated to the end of the scene.

My guess, besides maybe setting the wrong tone for the sequence, is that the Duelists didn't work in this spot due to a combination of motion and angle - depending on how they were positioned in the scene, the figure could have obscured his gun, or the twirling motion of the figures could have sent their capes flying out in such a way that revealed the effect from the perspective of the Doombuggy balcony. Since Mantle Guy stays put and only moves his head, there would be no danger of this figure revealing itself as it moved.

The next ghost we see is an old lady reading by the fireplace. She rocks in her chair and, at Disneyland, she appears and disappears, but in Florida she just sits there, half-transparent.

The "little old lady" ghost has always struck me as odd. Imagine the scene how it would have played originally - we see a chair pulled up by a roaring fire, and a flickering lamp, and a dusty old basket of yarn and knitting needles on the floor - then the ghostly old lady appears. There's even a cobweb-covered tea pot and cup sitting by the table. Is the implication that she died in the chair, and that's why her stuff is still there, abandoned?[57]

I suspect she appears and disappears at Disneyland because she was intended to appear simultaneously with the Duelists; upon their relocation, her lighting effect was never adjusted. This means that the ride designers hoped to make it seem as though the ghosts were blipping into existence before your very eyes following the séance, which is a neat idea, and simply doesn't exist in the *Mansion* as it is today.

If we were supposed to see the Mantle Ghost and Old Lady appear at the same time, then the effect is muddled; as the cars scoot by the two ghosts seem to appear and disappear randomly. The cars would have to be moving much more slowly to convey the idea that the ghosts are blipping into view.

And yet, I'm reminded of the Endless Hallway with its "thundering footsteps" effect: I've never been able to wrap my head around how an endless chain of cars was supposed to understand and enjoy the intended traveling sound effect. Unless, of course, they were moving very slowly. And yet, the speakers were actually installed and, presumably, the original version of the Endless Hall was tested in the field during construction.

Was the *Haunted Mansion* sped up? There certainly are very elaborate gags in the Graveyard that have never read quite right from the moving cars, gags that require trip after trip to understand. There's just a hint left, just enough to make you wonder.

The Ballroom has a terrific fireplace. Originally, the fireplace had a green flame effect inside it which was achieved by a simple sheet of plastic blown by a fan. In 2008, the plastic gave way for a new projection effect inside the fireplace logs which doesn't look much like a fire, but then again neither did the plastic, I suppose. I was always partial to the blowing cellophane for no other reason than that it was the last place to see the original version of Yale Gracey's "fire" effect from *Pirates of the Caribbean*.

Following the creation of a new version of the fire effect with more sophisticated lighting and using blown white silk for Disneyland Paris in 1992, all of the previous iterations were upgraded to the silk in the 1990s. Yet Yale's original cellophane version blowed on in the *Haunted Mansions*, green.

Gathered around the banquet table is a birthday party. I've never figured out how the idea for the birthday party happened. The piece of concept art most obviously based on the scene, by Davis, shows various ghosts gathering around a rotted banquet table with a drunk ghost laying underneath it. In some ways this art was realized in amazingly precise ways, down to the weird throw-away visual gag of a ghost just barely peeking up from behind the table. In other ways, the idea of a birthday ghost blowing out candles of a cake is one of those ideas that doesn't seem to come down to us in any traceable, obvious way.

Further complicating matters, the Birthday Girl, in hair style, hair color, and dress color, bears a striking resemblance to the Alligator Girl in the Stretching Room - but the figure as it appears in the attraction and the final painted portrait are entirely dissimilar in any other way, so this is more likely a coincidence. Perhaps the only thing lying behind the concept is the comedy inherent in the idea of a ghost celebrating a birthday - or perhaps, as some promotional material phrases it, a death-day. Arguably, this one-off gag simply muddies the waters of the logic of the attraction - are the ghosts materializing because of your "sympathetic vibrations", or because there's going to be an awesome birthday party?

Thankfully, Birthday Girl's guests are a little more interesting.

There's a King seated at the table, and not at the head of the table. No, this King is perfectly content to sit at the sidelines, letting the Victorian birthday girl lead the festivities. This is the first appearance of a minor but very interesting theme on egalitarianism which runs through the *Haunted Mansion* and will be further developed in the Graveyard.

How strange and quite unlike our expectations the ghost population of the *Haunted Mansion* turns out to be once they are visible! There are total oddities like a stern admiral, telescope in arm, who floats into the Grand Hall out of the hearse "taxi". Another is a floating, rakish gentlemen with a vibrant red rose extended in one hand. Then there are the "banshees" which fly in through the broken window, which consist of nothing but ragged sheets in human shape with ghoulish, bony arms extended above their heads - true nightmare figures which remind me of M. R. James's *Oh Whistle, and I'll Come To You, My Lad.*

Of special interest is the strange ghoul seated next to the King who commands the King's interest because he's barely peeking up from behind the banquet table. I must admit that even I can't explain this joke - is he a ghost afraid of other ghosts? Whatever the rationale, he used to wear a Derby bowler, at least at Disneyland, and has the same face as the Organist figure. Another detail that can only be seen when you're actually standing in the scene - his banquet table chair is knocked over on the floor behind him. I especially like this figure because his hands which grip the Ballroom table aren't actually attached to his body!

One nice detail still at Magic Kingdom but lost at Disneyland[58] is the huge cobweb which covers the rear of the Ballroom table. It's really a subtle bit of showmanship - it demonstrates that the ghosts can appear inside the web without moving it. Like the furniture strategically placed so that the Ballroom dancers appear to dance straight through it, it's another little touch of an old-fashioned magic trick.

Seated at the head of the table is Julius Caesar. In one of the most interesting touches in the scene he first appears looking up directly at the passing Doombuggies, then turns to look at the Birthday Girl before vanishing. This definitely seems to make good on the pre-publicity for the attraction's claim to be a "retirement home for ghosts" and the Ghost Host's reference to "several prominent ghosts who have retired here from creepy old crypts all over the world". And there he is, the only ghost in the whole *Haunted Mansion* you can identify immediately and on sight - the ghost of Caesar.

Okay, you object, how do we *know* this is the ghost of Julius Caesar rather than just any old Roman senator wearing a civic crown? After all, there's no knife sticking out of the guy's back to tip us off.

The answer lies in understanding what motivated Marc Davis to put the Roman there in the first place. Although there were Disney attractions which allowed for a much more leisurely envelopment of comedy - The *Carousel of Progress*, for example, or Marc's scenes designed to sit along the Rivers of America - generally speaking, Marc knew he was working for an audience where clear visual communication was the top priority. The jokes, gags, and visual concepts in the *Haunted Mansion* have to be fired off at spectators who are passing them at a rate of 2.5 feet per second. The deadline for comprehension is measured in seconds. There's no room for reinventing the wheel here. If it's a dead Roman, then it's gotta be *the* dead Roman - Julius Caesar.

Furthermore, remember that Marc was the main person on the *Mansion* development team who was cracking open history books to populate the *Haunted Mansion*. Caesar's Ghost is a character from the classical ghost tradition, most especially Shakespeare's tragedy *Julius Caesar*. Shakespeare's play depicts Caesar as a rational but haughty man who's murdered by his best friend halfway through the play. From that moment on, Caesar becomes an avenging spirit, hounding the minds and conscience of the conspirators, who die shrieking his name. In a Shakespearian canon overstuffed with avenging spirits, Caesar stands at the top of the pack. Also, if you are inclined to believe that "Welcome, Foolish Mortals" is X. Atencio recalling Puck's "O what fools these mortals be!" in *A Midsummer Night's Dream*, it's only the second Shakespearian allusion in the *Mansion*.

Yet more specifically we can see Caesar's Ghost here as part of the retinue of classical sources Marc tapped in his *Mansion* research - not just Medusa and the Gorgons, but operas (*The Flying Dutchman, Bluebeard's Castle*), literature (*A Portrait of Dorian Gray, Dracula*) and classic myth (*Faust*). Very few made it in, and even fewer into the Disneyland model of the show, yet here sits Caesar.

Or, if that does not convince, then most audiences in 1969 would have associated the Ghost of Caesar not with Shakespeare, but Superman - "Great Caesar's Ghost!" was constantly bellowed by John Hamilton on TV's *The Adventures of Superman*. If you have difficulty reconciling imagining Marc Davis cracking open Ovid and putting in a reference to the George Reeves Superman, get over it - this is a guy who painted *Moby Dick* canvasses in his spare time and who also made sure than the Cleopatra in *it's a small world* was posed and animated to recall Elizabeth Taylor.

A favorite of the Ballroom ghosts is the drunk under the table. Most people know enough to lean out to see him, but how many notice the careful placement of a tipped over chair which perfectly occludes the reflection of the legs?[59] Disneyland actually has a bottle of wine down there with him; it's a charger of champagne and the brand name on the label is blacked out with a felt tip marker!

I don't think Florida ever had the bottle, but both *Mansions* feature a tiny detail you have to be actually down in the Ballroom show scene to notice: the tablecloth above the legs is stained with lots of red wine!

The wine glass on the table above the legs is supposed to be tipped over, but it often isn't. The plates, cups, and cutlery on the Ballroom table are not glued down, and Cast Members have a habit of going in and messing with them. This is how the famous "hidden Mickey plates" came about... Maids and Butlers would go down into the ride and place them like that, and Imagineering would change them back during their inspections.[60][61]

While the front half of the Ballroom is more or less devoted to the business of making the ghosts visible and providing lots of disparate, interesting types of ghosts to fill the scene - the drunk Egyptians up on the chandelier, the old lady by the fireplace - the back half of the scene is both less fully populated and devoted to the realization of one large idea instead of lots of tiny individual ideas. In the largest room of all in the *Mansion* the largest spectacle unfolds as a genuine nineteenth-century waltz, in all its finery, steps out on the dance floor. Transparent men and women whirling and twirling in gorgeously bright, frilly, transparent skirts, dancing through dusty old furniture. It's an image simultaneously indelible and beautiful, one of the few moments where the attraction tips over into a suggestion of a lament for a bygone time.

The dance is accompanied by a deranged waltz played on a massive pipe organ of the style perhaps best thought of as residing in a cathedral. This is a total fantasy - we've seen evidence of eccentric excess in the construction and contents of the *Haunted Mansion*, but the pipe organ here is the sort of thing only found in a concert hall, or the Paris opera house. It was Lon Chaney's *Phantom of the Opera* which fixed and immortalized the concept of a spook or specter who plays a pipe organ. The *Haunted Mansion* isn't an opera - at least, not yet - but our phantom here is as certainly descended from Lon as anyone.

Marc Davis would've been twelve when *Phantom of the Opera* was new, and he certainly saw it - everyone did. It's another case where the *Haunted Mansion* most obviously appears to be an extensive catalogue of every horror trope as anything else; if there's going to be a waltz, of course there will be a mad organist.

There's something else at work here too, and it helps contribute to the sense of the significance of the visual of the pipe organ. This is a huge instrument. It fills an entire wall of the largest room in the house. And we've gone through practically the entire house before we can see it. Were this a genuine mansion, when that thing was playing it would be heard through every single room in the house.

Generally, the *Haunted Mansion* will show us the source of a piece of music. It doesn't have a "cinematic" soundtrack in the way that, say, *Pirates of the Caribbean* does: largely, if we hear a piano being played, it shows us the piano.

The noteworthy exception here is the "Wedding March" played in a minor key in the Attic since 2007; but that piece of music was recorded to accompany an effect at Disneyland which was not duplicated at Walt Disney World, so even that is exempt. And, to the ride's credit, it sticks to this all the way until the graveyard, where a subtle underscore of organ, guitar, and chimes is heard. But from the moment we entered, we've been hearing that damn organ.

The Ballroom organ is, in fact, our first sensory experience of the *Haunted Mansion*, playing as it does in the Foyer. Generally, even with a decaying portrait on view, there isn't anything explicitly supernatural that happens when we first enter the house. A spooky organ is playing, but that could very well be from a flesh and blood person a few rooms over. A voice comes from nowhere, but that could be somebody hiding behind a curtain or something. At Disneyland, this sense of potential normality is even stronger, as their Foyer is dust and cobweb free, and has no haunted portrait. It's just a room in an old house, no different than if we were on a walking tour of a historical mansion.

Most visitors simply write off the organ heard in the Foyer as a soundtrack, instead of a bit of foreshadowing of what is to come later. Those of us in film studies have a ten dollar word for this term: *diegetic*. In film, diegetic refers to a sound, effect, or situation motivated by the internal universe of the film, and anything not part of that holistic world is "non-diegetic". For example, John Williams's famous shark theme from *Jaws* is non-diegetic, but Chief Brody listening to the radio on the beach is diegetic.

I think most people walk into the *Haunted Mansion*, hear the organ, and think "ah, of course, the requisite spooky music" and tune it out until this moment. But if you listen carefully, that organ follows us everywhere we go: it whistles on the wind through the Great Hall, thunders through the Portrait Gallery, Library, and Corridor of Doors, and is even faintly present in the Load Area. And suddenly: there it is, in front of us. What we previously took for granted is now in plain sight, and the *Mansion* has it both ways: it's simultaneously diegetic and non-diegetic, because it's a real organ - played by a ghost!

This makes the Ballroom one of the great "discovery spaces" in themed design. Not only can we not anticipate that anything of this scale is contained inside that tiny house, or that the ghosts will look so spectacular when they appear, but waiting for us at the end of the room is a final little frisson as we realize we're finally seeing who's been playing that organ. It's surprise, spectacle, beauty, comedy, and overwhelming scale - and it's all over in less than a minute. Top that.

There's one touch of foreboding that most do not register. The Ghost Host indicates that he's expected at the party - and leaves us alone. Although never exactly reassuring, the Ghost Host has guided us past many dangers in the *Mansion*, and is so far the nearest we've experienced to a benign ghost. And without him, like Bluebeard's wife in the elemental horror story of the Western world, we'll stumble into the room the grand tour would almost certainly not have included - the monstrous Attic.

Interestingly, we originally were to see the Ghost Host actually in the Ballroom - back when the Ghost Host's role was going to be filled by the black raven. Disneyland has a raven perched on the railing overlooking the dancers, and Florida had him too at one point.

Now, we don't know enough about how the raven would've worked to guess how differently the show would have played this way; it's easy to imagine the bird talking to us in the Foyer and Stretch Room, but would its narration for each appearance have been piped directly into the Doombuggy? Would the raven have left us too, only to rediscover us on the graveyard slope instead of at the end of the scene? Or would there still have been a Ghost Host and a raven, and they would've played off each other in a way similar to what's heard in the *Story and Song* LP?

What happens next is crucial to understanding the flow of the attraction, although it happens silently and unremarked. We've progressively moved from being on a guided, controlled experience -

directed by the house staff, greeted by the Ghost Host - to an unguided experience, until finally the Ghost Host abandons us in this spooky old house. Without him, we make a sudden turn and stumble across the scariest room in the house - the place we were never meant to see. It's the dark heart of the ride.

11. THE ATTIC: HINGE

Where the sound of a beating heart echoes through a musty room filled with monstrous memories - 1975 Haunted Mansion Cast Member Training Guide

The Attic in 1969 and 1971

Act 3 of the *Haunted Mansion* has been anticipated since we first laid eyes on the building, yet the climax itself is split between the Ballroom and Graveyard — and the Attic is the wedge between them.

The tonal shift the ride undergoes here draws attention to the central role of this room in the ride. Yet the Attic is the most misunderstood room in the *Haunted Mansion*, both by riders and the various stewards of the attraction over the years. In fact, for the past twenty years this simple scene has changed more than perhaps any one area of the entire house.

This is because the basic concept of the Attic was "the one that got away" back in 1969. The ghost bride has always been there, and the scene has always revolved around her, but as of late Imagineering has been bringing her groom (or grooms) back into play, in the form of the infamous Hatbox Ghost.

But these are just details of a larger picture here, a picture we run the threat of losing in such a small space. Observe, for a moment, how the layout of the show scene was dictated by elements which are no longer there. There's a large, sharp turn that the Doombuggies make about halfway through the scene worthy of attention. That whole turn is motivated by the fact that right by the cars, in the original 1969 version, there was the ghost bride, and thanks to discoveries of photos in the last five years, we know that the figure as painted had a decayed skull for a face. The cars would then head directly towards an open window, passing the Hatbox Ghost along the way.

There is not a single moment elsewhere in the ride when the cars make such a dramatic turn. That was *the point* - the ride path was *motivated* by our reactions to these two figures. Upon seeing the ghost bride with her skeleton face, riders are expected to turn tail and literally flee the house. As this happens, her groom appears - both to pay off the Bride, possibly threaten to block our way, and confirm our suspicions. The bride who looks like an angel of death is indeed a murderer.

How the Imagineers achieved this at the original Disneyland house was nothing short of brilliant.[62] As we entered the scene, off to the right, amongst the junk was a small table with a hatbox sitting on it. The hatbox was open, and its hat was sitting on the table next to it, visually establishing that the hatbox clearly did not contain a hat. And

11. THE ATTIC: HINGE

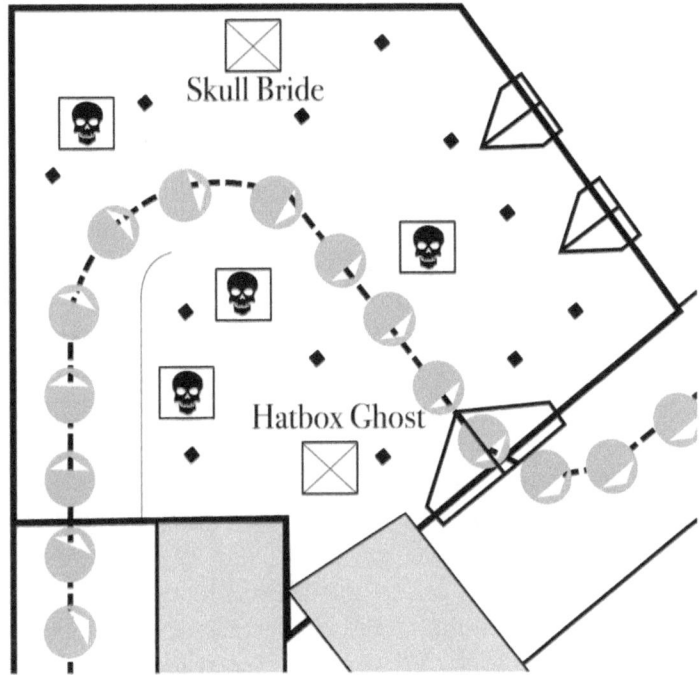

Disneyland Attic August 1969

horror clichés tell us that if hatboxes don't contain hats, then they do contain... severed heads!

Just at that moment, a skull would leap up out of the hatbox and scream. Terrific scare, and it establishes the crux of the scene to come. Right up ahead, ghouls leap out of open trunks, another likely hiding place for bodies in the musty corridors of an imagined Victorian horror house. We understand that dark deeds have been done in the creepy old place, and right here is a scary skull-faced lady with a candle who looks like suspect number one. And her heartbeat - the beating heart that we can see flashing red in her chest - fills the room in the same way her crimes do. The confirmation came when the Hatbox Ghost appeared, holding up a hatbox and grinning. His head would vanish and appear in the hatbox in time with her heartbeat.

And the Hatbox Ghost was clearly an old guy, his shaking hand supporting himself on a knobby cane. The Bride's appearance in the afterlife was clearly modeled on her amorality, while the Hatbox Ghost represented an undesirable companion. We all know, or at least we think we do, why beautiful young women marry much older men. The entire unsavory marriage and heads in hatboxes angle would seem to come from the 1935 stage thriller *Night Must Fall*, where an erratic young man insinuates himself into a family and is eventually revealed as a murderer, carrying around the head of his previous victim in a hatbox. The show was filmed in 1937 and again in 1964, shortly before Marc Davis began work on the *Mansion*. If this is indeed the inspiration, then Marc characteristically flipped the genders of the assailant and victim, murderesses being something of a leitmotif of the entire attraction.

Of course, by far the most famous thing about the Hatbox Ghost is that he didn't work properly, and was removed after two weeks. At that point the Bride was moved to his old spot near the exit of the room to give the scene some sense of completion, but just for fun let's imagine how *differently* we would interpret the Haunted Mansion had this effect worked as planned.

Since 1971, riders have been misinterpreting the Master Gracey grave out front to mean "Master of the House", and looking for some ghost inside to represent this name, most have chosen the young guy in the "Aging Man" portrait to fill the role. I mean, it's understandable, he does look kind of like a "Master Gracey", doesn't he?

But now imagine a world where the Hatbox Ghost *did* work and suddenly we have a creepy old guy upstairs who clearly was knocked off by the young wife who, we may infer, was motivated by great wealth. And here we are, at the top of a house which is itself a display of great wealth.

We could even, for example, believe that these spirits materialize inside this old house in the Attic because all of their old stuff is up here, their material belongings, the trappings of wealth. The fact that this is a genuine aspect of real ghost phenomena would only seem to support this conclusion.

So the Attic, and the inhabitants thereof, is a crucial scene in the ride and the disbanding of its central idea is a huge interpretive loss. We've been wondering since we saw the old place who could possibly have built it, and we've learned it's now a retirement home for ghosts. But our guide has left us, and we come across all the secrets of the old place locked away in the Attic. The *Haunted Mansion* once housed a murderer!

The thing about the *Haunted Mansion* is that it invites this sort of speculation by distinguishing itself to be an experience which unfolds in a clear, direct, and logical fashion. The fact that it has internal logic is more or less accidental, but profound. The human impulse for control and order means that any trace of a larger pattern encourages redoubled efforts to ferret out the logical ties in the whole experience, but in the case of the *Haunted Mansion* these ties are not formed by any larger plan but by chance, intuition, and convenience. But it isn't an experience like, say, *Mr. Toad's Wild Ride*, where the illogic piles up on itself deliciously. The *Mansion* nearly commands riders to, as they say, "fanfic".

WED Enterprises knew the power of their images, and one of the reasons why *Mansion* works so well is the way in which they dispensed them with ruthless economy. The art of the themed show is ultimately a nonverbal one.

The Attic in 1995 and 1996

> *I have always believed that the story is the thing that is really first, and the animation is the thing that tells the story. The background has to support all of that, it has to add the proper mood and give the characters the proper space and lighting to work in. But the backgrounds had to be balanced carefully. You can't make them overdone to the point of being distracting.* -
> Claude Coats, Disneyland Inside Story, Pg. 193

And so for decades, riders were left to ponder the exact significance of the ghost bride, but no resolution would ever present

itself. As time went on, the Bride looked less and less like a murderess and more and more like a victim. The scary skull face was abandoned in the mid-70s and now her face was enigmatically black, with two glowing eyes peering out of a veil. Was her heart beating or broken? The Bride became a visual contradiction; her beating heart and searching candle suggests a victim of some sort, which her eerie glowing eyes and lack of a face seemed to thoroughly refute. At the dark heart of the ride was a real mystery, and in some ways it was perfect.

At least, the Bride was. And although she was alone up there in the Attic now, the Bride was not the whole scene, and at least as important were her co-stars, those screaming pop-up ghouls.

At Disneyland, all of the Attic pop-ups came up out of hatboxes or trunks. This was a visual setup for the murder-mystery represented by the Bride and Hatbox Ghost.[63] I don't have as much visual documentation of the Magic Kingdom Attic scene as I'd like, but its story may be told this way.

To begin with, the props in the Florida Attic always seemed chosen with a bit less care than those at Disneyland; you can chalk that up to either the relative distance of the Walt Disney Studio prop warehouse or just plain old experience; the second time around they knew they wouldn't need stuff that was carefully chosen because most of it would simply fade into the background bric-a-brac.

What's different here in Florida is that the popup ghosts didn't just leap out of trunks. Two did, but just as many emerged from behind large piles of furniture, which changes their meaning in relationship to the Bride quite a bit.

Florida's popups remained concealed behind furniture carefully pushed together so that they seemed to rise up from behind large steamer trunks, or an overturned chair. One variation used a large chest of drawers to conceal the pop-up figure; the bottom drawer was pulled out, and various bits of cloth were trailing out of the drawer. Unseen to riders, the bottom panel of the drawer had been removed, and the ghoul appeared to pop up out of it!

There have always been a few white, folding rattan screens kicking around up there... an identical one once stood near the Hatbox Ghost at Disneyland, and another one has been rattling around on the second floor balcony of their *Haunted Mansion* facade forever.[64] Some of the larger pieces are very similar to those at Disneyland. Both houses have large brass railed bed headboards, both have precarious stacks of books and tea cups, and both have small baby carriages. However, the bulk of the "fill" for the Attic was likely, based on the look of it, purchased in Florida, and a lot of it was not especially vintage.

Also unique for the Florida house, a few of the props appeared to be specially fabricated for the Attic scene. There was an open steamer trunk with giant piles of old documents, maps, and books visible inside; out of another trunk a long length of thick old nautical rope seemed to coil. Throughout the scene, gauzy veils hung here and there on hat racks or old dress forms, teasing the ghost bride to come. Most trunks had visible peeks of what appeared to be dresses hanging out of them; the most impressive was run through with two huge, medieval-looking swords. Under show lighting this was very difficult to see, but these touches do show an eye sympathetic to the sort of imagery that would suggest a musty old attic filled with dark secrets.

The real trouble is that there ended up being a lot of stuff, and nearly none of it was actually bolted down in place. Photos taken by Mike Lee in 1992 show the Attic in complete disarray, with broken props, others thrown haphazardly into piles, and the pictorial nature of the scene greatly reduced. What had begun looking like a room packed with forgotten things now looked more like a junk shop. The pop-up ghosts no longer wore the white shirts they had begun with, but simple black cones of fabric. Then, in 1996, came the Big Change.

11. THE ATTIC: HINGE 209

The biggest change in the Big Change came with the introduction of a new Bride figure. No longer would the Bride simply stand on two transparent plastic legs; now, her entire lower body was removed. Her upper body was placed on a winch arm behind the figure, so she would appear to float up and down. She was given a face, and actual eyes that glowed instead of two round yellow headlights. The veil was removed, and she was given a huge, crazy hairdo. And as the final touch, a long train stretched behind her, complete with an assortment of fans to ripple the train and billow the dress.

Now, dear reader, if you are reading this book and never saw this Bride in person, you've likely already pulled up a photo of her online and you're scratching your head. A blue face? Is she smiling? And did a bomb explode in her wig?

I assure you, she looked a little better in person than flash photos suggest. What few photos show was that her face was painted in such a way as to appear inscrutable and darkened, so the smile simply was not visible. Also, when she was bobbing up and down, that crazy wig gave the impression that her hair was levitating, as if the whole ghost was floating and billowing in some impossible wind.

But was she really scary? I mean, one thing about "Miss Wind Power" - as Mike Lee called her - was that she looked *huge*, and she looked like she was floating straight towards you. But she also had a recognizably human face, and those glowing eyes still came right out at you. The effect was more pathetic than scary. Bride '96 looked lonely and lost.

But Miss Wind Power was not the most dramatic change in the Attic. The background here is that Disneyland had refurbished their Attic in 1995 in an attempt to add more of a story to it. Disneyland kept the look of their Bride, but zeroed in on their popups as a weak link in need of renovation.

Each ghoul now would rise and say "I do!" in their own distinct voice, and the sequence of the figures was altered so that they rose in order a few seconds apart, starting at the back of the Attic and heading to the front.[66] Along with this, a broken down harpsichord played by a shadow-ghost appeared about halfway through the scene.

The "I do!" ghosts changed the meaning of the Attic once again, demonstrating how the pop-ups and the Bride retain a reciprocal relationship even in the absence of the Hatbox Ghost.

It's possible that the Imagineers intended to clarify that the pop-ups hidden in trunks and hatboxes were former victims, but the final result implied otherwise. Each pop-up had a unique personality; the first one up, out of the hatbox, would shout "I do!" loudly and quickly. Others would say it slowly, or with a lot of echo. One of the five would laugh manically afterwards. It was *Imagineering Junior Voice Acting Fantasy Camp* at its worst. The overall effect was that the ghosts were mocking the Bride, who now became a figure of tragedy.

Were the ghosts mocking the Bride? Or were they enacting a revenge? After all, the Hatbox Ghost is a figure of revenge from beyond the grave, revealing the Bride's crimes for all to see. Were we intended to think of the leaping ghouls as murdered lovers? Are they former husbands?

I float this idea because Magic Kingdom has to have gotten their idea to make the pop-up ghouls in their Attic into grooms from somewhere, and Disneyland is the most likely culprit here. Because besides installing Miss Wind Power in 1996, that's just what they did.

Each ghoul was given a top hat, tiny jacket, bow tie, and button down shirt with tiny red flower, all in colorful purple and green. No shouts of "I do", they all just popped up and screamed like they always did. And with Miss Wind Power being the friendliest looking Bride yet, the dissonance between the Bride and the cartoonish pop-ups was never as deeply felt. And without the trunks and hat boxes - the signifiers of concealed bodies - why were all these grooms hiding behind objects in a musty old attic?

Which brings us to the real thing which derailed the 1996 edition of the scene. Again, much like the changes wrought on the Bride and pop-ups, it was done with the best intentions, but it singly destroyed the Attic's credibility.

None of the stuff in the Attic was nailed down; it never was and still is not. In 25 years, a lot of the furniture in the Attic got wrecked by Cast Members and routine maintenance. In the bad old days of the Walt Disney World College Program, it was once customary to ride the *Haunted Mansion* and toss your black work shoes into the Attic on your last day. Shoes were regularly removed and retrieving them took its toll. It was time to refresh the props in the Attic.

Nearly everything was pulled out, repaired or repainted, or discarded. New props came in, and not all of them were appropriate. The harp in the Séance Room was replaced with a new model; the old one was hung up in the Attic. It was joined, inexplicably, by such items as two saxophones, silk plants, bolts of fabric, a box kite, Asian statuary, and even a hitching post from Main Street. None of it made any sense.

But the *coup de grâce* was the way the Attic was set-dressed in 1996. Areas which once had items carefully pushed together to hide the pop-ups were now just open floor space. All it took to spot a hidden pop-up ghost was to lean forward a few inches. The entire element of surprise was lost.

And, finally, the scene was grossly over-lit. The original Attic was lit very simply. Most of it was in darkness. Each pop-up had an ultraviolet spotlight to catch them only on their rise. The rest of the scene was lit with pocket lights, blue toned, hidden amongst all of the clutter and giving some definition to the setting.

Because the new Bride required a small army of backlights, the total lighting package was adjusted in 1996 to be quite bright, relying heavily on ultraviolet fluorescent lights to illuminate the scene. The original effect of a ghost leaping into view in an Attic filled with broken furniture and lit by moonlight filtering through broken windows was lost. Tokyo Disneyland is the last place to enjoy the original lighting scheme.

Refurbishments on both coasts, intended to complement and clarify the Bride figure, ended up unbalancing the Attic scenes in different ways. Disneyland's version succeeded but ended up turning the Bride into a tragic figure. Magic Kingdom's ended up with a slightly friendly looking Bride and a bunch of pop-up spooks whose appearance and execution was far below the standards of the rest of the ride. Both "new" Attics lasted about a decade and provided good reason for a new wave of Imagineers to reboot the Attic more dramatically, which is what they did.

The Attic in 2005 and 2007

Constance came to Disneyland first. For several decades now, Imagineering had been messing around with the possibility of combining audio-animatronics and projection to allow for a greater range of facial movement - the original such figure premiered in 1998 at Magic Kingdom inside *Buzz Lightyear's Space Ranger Spin*, and others have appeared in Dead Man's Cavern at Tom Sawyer Island and the *Seven Dwarfs Mine Train*. In the mid-aughts, Disney in general was pushing towards projection technology and away from their traditional art form of dimensional animation. *Toy Story Midway Mania*, in development concurrently with Constance, was nothing but 3D screens.

If there's something to be said for the original Bride figure, it's that she was dimensional, and one of the most effective dimensional figures in the ride. Her face was darkened, but you could still see that it was an actual shape behind that veil. Her heart beat could be seen through her body because the light was *actually inside* her torso, and her arms were filled with strangely sparkling lights. It's hard to achieve the effect of making a physical, dimensional, fiberglass object appear to be hazy and indistinct, but in her best moments the original Bride did that.

Constance, the new Bride, is basically a dress form with a lot of gauze layered over her. Her face is projected on a rounded, smooth surface, not at all like the custom-sculpted blank faces used for similar effects elsewhere in the *Mansion*, which allow those effects to be seen from all angles. This meant that views of her profile had to be carefully covered with curtains. Yet, under show lighting, with fans pumping that gauze around, it would be unfair to say that Constance doesn't look reasonably good.

The move to bring her east to Magic Kingdom began almost immediately. Miss Wind Power looked pretty impressive when all of her many moving components were working, but "when" had become an increasing liability in the years following her appearance. The Attic had been a sore spot for a long time, and unlike at Disneyland when Constance appeared, the whole room was cleared and rethought.

The 2007 version of Constance was an improved model. She was given a much more detailed wedding dress, brocaded and jeweled elaborately. The Disneyland Constance had only one kind of arm movement: both arms would rise and a hatchet would appear in her hands. Walt Disney World's version switches between one-arm and two-arm motions, allowing her to occasionally flash a ring at the audience. Disneyland's version stares straight ahead the entire time, possibly at some distant Doombuggy, but the effect looks entirely unconvincing. Magic Kingdom's version can actually turn her head slightly to look directly at passing cars. It's a much more effective presentation.

The effect that Constance brought with her, the five portraits of her husbands, is deserving of some accolades. If Constance doesn't work great for everyone, then the portraits are almost universally liked. Much like the new changing portraits, it's done with a change-o picture in two layers. The top layer is illuminated by a light up in the rafters, which then dims as an internal light inside the picture's frame is brought up to illuminate its "changed" state. The two layers are sufficiently close together, and far enough away from the cars, that we perceive the two layers are existing in the same place. The changing portraits from earlier in the ride operate in near-darkness because the changed image simply shines through the rear of the canvas; these Attic portraits require much more light. One nice detail as a result of this is that the material the portraits are printed on appears to physically decay as the husband's head vanishes.

But despite these new special effects, by far the biggest success story in the 2007 version of the Attic can be attributed to the set dressers. As in 1996, everything was cleared out and re-installed, but this time all of the inappropriate bric a brac introduced in the 1990s was discarded and new items were purchased from antique dealers. It may be too much to suggest that *everything* in the Attic is Victorian, but per the original designers' intentions, it all is appropriate and legitimately old. To those who enjoy scouring through old stuff and clever set dressing, it's the most impressive Attic effort yet.

We are meant to understand that the stuff around each husband is their belongings; one of the nicest touches is that when we see the "Reginald" portrait, about halfway through the scene on the left, we can also see the chair that Reginald is sitting in and the cane he's holding right there to the left of the portrait. There are touches like that throughout. Each scene - one for each of the five husbands - has a small, telling detail, and the richness and extravagance of the furnishings around each portrait improves as Constance chops her way up the social scale.

As we enter the scene, there are two old fashioned-style champagne coupes on a table; one is knocked over. Nearby, under Frank's portrait, there are two ceramic figurines of a man and woman; the man is knocked over and the head is broken off. There's a bronze oriental statue over by The Marquis's portrait, no doubt indicating international travel.

Most tellingly, right as the cars exit on the right where the old beating heart Bride stood, there's a pile of five hatboxes. Nearby, a hat rack stands with five hats on it, and if we look closely, the five hats are exactly the ones worn by her five husbands in their portraits. And if we know that the hats of the husbands are not in those hatboxes, then what is...?

Constance herself is surrounded by a lot of old wedding decor.[67] There's a decorative candle holder and, befitting candles left up in a hot Attic for generations, the candles are warped and melted into a shape which suggests a reaching claw. What's disturbing, however, is that the candles are melted as if they're melting *away* from Constance, as if her mere presence is evil enough to melt wax. There's a statue nearby positioned so as to apparently shield her eyes from the ghost. These touches are just naturalistic enough to suggest random happenstance while still being expressionistic enough to make their intent clear. To my eyes, it's the scariest thing about the whole scene.

The Attic: In Richer and Poorer

Does the *Haunted Mansion* lack a feminine perspective? Dan Olson thinks that the *Haunted Mansion* is a more masculine experience - you're alone in a creepy old house, just you against the ghosts, while *Phantom Manor* depicts a personal tragedy with a relatable character which makes it more feminine. But even if you agree with this perspective, there's a trap waiting at the end of both rides.

Because the fact is that the *Haunted Mansion* depicts an ultimately reassuring message about the afterlife, while *Phantom Manor* unambiguously depicts a world where the innocent suffer for no good reason and Evil Wins.

Most of the residents of the *Haunted Mansion* are Happy Haunts. There was, until the mid-naughts, one exception to this rule: the Beating Heart Bride. Depending on the era and your own perspective, that figure could be tragic or maniacal, but the fact remains that, as originally intended, the Attic dramatized a salient point of the *Mansion*'s conception: justice is being served from beyond the grave.

The *Haunted Mansion* doesn't do any moralizing for an attraction which is entirely about death, except in the Attic, where the Bride was absolutely originally intended to be a figure of evil. She may have successfully lopped off her husband's head and hidden it in a hatbox - and, we may assume, inherited the big old house - but now they're both dead and he's won. That's why the Hatbox Ghost is smiling and holding up that hatbox; he's revealing her crime for all to see. And she gets to spend eternity not at the big party with everyone else, but hanging out with her murdered groom in a scary old Attic. That's an amazing moralistic conception, and it's the darker shading that the light requires.[68]

The Constance scene is an attempt to return to the *Haunted Mansion* the dimensions of this original conception. *Mansion* fans may debate the merits of the scene, but the scene's designers would rightfully point out that it brings the 2007 Attic scene as close to the original conception as possible without bringing back the Hatbox Ghost. Connie even stashes her husband's heads in the same places as her predecessor. And yet, can we really say that, in Constance's case, justice is being done?

In the wedding portraits, it's hard to read Constance's expression: she has the same tight-lipped, controlled look we associate with real-life serial killers. In comparison, it's clear that her ghost isn't so much mischievous as *completely deranged*. She grins and leers and reveals to all who pass by what her crimes were. Now, being scary and crazy may be sufficient "punishment" in the end, but what's missing here is some word from her grooms. Even if they're the ones causing their heads to vanish in the portraits, that doesn't really qualify as justice. The function of the wedding portraits and also the discrepancy between Constance in those photos and Constance the unhinged maniac ghost seems to be the same impulse which causes the portraits earlier in the attraction to transform: the gap between appearance and reality.

Thing is, it's *too easy* to admire Constance's murder spree. Her husbands look like buffoons. She buys herself a new expensive pearl necklace for each one of them she offs. Instead of becoming an illustration of "you can't escape from your crimes" - the same moral lesson imparted by Disneyland's *Pirates of the Caribbean* - Constance becomes a figure of humor, success. The line between her maniacal ravings and gloating is tissue thin.

But really, the weakest choice made by the Constance team was to try to tie the whole thing back into the classic Marc Davis "Widow" portrait from the Stretching Room. Take a look at that final portrait right near Constance - she's holding a rose and she's married a guy with a big handlebar mustache named George. We're intended to connect this to the Stretch Room portrait we saw just as we entered.

Now even if we write this off as an Imagineering in-joke and basically harmless, almost no rider actually makes the connection. As a result it qualifies to me as what I'd describe as "extratextual". It may *reflect* on an interpretation, but knowing it in no way improves the ride experience.

I'd argue that everything we need to know about the *Haunted Mansion* may be gleaned from riding the attraction and simply *looking*. If it doesn't work visually, or if it requires the appearance of an Imagineer waving a piece of paper to explain it, then I feel no reason to include it in my interpretation. The George-Constance connection, to me, is much like being told that the skull in the headboards of the bed in Disneyland's *Pirates of the Caribbean* is real, and was given to Walt Disney. Such facts only mean as much as you're willing to allow.

The Constance story opens other cans of worms, as well. Even if we accept the idea that George Hightower owned the house before he became Constance's last victim, it shuttles aside the widely believed fan theory that the *Haunted Mansion* is the home of a family named Gracey. That may be a piece of fan lore, but it's embraced by official park merchandise, the 2009 expanded attraction queue, and the 2003 film.

Nor does the story explain why Constance's portrait of her as an old lady would be hanging in a room which the Ghost Host himself describes as "paintings of some of *our guests*".

Now, it's *possible* to excuse this logically. Perhaps she waited a long time before finally deciding to off George for the money. Having become rich, she could have laid low for a long time before resuming her murder spree.

We also know from real life hauntings - as well as ghost lore and literature - that ghosts need not appear as they did in life when they died; they can look young, old, or not human at all. But the problem isn't that the difference between the wedding photo in the Attic and the portrait in the Stretch Room doesn't match real life, it's that it doesn't match *the rest of the ride*.

Given what we know about Marc Davis it seems extremely likely that he cracked open a few books on the supernatural before beginning work on the *Haunted Mansion* - perhaps modern ghost accounts like those of Hans Holzer, or classic ghost stories by M. R.

James, whose *The Mezzotint* seems to prefigure the changing portraits of the final ride so well. Given *any* exposure to ghost lore or legend, Marc would have observed the rule that ghosts can appear in any form.

The thing is that he intentionally *didn't* go in that direction. Davis simplified the visual logic of the attraction by posing his ghosts and ghouls as they appeared *when they died*. Everything was organized around the visual logic of the stretching portraits: here's a normal person, with a morbid surprise below them. That's why we understand the duellists joke in the Ballroom, despite logically making no sense (why would anybody paint or display such a portrait?).

All of the extraneous conceptual clutter is pulled out of the joke: their appearance in the portraits matches the appearance of their ghosts which replay the moment of their deaths. All we have to do is connect two dots and the concept just naturally unfolds itself. It's the same *visual* logic applied to the short hitch-hiker at the end of the ride: this guy died in a prison so he's a little old man with a huge beard holding a file and a ball and chain.

Constance is the *only* ghost in the *Haunted Mansion* that we have to make logical exceptions for, and the backstory she brings with her attempts to impose order and logic on an attraction which operates on dislogic and mystery. Practically everything we see before the Attic and after the Attic is dreamlike, abstract, and open to interpretation. Constance's scene, with its projected faces, rambling narration, and on-the-nose visuals, feels like it dropped out of another ride entirely.

But the central role of the Attic should not be ignored. The *Haunted Mansion* is wedded to it, in richer and in poorer. The whole ride pivots around this short sequence. And, if Imagineering manages to get it right one day, I believe that its role as a key conceptual component of the *Haunted Mansion* instead of an awkward afterthought will be widely recognized.

12. THE GREAT INDOORS

But as the 'doom buggy' winds its way up into the attic, past the vestigial bride, the scene shifts to a cemetery, outside the Mansion. The terror arises as much from the violation of dramatic unities, the abrupt turning inside out of the building, as from the graveyard tableau itself. [..]

By switching the point of view spasmodically from interior to exterior, however, the movie metaphor is deepened and amplified. Instead of the bookish, linear narrative of Main Street, the Mansion opts for the cinematic jump cut. Continuity and Reassurance are first established

12. THE GREAT INDOORS

> *and then abruptly denied, for an emotional effect that floats free of narrative and hovers in the air like the disquieting scent of a burning city.* - Karal Ann Marling, Designing Disney's Theme Parks: The Architecture of Reassurance

Moving outside the *Haunted Mansion* is a key moment; in fact, it may be *the* key moment of the entire ride.

Once again, we are up high and looking down on an expanse filled with ghosts; notice, for example, that the exact same railing which divides the Doombuggy balcony from the Ballroom again reappears, as if we're going to continue to scoot placidly along it. As the Attic demonstrates, however, we cannot remain unobserved for long, as the main surprise of the ride is suddenly revealed as the cars tilt backwards and proceed down a steep hill to ground level. This is the nearest the *Haunted Mansion* gets to attempting a physical thrill, and it still takes people off guard, because although the cars have been steadily and methodically ascending through the house, now we are given no choices but to come down and join the party. The only escape route is through a teeming horde of ghosts.

This is it. Until now the *Haunted Mansion* has been a constant and building conceptual pattern, and although it's been impossible to guess which room will come next or what will happen inside it, we have been presented with a building crescendo of interior spaces — until the ride pulls the rug out from under us here and we go tumbling backwards into the Graveyard.

This is the point where most dark rides, most haunted houses would end. We have entered the house of our own free will, confronted the horrors, and escaped. But our escape isn't really an escape at all, and it's in this final sequences that the *Haunted Mansion* most radically diverges from tradition and, in the process, brings to the table its own unique perspective.

What happens when we enter the *Haunted Mansion*? What's the larger pattern? We enter afraid but we leave laughing and enlivened, and not simply because we made it through to ride another day. The passage through the house turns it into a friend. What looks imposing and intimidating at first almost smiles down on us as we leave, and it's because the *Haunted Mansion* presents us with a reassuring story about that least reassuring of subjects: death.

In this case, we enter and are subject to illusions and frightening glimpses of supernatural activity, perhaps lending credence to our qualms about entering. The deeper we go, the more overt and frightening these manifestations become, until we're sure that there's something horrible just on the other side of that door, inches away, trying to break through and --

But then we attend a séance. The spirits are materialized and their first order of business is - a huge party. Kings and Queens mingle with commoners. Knights and prisoners sing happily alongside their executioners. These are the happiest, most well-adjusted ghosts you've ever seen. The good get to party in the afterlife; the wicked's deeds are revealed.

This is by far one of the most egalitarian expressions of a philosophy about death in American popular culture. Is there anything more reassuring than showing that death will not only be overcome, but you can still have fun afterwards too?

The Graveyard is where this philosophy comes to the forefront in the ride, and where I think the key conceptual innovation of the *Haunted Mansion* is, the thing that gives it the uplift at the end. Consider the Caretaker: the poor guy is terrified, yet, the scene is a funny one. Why is this? Didn't we feel a lot like him only a little bit ago? Seeing somebody scared out of their wits isn't funny if you yourself are scared out of your wits. It's because we've joined the party now.

At Disneyland, the *Haunted Mansion* anchors the north half of what was the greatest theme park "land" ever built - New Orleans Square. Anchoring the south half was *Pirates of the Caribbean*, an attraction which forcefully demonstrates that the wicked cannot outrun their fate. Much like Constance up in the Attic, there was nothing reassuring about those ghosts. We didn't even see any; only rotted bones and voices of condemnation remained. *Pirates of the Caribbean* is a **morality** play, about doomed criminals.

12. THE GREAT INDOORS

The *Haunted Mansion* is both the flip side and corrective to this, which is why they work so beautifully together. The *Haunted Mansion* is a **mortality** play, where we face down death and then death makes a silly face at us. Death isn't the end. It isn't even all that bad. The morality play and the mortality play hold down either end of the most ideologically complex and beautiful area in theme parks.

And so in this case, the descent down the hill and out of the house is both a conceptual and literal change of perspective - "look again", we're encouraged. And the pattern breaks along with the attraction's dramatic unities, to reveal something playful that was there all along.

Where did this unexpected note of egalitarianism come from?

Let us consider the group of Disney attractions which most directly approach the subject of "civics", a loose group I like to call the "America Attractions". The first was *Great Moments with Mr. Lincoln* in 1964 and the last was *The American Adventure* in 1982. In between came *America the Beautiful*, *The Hall of Presidents*, and... *America Sings*.

Marc Davis had worked on the character animation for Mr. Lincoln in 1964. He had done some of the earliest sketches for the mechanics of a human figure, breaking down the movements of a man standing up from a seated position to work out the basics of how much motion could be replicated. Marc said to a television program in 1984: "I did a number of things of how simple things work in anatomy - how perhaps a mechanical hand could work. This was rather naive in thinking because really our problem was not to create a mechanical man but to create an illusion. We had great technical problems getting the character to move properly in New York, and god, he would be going great - then all of the sudden he would do a great jerk - or decide to sit down!"[69]

During testing, Marc turned to the show's producer James Algar and quipped "Do you suppose that God is mad at Walt for creating Man in his own image?"[70]

Algar went on to write and produce the original 1971 version of *The Hall of Presidents*, a remarkable show building on the *Mr. Lincoln* experience. *The Hall of Presidents*, along with *The American Adventure*, espouse the "Great Man" theory of history - titanic Americans striding across a colossal dreamscape.

America Sings is a poor fit with these shows, and that along with its strange placement in Tomorrowland branded it as a problem attraction amongst the generation of Imagineers who built EPCOT Center. *America Sings* was eccentric, energetic, irreverent, and just plain weird.

Which was the point. Marc cultivated in *America Sings* not the "Great Man" history of the United States, but a people's history. As Sam Eagle said in his opening remarks, "[These] were the songs that people brought from their native counties. Sometimes it was happy, sometimes it was sad."

America Sings mixed up popular folklore and popular humor to tell the story of America's growth toward the 20th century. A retired Kentucky colonel rocked on his front porch while a scurrilous fox bootlegger ended up in jail. Deep South foxes and hens gathered "Down by the Riverside" to "study war no more". Drunks sang in a Western saloon. A showgirl pig belted out the early black America anthem "Bill Bailey Won't You Please Come Home". Temperance songs counterpointed drunken policemen. Hippies sang "Shake, Rattle and Roll". Absolutely nowhere did George Washington or Abraham Lincoln appear.

America Sings was unique for insisting on the diversity and complexity of America, not through high-minded words, but through actual direct representation. Marc made room for both the wealthy, and the dispossessed and downtrodden. *America Sings* insisted that history belonged to everyone. Where *The American Adventure* offered a John Steinbeck quote about diversity, *America Sings* gently reminded viewers to the tune of "Yankee Doodle": "To make these songs ring true, people came from every land to mix these tunes for you. So we should all remember, as history moves along, that everything is better now for someone wrote a song."

It's this broadly temperate, open hearted attitude we see enacted in a quiet way in the *Haunted Mansion*. While the band from all corners of history plays, royalty rides a teeter-totter under the dead oak tree. Marc's art turned the house of horrors into an affirmation that after death, everybody of all classes gets to live in the big house on the hill.

According to persistent rumor, some people think that when we turn backwards and head down the hill to the graveyard in the *Haunted Mansion* that we "fall" from the Attic to the ground level and *die*, which is why the Caretaker looks afraid.

Now, there are some early *Haunted Mansion* publicity documents describing how riders "fall" through a thicket of trees to reach the Graveyard. Of course, just because somebody in WED described it that way doesn't make it true. They could just as easily be reaching towards an obvious conclusion based on seeing the ride (or model) in person.

To these eyes, the descent represents nothing but an attempt to do something new with the Omnimover system. So far, they haven't really done anything not already done in *Adventure Thru Inner Space* - the cars have gone up and down slopes while remaining upright, pivoted, and moving backwards, so actually tilting and sliding down a hill would have been as unexpected to that audience as it is to modern audiences.

It's an abstract experience, moving backwards down that hill. Are we falling? Descending a staircase? Walking down a hill? It actually doesn't matter, because it's a dramatic cinematic move, the equivalent of a camera tilt.

Camera tilts are also reveals. At Disneyland, the reveal is of a cluster of menacing, Snow White-style trees on both sides, seemingly reaching for the cars as we travel past. Overhead, the Raven is perched in an overhanging limb. It's a terrific reveal, and made even more impressive by the fact that it was not, for whatever reason, repeated in Florida.

Disneyland's movement draws our attention up, to the ceiling, where the Raven is perched, while Florida's draws our attention away from the slope and off to the right. Literally everybody looks off to the right in Florida, because the trees are thinner and de-emphasized. They still reach towards us with claw-like hands, but this may be too subtle for many. And because off to the right is the only thing to be actually lit in the Florida descent: the outside of the house.

The two key legends about this section of the ride, interestingly, come from the two coasts and could almost seem to be in competition with each other. The concept of "falling off the roof and dying" comes from Disneyland, and the reason we know this is because the corroborating piece of evidence - the Caretaker looking terrified - is staged in such a way at Disneyland that he seems to be *directly facing you.* Magic Kingdom's Caretaker figure is rotated to directly face the graveyard in a way that makes it unambiguously clear that he's afraid of what lies directly ahead.

The myth Magic Kingdom contributed is that the "back" of the house we see from the Graveyard does not match the "front". We know this came from Magic Kingdom because at Disneyland there's next to no way to actually see the "Attic exterior" facade they built.

The concept of there being a discontinuity between the "front" of the house (as seen as we enter) and the "rear" of the house (overlooking the graveyard) is intriguing. Many describe the "rear" of the house as being a "clapboard" facade, but it actually has no surface detailing besides the roof whatsoever. The roof is indeed made up of wooden shingles, which do not match the slate shingles on the front facade, but again these cannot be examined in any detail - they're painted flat black and modeled entirely with a green light.

For those who notice this detail, perhaps what can be said is that the "rear" of the *Haunted Mansion* lacks the intricate stonework seen on the front, and that two dormer windows we see don't match the front elevation. But really, who is to say what the rear side of the *Haunted Mansion* looks like, anyway?

Instead of fixating on continuity in a ride which otherwise dispenses with it, let's think of it this way: what we've got here is an example of the *Haunted Mansion* team's belief in "visual economy".

They want you to understand that you're looking at the rear architecture of the *Haunted Mansion* in less than a second, and nothing indicates "roof of an old house" more clearly than shingles, a sloping roof, and dormer windows. 100% of riders understand it immediately, even if 30% of them keep riding and eventually realize it makes no sense. That's little rear ride facade is a testament to the illusory power of the attraction's visuals.

The Graveyard presented in the *Haunted Mansion* is a large public cemetery enclosed in an iron spike fence with a gate we enter through. The graves are done in a vernacular American eighteenth century style, quite unlike the Victorian tombstones we saw by the entrance.

As a young rider, a huge graveyard right behind an old house I could understand - we had plenty of colonial graveyards in New England, and the style of tombstones matched what I expected from reality.

What didn't match up, and what puzzled me, was the fog. Where I came from up in the Berkshire mountains, our fog was more like a mild haze that became a heavy wall at a certain distance, thick and white. What it didn't resemble was the delicate sheeting seen in the *Haunted Mansion*, and as a result I always thought the effect looked unrealistic.

Then I moved to Los Angeles for a year and late one night was driving home from Disneyland. I'd been on the *Mansion* several times and was just turning west onto Wilshire towards the bay when I realized I was looking at the real life thing. The fog had rolled in off the ocean, and hung between the buildings like a delicate tissue. In the very distance, I could just make out the sky. Growing up inland I had never seen marine fog before.

Yet seeing this also put me in a mood that was moving and almost impossible to put into words. I was seeing what Yale Gracey had seen so many years ago and carefully recreated on an indoor set. I had to wonder if he too had driven west on Wilshire one night and been struck by the beauty of the coastal Los Angeles fog.

Maybe the most beautiful thing about the Graveyard set is its huge back wall, which cannot really be appreciated from the Doombuggy unless the scrims are very, very, very clean. The entire rear wall of the scene is composed of a carefully aligned projection of ominously rolling clouds[71] interspersed with the occasional sequence of rising ghost effects. It's a huge backdrop of nearly 50 feet of a moving sky, and is jaw dropping to see in person.

The lighting scheme of the two *Haunted Mansions* diverges most radically here in the Graveyard, and one way we can observe this comes down to understanding the way WED was trying to decide how to visually represent ghosts.

Generally speaking, the ghosts at Disneyland are represented as glowing green or blue but otherwise appearing in a room that appears to be lit normally, i.e. with yellow and white lights. This is

12. THE GREAT INDOORS

the reason why the Disneyland ballroom ghosts are green and blue but appear in a room that appears to be lit by candlelight; it's so they don't look dissimilar to the ghosts we'll see later in the ride.

This means that the Disneyland Attic and Graveyard scenes use lots of incandescent lights, but try to create pools of darkness where the UV-sensitive backlight ghosts can appear. This means that lots of scenes at Disneyland are cross-lit with two kinds of light, so on one hand you get, say, gravestones and earth that appear to be lit with yellow and amber light but which have a glowing blue person standing inside them.

Just two years later, they had tossed out the whole idea of visually unifying the ghosts from scene to scene. The Florida Ballroom ghosts appear white, because the color reflects better on glass. The Attic and Graveyard are lit with pretty much exactly the same strategy: UV light to illuminate the spooks with small pocket fill lights stashed here and there to light up details of the scene. This means that the Attic and Graveyard in Florida ended up being much darker that those at Disneyland, yet Disneyland's graveyard has a wonderful sensation of really being in amongst the old sunken graves that Florida can't quite match. It's hard to see the dead grass floor covering in Florida, and you generally only get silhouetted impressions of the headstones. The overall effect is a scene very dimly awash in moonlight and primarily illuminated by the glow emitted from the ghouls themselves.

Why abandon a perfectly good and ambitious lighting scheme? Because it gave WED lots of problems. The Disneyland Graveyard, unless it's in absolute top condition - which the realities of running a theme park all but preclude - is just too much to give the ghost figures a fighting chance to come through. They're standing in the shadows of a well-lit set being viewed through a scrim - the slightest variation in those conditions or light leak, or a bit of dust on your scrim, and your ghosts become muddy, difficult to discern figures.

Florida's lighting designer solved this problem by dropping the ambient light to almost nothing. There's nearly no light illuminating the area between the cars and the scrim, giving the

Florida and Tokyo graveyards their distinct "silhouette" look. In addition, the ghosts have been moved forward to be right against the scrim - sometimes, mere inches. The overall darker lighting scheme and proximity to the cars give the Magic Kingdom ghosts the absolute best chances of being seen.

As it happens, although the Haunted Mansion in both forms is very much a Claude Coats show, Marc was on-site in Florida in 1971 overseeing *Jungle Cruise* and *Country Bear Jamboree*, and often dropped by Haunted Mansion to make suggestions on the Graveyard. Although it's impossible to know for sure, the idea that the Florida show's vastly improved Graveyard may have come about partially due to Marc's perfectionist tendencies is a pleasing one.

Maybe the oddest thing in the *Haunted Mansion* is the small Mummy tableau near the end of the graveyard. Marc Davis was a master of the one-glance gag. A top shelf Marc Davis gag, like the duelists in the Ballroom, is a beautiful thing.[72] But I can't think of any other Marc Davis joke which is as confounding, yet also actually got into an attraction, as the Mummy. It's strange, and it's over before you have a chance to decode it.

The Victorians loved the ancient world to such an extent that it's easy to forget that they were the first generation of the modern world. An expanding leisure class meant booming populations of collectors and hobbyists, and technological advancements in printing meant expansive volumes with elaborate illustrations could be produced and purchased affordably. As a result, a great many Victorian tastemakers with too little to do could purchase at popular prices unusually opulent printed editions on such matters as ancient Grecian art, or Sir Walter Scott-ian medieval England, or new discoveries in the ancient art of Egypt.

This real-world influence is all over the *Haunted Mansion*. There's the absurd neo-romantic Castellated facade of the Florida house, but the tall Grecian columns and wrought iron traceries of the California house are as strong as the statement. Is there any point in history when the Victorians didn't seem to be racing towards their destiny as the template for ghost lore? Even their most modern and fashionable houses looked like tombs.

In 1799, Napoleon's army was digging in Egypt and accidentally uncovered the Rosetta Stone. Once the stone passed from French to English control and was brought to London in 1802, it sparked a craze for all things Egyptian. If you've ever been wandering Central Park in New York and wondered why there's an Egyptian obelisk in the park for no apparent reason, it's because of Victorian Egyptomania. There's another in London near Westminster Abbey and another in Paris, and collectively they are known as "Cleopatra's Needles".[73]

The "Needles" touched off a fashion for Egyptian funerary art, and to this day American cemeteries are dotted with once-fashionable funerary obelisks, a form of gravestone once unknown in the Western world. The Florida facade is covered with them and they help create the impression of the house as a gigantic tomb.

Even wealthier and more fashionable Victorians erected tombs in the Egyptian style, which explains the neo-Egyptian crypt we see in the Mansion behind the Mummy. One bizarre social event of the era was to procure a real mummy, lay it out on the table of the drawing room, and host a mummy unwrapping party.

And so here we're given an interpretive choice. Either the *Haunted Mansion* Mummy is a legitimate mummy brought over to the New World for social or scientific use and then re-buried in a public cemetery in an Egyptian-style tomb, or some Victorian crackpot paid to have his body bandaged up, placed in a sarcophagus, and placed in an Egypt-style mausoleum. What's alarming is that both of these possibilities are equally legitimate.

Mummy re-burials in the New World are actually fairly common. Poorly preserved mummies which either had simply crumbled or been poked at too much by the Victorians could not be offered to museums and were simply buried in the public cemetery. A two-year-old Egyptian prince who died in 1883 B.C. - Amun-Her-Khepesh-Ef - is buried in Middlebury, Vermont.[74]

If that's how a mummy got to the New World, what about his companion, the old guy? He wear a cowl with a hood, and has a long beard - signifiers of a mystic, perhaps a wizard or alchemist - a figure of antiquity who dabbled in the Secrets of the Universe. It would make sense that a figure of venerable learning would want to speak to a mummy. After all, one reason why the Victorians loved mummies is because they imagined that they could, through Spiritualism, contact the souls of the departed and thus learn the secrets of the ancient world.

So is the joke that this ancient seer is here confronted with an actual living mummy but is too old and deaf to hear what he says?

But the likelihood of this gag being tapped to appear in the *Haunted Mansion* based on such esoteric knowledge is unlikely. I'm convinced that what I outlined above is what was running through Marc Davis's head when he conceived of the joke, but why did that sketch get pulled out of the pile for inclusion in the final show?

Much of the material chosen for the *Haunted Mansion* seems to have pulled simply because it was amusing, visually understandable, and somewhat spooky. The Mummy is one of those really puzzling details that stays with you, and perhaps that argues best for its inclusion.

12. THE GREAT INDOORS

Near the Mummy is the only thing in the Graveyard which I think is legitimately chilling: the oft-overlooked bicycle ghosts.

What are the bicycle ghosts? Well, depending on how carefully the lighting in the Graveyard has been maintained and how dusty the second scrim is, it may be next to impossible to see them. They circle around on the hill up behind the tea party and crashed hearse. The best spot to see them is actually probably from the top of the *Mansion* once you exit out from the Attic window; it's easy to spot all four of them spinning around way at the back of the scene from there. There are two single riders and two sharing a tandem bicycle.

What do they look like? Your best shot for seeing them is to ride again and take a close look at the ghosts which fly in the ballroom window; it's the same figure. It's like a sheet draped over an invisible human form with two long, bony arms jutting out with reaching hands.

That's scary enough, but the cyclists have *ping-pong ball googly eyes* inside the hollow form of the sheet, and they're painted to appear to be looking at the Doombuggies as they spin by. It's supposed to be whimsical, but I find it to be completely unnerving. Until the 1980s, the cyclists would emit long, drawn out moans as they made their rounds.

There's a long, dark hallway that goes under the Graveyard for emergency evacuations. The access staircase is hidden across from the Singing Busts behind the crypt with a bulge-o brick front. You go through a dark tunnel under the scene, pop out along the back wall underneath the 10 x 10 sky projectors, then climb a staircase to a platform that leads to the exterior exit door. Alongside that platform, you get a great view of the bicycle ghosts making their rounds just inches away. It's hard to stand there, with those hollow sheets and googly eyes staring at you as they zip past.

The *Haunted Mansion* opened in 1971 with twelve pop-up ghouls. They lurked inside trunks in the Attic, where I argued they played a major interpretive role in the attraction. They linger on in the Graveyard, where I would argue they once were, and still are, important figures.

There is not much love in the world for these minor inhabitants of the spirit house. For one, they are not a special effect - the *Haunted Mansion*'s true stock in trade. Second, they are relatively close to the funhouse apparatus which, as of 1969, had been haunting local amusement parks and fairground Ghost Trains and Wacky Shacks for around 40 years. For these reasons they are often objects of scorn for being below the standards of the rest of the show.

But there is no harm in pointing out that Disney appropriated certain aspects of a very rich American tradition of amusement parks - a rich American tradition which is all too often ignored in studies of Disneyland and her progeny. Just as *Mr. Toad's Wild Ride* and especially *Snow White's Adventures* took the form of dark rides not unlike any number of non-Disney spook houses, the familiar presentation is *part of* what helped frame the audience's expectations for these attractions.

But *Mr. Toad* and *Snow White* were beautifully mounted experiences in a genre they helped abolish. To cite another example, the Magic Kingdom *Jungle Cruise* kicked off with a leafy variation on the traditional Tunnel of Love, and of course the trip behind the waterfall at Schweitzer Falls had been a stock in trade for old mills and log flumes for generations.[75]

It is where these Disney attractions connect to a larger native tradition of amusement parks, world's fair, amusement piers, Atlantic Cities and Coney Islands that the difference between what Disney did and the rest of the world did becomes important. Anyone who had actually boarded a spook house at a local carnival would immediately see and understand this world of difference.

Ironically, Disneyland and the Magic Kingdom are places where these established traditions, expanded and elaborated, could have lived on. Coney Island is today but a pale shadow of her former glory, and rare is the person today who has actually been on a real Wacky Shack or Phantasmagoria at their local amusement park. The Disney versions have driven the originals to the verge of extinction, and today the points of connection between the Disney tradition and the earlier traditions are often our only point of connection to a larger, and vanishing, world of American entertainment history.

The *Haunted Mansion* is really the best Ghost Train ever built. You don't ride in Pretzel Amusement Company cars and you don't zip past dancing skeletons and women being sawed in half, but there are a number of eerie echoes between the *Mansion* and the earlier attractions which become a part of the texture of the whole experience.

The true precedent for the *Mansion* pop-up ghoul was one of Pretzel Amusement Company's most famous "stunts", known as the "Jersey Devil". A simple paper mache head impaled on a rod, when the car would roll near the Jersey Devil's black painted box, the wheels would depress a lever set in the floor which would both send the Devil shooting up on his pole and connect an electrical circuit causing a light to turn on. When the car rolled away, the lever would reset and the light would turn off. Pretzel Amusement Company sold the same gag with skull and witch faces.[76]

Which isn't too far from the MAPO pop-up ghoul of 1969. But what separates the pop-up ghouls in the *Haunted Mansion* from the Jersey Devil lurking in the dark corners of some Pretzel ride seventy years ago is **context.**

Compared to the paper mache creations of the Pretzel company and Outdoor Dimensional Display, Blaine Gibson and the rest of the WED model shop did a bang up job sculpting the array of faces which leap up at us from behind tombstones and out of trunks. It's too bad that these sculptures must be seen only fleetingly, because when painted properly, given proper wigs and sensitive lighting, they're memorably effective.

Each ghoul rises at the conclusion of each verse of "Grim, Grinning Ghosts". It still is this way, but the reasons **why** this happens is our clue to unlocking the secret of the importance of these figures to the larger Graveyard scene itself.

When Buddy Baker wrote "Grim, Grinning Ghosts", he was drawing on a diverse tradition of nominally spooky songs of the 20s and 30s like "Mysterious Mose", songs inspired by a rumbling of the horror train already headed down the tracks. "Mysterious Mose" lightly kidded the popularity of Lon Chaney and *The Bat*, and so became a signpost for the popularity of the cinema of the fantastic. And early on, "Grim Grinning Ghosts" was called "The Screaming Song".

Not to put too fine of a point of it, but have you ever noticed that the lyrics to "Grim Grinning Ghosts" are extremely literal? I mean no disrespect to X. Atencio, but notice that lyrics like:

When the crypt doors creak and the tombstones quake
Spooks come out for a swinging wake

Or:

Now don't close your eyes and don't try to hide
Or a silly spook may sit by your side

Describe things have happened or will happen on the attraction? Observant riders will see plenty of creaking crypt doors and quaking tombstones and rising spirits in the Graveyard scene. Once we've noticed that "Grim Grinning Ghosts" is quite directly referencing things happening in the attraction, statements in the lyrics like:

Creepy creeps with eerie eyes
Start to shriek and harmonize

...start to look suspicious. There's plenty of harmonizing happening in this "Screaming Song", but shrieking?

Well, there *was*. There still are speakers hidden in the front of every tombstone these happy haunts leap up from behind. Each ghost had an individual sound effect as they came up - a grunt, scream, groan, or laugh.

There are several excellent recordings of the Disneyland *Mansion* in the 70s, made by Jaime Maas and "Guy the Ghoul", where these vocalizations can be heard very clearly. This repetition, with a ghoul popping up in front of each graveyard tableau between verses, allows there to be some formal continuity between each cluster of ghosts in the graveyard. The ghoul pop-ups aren't just cheap scares throughout the scene, they were actually *the thing that structured the Graveyard finale*, a unifying thread just as much as the song. Like everything else in the attraction, the leaping ghosts were conceived with a purpose.

Plus, they were *scary*. The *Haunted Mansion* is no slouch in creepy ideas and images, but the pop-up ghosts represent the only *really* scary thing in the whole ride. That they appeared only in the final leg of the attraction was significant and speaks to a structural progression which was carefully thought out and artfully realized. And they really should still be screaming as they leap to this day.

How old is the Graveyard the scene takes place in? Despite early publicity describing it as a "private graveyard playground", it's clear that it's a separate public cemetery behind the old house, with its own gate and fence. It's the "old boneyard" which invariably accompanies any truly haunted house in pop culture.

We can date it pretty conclusively based on the style of the gravestones, and so we can also tell that it pre-dates the house itself. So the scared guy we passed on our way into the cemetery is probably The Old Groundskeeper. Not the Caretaker of the *Mansion* - the wait staff still hanging around to take care of the ghosts fulfill that function - but the groundskeeper of the Graveyard. He fits the description - shovel, lantern, dog, big scarf. In California he truly is "The Old Groundskeeper" but in Florida he's a younger guy, with a Don Knotts kind of look to him, freckles, and a baseball cap.

We pass him holding his shovel and then once we're down into the Graveyard we see an old hearse stuck in the mud. There are actual wheel tracks veering off the Doombuggy track leading to it, and the coffin is spilled out the back and its occupant is sitting up and having tea.

So let's work backwards in our logic here. We see a hearse and a coffin, and earlier we see a cemetery groundskeeper with shovel. Now unless we place a *lot* of stock in the invisible-horse hearse out in front of the *Haunted Mansion* - and I don't - this is our *second* interrupted funeral.

It's easy to imagine the scene: the hearse slowly pulls into the public cemetery deep in the woods behind the spooky old house. It's raining lightly, and the hearse leaves a muddy trail as it makes its way to the family plot. There's a short service, but everyone leaves quickly - the old cemetery is spooky and it's getting late, but everyone's wary of the spooky old house just on the other side of those trees. Eventually only the old caretaker is left alone with his dog, and by lantern light he goes to work until...

The graveyard is old. The above ground sarcophagi are all cracked and broken, and the place is overrun with shrubs and wild plants. So what, exactly, is our groundskeeper taking care of? Burials in the old cemetery must be uncommon, and there's that weird

Egyptian crypt that nobody likes. He could be a grave robber (unlikely, but worth considering), or perhaps a treasure hunter. Or maybe he's just one of those caretakers who hates sticking around the place at night.

We know the guy was getting set to bury that coffin sticking out of the back of the hearse because he's holding a shovel, something I doubt anybody would be doing unless they planned to use it. It's a nearly subliminal setup for a payoff to come much later in the scene, and one of the most subtle delights of the *Haunted Mansion*.

Yet the Caretaker raises a question, and it has to do with his hat - at Disneyland he's an old guy with an old fashioned style hat and at Magic Kingdom he's a young guy with a baseball cap. He's burying a toe-pincher style casket that's spilled out of a horse-drawn hearse. What time period is this?

At Disneyland, the time period strikes me as today. Disneyland is laid out in such a way that the individual themed areas aren't really screened off from each other but bleed together - while entering the *Haunted Mansion*, we can see *Big Thunder Mountain*, *Splash Mountain* and the *Matterhorn*, none of which "belong" to New Orleans Square. Once we get inside attractions they play by their own rules, but the open spaces of Disneyland are aesthetic free-for-alls where we are nowhere else but Disneyland.

It's tough to say the same for Magic Kingdom. Largely, the Magic Kingdom themed areas are screened out from each other much more carefully. Architecture that spills over from other areas, like Cinderella Castle, has been painstakingly matched with other architecture inside the area so it presents as little of an intrusion as possible. There's a famous detail, popularized in *The Imagineering Field Guide to the Magic Kingdom* by Alex Wright, that WED decorated the facade of the Sunshine Pavilion with carved water buffalo, knowing they would read as western longhorns from inside Frontierland.[77] Nobody inside Magic Kingdom who's walked through colonial America to get to the *Haunted Mansion* would suggest that we are still in "today".

Then when are we? We've got a mansion which I've dated as being circa 1850. Then there are two horse drawn hearses that need accounting for - one out front, the other in the cemetery out back - plus an abandoned funeral sitting in the Conservatory upstairs, and a skeleton still hanging in the cupola.[78]

The Caretaker at Magic Kingdom is wearing a baseball cap, but all that means is that we can safely date him to post-1900. There are still horse drawn hearses in use, but we already know that this is a very isolated area. How long do we have to allow for to account for the level of decay we see inside the house? Twenty years? Thirty years?[79]

I like to think of the *Haunted Mansion* as taking place "sometime in the twentieth century", but specifically with an emphasis on the earliest years of the twentieth century - pointedly, the same years when Marc Davis, Claude Coats, and their WED associates would have been children, shrinking past their own neighborhood haunted houses.

This is why it is necessary to place such an emphasis on the formative horror culture of that era - the 20s, 30s, and 40s. This is why it is important to know *The Cat and the Canary*, and Lon Chaney, and "Mysterious Mose" when talking and thinking about the *Haunted Mansion*. It may be the ultimate haunted house from everyone's childhood, but that also means it's the ultimate haunted house from the childhoods of the men who built it. Creators who went to the local cinema and thrilled to comedy mysteries where clawed hands reached out of sliding panels to grasp helpless heroines.

The *Haunted Mansion* is, at its core, an Old Dark House thriller. It belongs specifically to that genre, and within that genre and the other genres it codifies and combines - the gothic romance, the fireside ghost story, and the amusement park *Laff in the Dark*. This is why the 2003 *Haunted Mansion* film failed to evoke memories of the attraction it was based on - it got the film genre wrong.

WED Enterprises built the ultimate haunted house, and they stuffed it full of mysteries, threatening images, dark deeds, and amusing comedy. The see-sawing tone of the attraction, the sliding panels, the sinister servants, the cobwebs, and the decaying grandeur of the place all speak to formative thrills on hot summers at the movies - the distinctly American character of the Old Dark House thriller.

As we pass out of the Graveyard and the Ghost Host returns with a cheerful "Ah, there you are!", Act 3 of the *Haunted Mansion* comes to an end and we enter what amounts to an extended coda. Right as we're leaving, off to the right, is the visual equivalent of a grace note from an orchestra - one final joke to go out on.

Throughout the *Mansion*, we've seen ghosts attempting to escape from confined spaces: coffins, locked doors. This only accelerates once the jamboree begins and we get down in the Graveyard; Madame Leota must have been really good, because she's also managed to bring back practically every occupant of the nearby old cemetery. Sarcophagus lids shift back and forth, tombstones push up and down - everyone's ready to join the party.

As we enter the cemetery, sharp eyed viewers will see that the crypt back behind the Graveyard Band has a bricked-up front that's been broken through - a cleverly accomplished painting, for those who appreciate that. The Flutist is sitting up in his own sarcophagus, and the drummer is using its lid as an instrument. WED has established the pattern here in this first scene: expect these ghosts to be pushing their way out of their graves. It's like the scene in *Thriller*.

And our expectations are rewarded with a succession of crypts with what I call the bulge-o fronts, as if a force inside is trying to push its way out. And at the very end, as we're leaving, we see one final crypt - and this time its occupant is bricking himself back in!

Almost nobody sees the setup for this pay-off gag, but those who do really appreciate it. And if we widen our scope to include the entire show inside the main house as part of the set-up for this gag, where coffins shake and doors groan under supernatural pressure, it's a pay off a long time coming.

13. OUT OF THE GRAVE

Following the pandemonium of the Graveyard, the *Haunted Mansion*'s focus narrows to a laser intensity as we pass into the crypt and before us stand the three Hitchhikers. They're visually complementary - there's a short one, a tall one, and a medium-build one. Their features are distinctive - the short fellow has a hook nose, the tall fellow is gaunt, and the medium one has heavy features and a hunchback. If this seems unremarkable consider how much less compelling and less interesting it would have been to have a short fat guy, a tall thin guy, and a "normal" looking guy.

They're arranged in a row, and placed up on a little platform so they're visually centered inside their framing arch. Behind and around them is the merest suggestion of a stone crypt, nearly negative space - it's a stripped down, effortlessly communicative visual.

The body language is impeccable. The short fellow has hoisted his ball and chain, indicating he's ready to travel. The heavy set guy has a carpet bag, and of course the tall guy has jauntily raised his hat, ready for a lift. The composition is balanced. The ghosts are complementary, expressive, and just the right level of spooky and funny. If we can boil down the *Haunted Mansion* to one visual, this is it. The ride designers sure felt so - they put this key visual on the attraction's poster and advertising. It's an unusual choice to advertise your attraction entirely on the basis of something that happens only at the very end of it, but the expressive power of three ghosts hitching a ride is powerfully associative.

It's also a distinctly American concept. The urban legends and rumors about phantom hitchhikers and ghost cars, indeed entire haunted roadways, develops from our love of the automobile, the size of the country, and the breadth of our interstate travel system. There's a wonderful freedom in knowing you can get in a car and go all the way across the country if you want to. But it's a long, lonely road - there's a suspicion that things can get mixed up and reality's wires can get crossed out there on a lost highway in the middle of nowhere. If road travel is a key American myth of the 20th century, the Phantom Hitchhiker is its flip side image.

There's the classic story of the young man who pulls over to pick up a pretty young girl in a rainstorm or on a back road late at night. He offers to bring her home, she gives him directions, but she vanishes before the car gets there. Upon discovering this the young man goes to the house the vanishing girl directed him to only to be greeted at the door by an elderly lady. He tells her his story and she explains that he picked up the ghost of her daughter, who was struck and killed by a car on that spot many years ago.

You know the story. We all do. It's been circulating in force since at least the advent of the automobile, and before that with the wagon, and horse-drawn carriage.

There are further variations. Stories are told of a red-bearded man who haunts a desolate stretch of highway in Massachusetts who pulls a similar vanishing act, only he grins grotesquely and laughs manically before disappearing. This same specter has been known to appear with his face pressed against the passenger window of cars traveling down the road at high speed.

Caryville, Wisconsin, has a phantom pickup truck which speeds by a haunted cemetery and schoolhouse. Central Florida has a "Dead Zone" on I-4 where phantom pickup trucks and a ghost car with its lights off sometimes drives against traffic; the highway was reportedly built over some graves in this spot. Scotland has a haunted stretch of highway, the A75, where phantom ghouls and monsters run screaming into the headlights of oncoming cars.

The hitchhiking ghosts play on these long-standing oral and folklore traditions, and offer us an opportunity to have a phantom hitchhiker story of our own.

Since the 1990s, three names have become associated with the figures: Phineas, Ezra, and Gus. These names have even become official: they're used on the official action figures from 2003, in the *Haunted Mansion Clue* and *Haunted Mansion Game of Life* board games sold at Walt Disney World, and these names were added to gravestones in the new exterior queue graveyard in 2011.

I suspect that the names derive ultimately from stories within the "Ghostly Gallery", a binder collecting backstories of the *Haunted Mansion*'s major ghosts written by Cast Members in the early 90s. These stories are basically fan fiction, and vary in quality from telling to telling. If the names descend from a legit source pre-dating these stories, I'm guessing it's nothing more than nicknames Maids and Butlers invented for these characters - the maintenance documentation for the ride calls them "Little Man", "Skeleton", and "Hunchback".

That may be a superficial distinction, but I worry that the fan names, besides being the sort of extra-textual trivia that already snowballs around this ride experience, obscure the visual grammar of the scene. Giving the hitchers name obscures their function as specific *types*.

Take a look at the tall guy. He's lanky. His hat is jauntily, ingratiatingly raised above his head. He's got a big smile and a bow tie. I always imagine that when he talks he sounds like Lee Tracy from *The Front Page*. This is a guy who wants you to think he's an okay fellow. He wants your confidence. Isn't there a name for somebody like that? A confidence man? A con man?

The hitchhiker trio are cleverly designed to evoke exactly three key types of hitchers we wouldn't want getting into our car on a dark and stormy night: the mysterious traveler, the con man, and the escaped convict. It's a murderer's row of suspicious faces, and it's far more interesting - and funny - concept than knowing their names.[80]

The typology of the hitchers plays into what was once the cherry on the sundae of the ride experience: when a ghost actually sat next to you in the car. This moment was both comic and genuinely spooky, because they could only be seen while you were looking in a mirror! It was really the perfect encapsulation of the tone of the attraction: is it scary or is it funny? It was both.

In 2011, a brand new digital projected version of this effect was installed, and the result is a mixed bag. On one hand it's nice to see the ghosts inside the car moving around a lot more - on the other the CGI models are a poor match for the dimensional ghosts we enjoy just around the corner. It's another case where new special effects appear to "interact" with the occupants of the car.

But the Hitchhiking Ghosts have always been interactive - and interactive on the rider's own terms. How many people, since 1969, have given the invading ghosts bunny ears, or kissed them, or "hugged" them?

That was true interaction; that was lightning in a bottle. Now the ghosts juggle your head with theirs, and riders don't really interact any longer, they just stare with amusement at yet another digital effect. While the original was limited enough to invite you to bring your imagination to the party, now WDI does all the work for riders.

Around the corner and up the hill from the Hitchhikers we pass one of the most enigmatic things in the *Haunted Mansion*: Little Leota, who floats above us, unexplainably tiny, calling out at us to return.

It's an arresting image for the attraction to end on, and it sounds a note of ambiguity which carries with us out through the exit of the ride. The ambiguity is even keener at Disneyland, where Leota waits for us literally just before the final door. She's been puzzling and unnerving riders for as long as they've been streaming through the exit.

X. Atencio has always claimed that Little Leota is based on a character played by Anjanette Comer in *The Loved One*, an elaborate dark comedy about the funeral business from 1965. The film is full of the kind of death puns that are the *Haunted Mansion*'s stock in trade, so it's possible that Atencio revisited the film in preparation for writing his script. In the film, Comer plays a pretty girl who loves working at a funeral parlor and lives in a house ready to collapse off the side of a cliff, a sort of predecessor to the Goths of today. But besides her enthusiasm for morticians, coffins, and death certificates, it's hard to see any connection between the two characters.

The projected face for the figure, when it was projected by 16mm film, had a leader strip for the film labeled "Ghost Hostess". In fact, there is such a reference in Atencio's script, although it was deleted from the final attraction:

> We have 999 happy haunts here, but there's room for 1000 - any volunteers, hrm? If you should decide to join us, final arrangements may be made at the end of the tour. A charming

'ghostess' will be on hand to take your application.

Here we are at the end of the tour and there's the "Ghostess", just as promised.[81] Hanging out in a crypt and taking ghost applications does sound exactly like something the Anjanette Comer character from *The Loved One* would do, but I think there's something else at work here.

Little Leota is sinister, but not in the obvious way that much of the ride is. She's sweet, almost disarming. But if we got ourselves into this mess by daring to poke our heads inside the old house on the hill, then Little Leota is the final gatekeeper. We pass by her easily, mere mortals taking a tour, but she's the one who's there to stop you from leaving if you become number 1000.

Also, in a larger sense, Leota adds some shading to the end of the attraction. Ghost stories are basically mysteries, and like most mysteries, the *Haunted Mansion*'s trajectory is from obscurity to clarity. What's in that big house? Is it really haunted? Are there such things as ghosts? What do they want? All of these questions are raised and resolved by the larger reassuring pattern of the attraction, but Leota sounds a note of caution. Her strange appearance and menacing tone implies that not everything is resolved, that the house still has mysteries it is not willing to let go of.[82]

But that isn't goodbye; we must still go about the business of unloading out of our cars and then proceeding back out into the park. There's almost nothing to look at in the Unload Area; similar to the Load Area, there is the bare minimum to maintain the setting, quite unlike Disneyland's beautifully sculpted crypt vault of collapsing stones behind a wrought iron gate. Yet in the last few hundred feet of the attraction, the Magic Kingdom *Haunted Mansion* rallies and ends on a subtle note.

It's the exit hallway, which is something like a decompression chamber between the *extreme* unreality of the *Haunted Mansion*

and the manifest unreality of everywhere else in the Magic Kingdom. It's a short hallway with a twisty layout - what first seems like a sharp turn to the right is a gentle curve, followed an unexpected turn to the left, and we are back outside.[83]

Interestingly, the idea that *Haunted Mansion* guests would begin their tour in an old house but eventually wind their way into a graveyard and then exit the attraction through a crypt seems to date back to the mid-sixties version of the attraction; the double-sided walkthrough being developed by Yale Gracey and Rolly Crump.

As shown by Dan Olson, when Disneyland's *Haunted Mansion* facade went up in 1963 and 1964 two mirror-image exit areas were built, one on each side of the attraction. The idea seems to have been to style these as very elaborate walled graveyards that the attraction would spill into. Once the two walkthroughs became one ride-through, the south-side exit courtyard became the current "side yard" waiting area and the north-side courtyard became the current exit area, although the final shape of the Speedramp exit precludes the notion of exiting directly into an area that allows you to wander amongst tomb stones.

So while Magic Kingdom's *Haunted Mansion* doesn't quite have the oneiric qualities of the ascent to the surface, the literal return from the tomb, it does have that terrific exit corridor. It's hard to convey the excellence of this short little jog in words, but with arched plastered ceilings, earthen brickworks, and high-set windows, with the sung refrain of "Grim Grinning Ghosts" by the singing busts - an atmospheric track that's totally swallowed up at Disneyland - it's all allowed to bloom into a uniquely mournful and spooky send-off. It's a slow release from the compression chamber of the attraction, more in keeping with the more leisurely key-up and wind-down which attractions are afforded at Magic Kingdom.

Most of Disneyland's attractions exit in a way not dissimilar to their cultural forebears: the attraction simply deposits you back out on the main thoroughfare somewhere not too far from where you entered. There are some exceptions - the long walk down the trellised exit at *Pirates of the Caribbean* is a major highlight, but the Florida park is where WED Enterprises really began to experiment with making the action of exiting an attraction into a bit more of an experience.

Ergo, we have a version of *Pirates of the Caribbean* in Florida which deposits riders into the sun-splashed depths of a Caribbean market. Here, the *Haunted Mansion* releases us bit by bit, through three distinct phases until we reach the "safety" of Liberty Square once again. The exit hallway is where the ghosts "say goodbye", an inverse echo of their slow, gradual introduction at the start of the ride. They began as shadows and end as voices, dimly echoing through one last, twisty corridor leading out to the sunlight.

Along the left wall of the exit hallway are three high, half-round windows, each with a drab little spiderweb wrought iron motif. For a long time these windows were frosted, and often let in a dim but appropriate sunlight. Originally they were clear glass, and the wooded hill that divided Liberty Square and Fantasyland and the bottoms of a great many tree trunks could be seen through the windows. I believe this was added to help compensate for the lack of a strong "underground" feeling in the Florida version's crypt scenes; while exiting, we can see that we are indeed traveling through a buried tunnel. If so, this was literally the *Haunted Mansion*'s final effect, and the opaque state of these windows means a bit of visual communication has been lost.

The exit corridor spills into a quiet courtyard of crypts which marks the original "exit area" of the attraction, long before the current entrance gate went up and claimed what was once general Liberty Square open space as the "estate" of the *Haunted Mansion*.

For the first twenty years of the existence of the *Haunted Mansion*, it was positioned at the end of Liberty Square separated from the nearest structures by very large oak trees. It was simply *there* at the end of the street. Yet the area around the Mansion unquestionably *belonged* to it: the wrought iron fences, flickering gas lamps, and crooked cobblestones announced the arrival of the supernatural as surely as an entrance gate, which it did not have. When the Magic Kingdom *Mansion* received its formal entry gate in 1992, the original exit gate was dismantled and the area where it once stood was re-paved.

There was just one piece of the exit gate Disney could not dismantle. It was the top of a hollow pipe buried in the ground, roughly the diameter of a dime. This was almost certainly a hole in the tarmac that a metal peg could be dropped into to "lock" the exit gate.

Next to it, embedded in the concrete, was a mysterious but separate rectangle. I've been told that this was actually the tip of a flat head screwdriver inserted between the pipe and the concrete in an attempt to jimmy it out, but the tip snapped off. After years and years of being walked over by tens of thousands of people an day, the two metal pieces smoothed over and began to look like they were attached. They began to look like... a ring.

13. OUT OF THE GRAVE

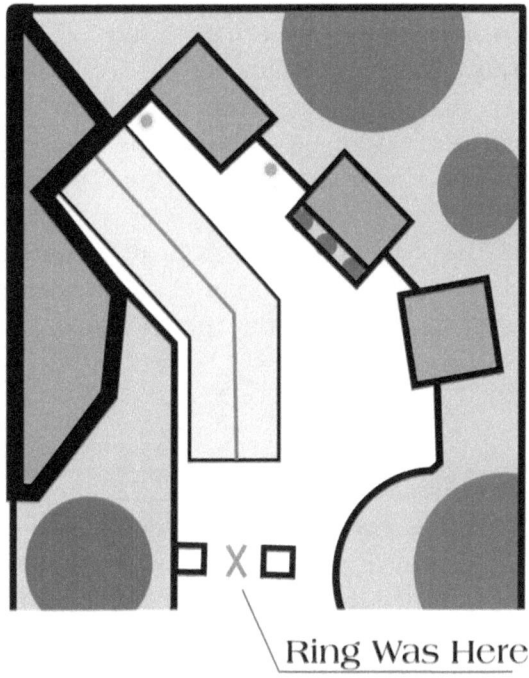

Ring Was Here

Once the internet really got rolling, the first discussions tended to center around the topic of theme park urban legends and trivia, of which the *Haunted Mansion* is fertile ground. At some point, the idea that guests "fall" backwards to the Graveyard and die got conflated with rumors about the Bride, and then the idea became that the trip down the hill to the graveyard is a *re-enactment* of the bride's suicide plunge off the top of the house to the ground below. The proof? As you leave, if you look carefully, you can see her wedding ring still embedded in the pavement where she died!

People *really* liked this idea. It was the perfect storm, including a location outside the house where a suicidal bride could realistically, and fatally, land. It became a tradition for some families to search for the ring after a *Haunted Mansion* ride, and Cast Members enthusiastically perpetuated the story. More often than not, one or more groups could be spotted aimlessly wandering the exit courtyard, looking for the elusive ring.

In 2007, Imagineering paved over the "wedding ring", probably not coincidentally with the arrival of the "Constance Hatchaway" bride. The fan uproar, however, was more significant than anyone expected. In defiance, some fans fabricated new stories involving circles in pavement, or perhaps jumped to strange conclusions upon hearing of the lamented "ring" and not finding it in the park.[85]

In 2011, the wedding ring was finally returned - but in a different spot. It now resides in a corner of the interactive queue, and it's an *actual* wedding ring with a stone, not the top of a pole.[86]

In 1992, Imagineering introduced the now-ubiquitous on-ride photo at *Splash Mountain* and gave theme park purists grief for about a decade in which seemingly every possible on-ride photo opportunity was exploited. Following the opening of a photo location at *Buzz Lightyear's Space Ranger Spin* in 2002, merchandise set their sights on the *Haunted Mansion* in 2003.

2003 is also notable for being the release of the highly questionable Eddie Murphy theatrical comedy *The Haunted Mansion*. In the film, a major sequence is set in a flooded crypt, and this crypt was earmarked to be the design inspiration for an on-ride photo shop located at the exit of the ride. Those three arched windows were going to become the off-ride entrance to the shop, themed as a wine cellar and crypt. The middle-most crypt was due to be replaced with the new outdoor entrance and exit.

Starting in the late 90s at Walt Disney World, the Merchandise division had enjoyed record years of profitability thanks to the 25th Anniversary "castle cake", the opening of Animal Kingdom, and the Epcot Millennium Celebration, and began to be granted more and more input into decisions about the parks. This came to a head in 2001, resulting in the construction of a gigantic sorcerer Mickey hat at the end of Hollywood Boulevard at Disney-MGM Studios (it housed a pin shop), and the simultaneous unveiling of the "Share A Dream Come True" parade at Magic

Kingdom. The parade floats would be styled to resemble giant snow globes - snow globes which, not coincidentally, would be on sale throughout the park.

But in 2001, following the terror attacks, new restrictions on liquids in air baggage effectively ended the market for snow globes at Walt Disney World. The subsequent national tourism recession eroded the power of the Merchandise division, and the *Mansion* shop never got off the ground.

Between 2003 and 2010, Merchandise continued to push for a *Haunted Mansion* shop. 2003 and 2004 saw the introduction of the most extensive, elaborate line of merchandise in *Haunted Mansion* history. The Yankee Trader shop was given over entirely to the *Mansion*. Board games, shirts, and a line of "action figures" in ride-accurate dioramas appeared. At this stage, the plan was to dig out the entire hill between the *Haunted Mansion* and Yankee Trader and create an exit directly into the Trader. By 2006, the Trader had reverted to housewares and again the idea died on the vine.

2011 saw the final nail in the coffin for the "buried shop" idea as the space between the *Haunted Mansion* exit and Yankee Trader was redeveloped into a new entrance to Fantasyland themed to *Tangled*, leaving the shop marooned by a network of encircling walkways.

By that time, Merchandise had changed their approach and now focused on deluxe collectors' items intended for adults and savvy consumers. In 2013, the Yankee Trader was repainted in a murky dark blue, and in 2014, Merchandise finally got their *Haunted Mansion* shop. Even all those years later, the proposed name from back in 2003 was still used - Memento Mori.

The *Mansion*'s exit courtyard is one of the most pleasantly contemplative areas of the Magic Kingdom. Here, fascinatingly, finally, the long-planned cemetery exit for the *Haunted Mansion* is realized. Three simple crypts sit off to the left amid some very evocative flickering lamps. The exit corridor reprise of "Grim Grinning Ghosts" still echoes dimly, but now its sounds are mixed with the general bustle of the park and the river, achieving a very evocative transitory space.

The first two crypts contain names which are all basic ghost puns, the kind of which are still written on cardboard front lawn gravestones around the country - I. Emma Spook, Paul Tergyst, etc. This is strictly formula, although the names do demonstrate a bit more writing chops than the standard issue 4H Club Haunted House gravestones. What I like about these is the weirdly lopsided, evocative script these are carved in. Not quite antique or modern but thoroughly strange and whimsical, it's evocative and owes nothing to any discernible source, especially with strange touches like "Dustin T. Dust" rendered with the "u" as a superscript above the name.

Sitting at the end of this courtyard is a crypt with a legend of extreme interest. These are the last words of the *Haunted Mansion*.

1440
BLUEBEARD

Here Lyeth His Loving Wives
Penelope Died 1434
Abigail   1435
Anastasia   1436
Prudence   1437
Phoebe   1438
Eugenia   1439
Lucretia

Seven winsome wives
Some fat, some thin
Six of them were faithful
But the seventh did him in

The Bluebeard crypt puts the bow on several motifs that run through the *Haunted Mansion*. There's the motif of wordplay, which is introduced as we move through the family cemetery at the start of the attraction. The "family plot" entertains while it establishes that everyone in this house is already dead, but the wordplay which begins on those gravestones continues with X. Atencio's thesaurus-laded script - where no stone is left unturned in the search for faintly absurd ghost-related puns.

There's also the motif of marriages that end in murder - a rich vein of folklore already tapped by all three of the creative teams who worked on the attraction over its ten year development cycle.[87]

What's especially interesting is this crypt's treatment of the Bluebeard legend - a French folk tale about a serial killer. In the version of the story most commonly read, recorded by Charles Perrault, the seventh wife who discovers the secret of Bluebeard is rescued by her brother on the brink of being slain; she buries the previous wives and remarries as a rich woman. The large crypt, the six wives buried within, the last wife's date of death missing - so far, this tracks with the source fairy tale.

But notice a key difference, that last line: "The seventh did him in."

The folk tale provides no real motivation for Bluebeard. He's a serial killer, and like many modern serial killers he keep mementos of his deeds around - in this case literally the putrefied bodies of his former wives hanging on hooks in the room where he slaughtered them. Presumably wives two through six were slain when they foolishly decided to look inside the "Forbidden Room" and learned the truth.

The *Haunted Mansion* has a "forbidden room" - the Attic. In the Bluebeard story, his "murder room" is in the cellar of the castle. Both basements and attics contain things we don't need, or perhaps want to forget, and are thus imagistically linked as private spaces where secrets may be stored.

An attic was chosen for the *Haunted Mansion* instead of a cellar, presumably because it dramatically makes more sense to enter the house on a ground floor and work our way to the top. And tellingly, the Attic is where the Mansion's own Bluebeard story is uncovered, and it's that revelation which motivates us, like the seventh bride, to flee the house.

Ken Anderson initiated the Bluebeard motif in 1959 and it was then developed by subsequent teams. In Anderson's *Ghost House*, the bride is named Priscilla and she discovers that her husband, a sea captain, is a pirate. He murders her by throwing her down a well. So far, so good: this is a typical Bluebeard story.

It seems to be Marc Davis who is responsible for gender-flipping the story, drawing in his concept art successions of cunning wives murdering doltish husbands. It's these cues *already existing* in the attraction that were drawn on by the design team which developed the "Constance Hatchaway" version of the Bride.

So what we're seeing here is a take on the French folk tale which contorts it to fit a specific *Haunted Mansion* pattern. This crypt is telling a story about a wife murderer who, quite to his surprise, *marries a husband murderer*. It's ironic instead of horrific, and we laugh, because Bluebeard got his just deserts.

This plays very nicely to an overall sense in the *Haunted Mansion* that justice may be served beyond the veil. The Hatbox Ghost reveals the Bride's crimes. Constance may have "gotten away with it" but her ghost confesses to it all.

Consider the dynamite guy stretching portrait - do we feel bad for him? Here's a guy wearing no pants standing on a lit keg of powder. Did he light it himself? Is he committing suicide? He holds a sheet of paper and wears a sash, suggesting a man of learning and position.

His lack of pants suggests embarrassment - has he been placed in a compromised position and sees his own recourse as suicide? There was an era in American history when a mere public insult was grounds for the suggestion of a fatal duel, a time that the *Haunted Mansion* emphatically belongs to. The dynamite guy, even in the portrait's unstretched mode, is not painted in such a way to invite our sympathy. It's very similar to the dynamite guy's mirror image - the quicksand man, whose crossed arms radiate confidence, but whose confidence is misplaced.

All of these reasons, I feel, contribute to the sense of completion the Bluebeard crypt invites, the feeling - for those who take the time to read it - that it wraps up the attraction satisfyingly.

One last point worth considering, and to do so we must detour back into history.

The Bluebeard crypt introduces one of the most problematic details of the *Haunted Mansion*, which is the 1440 date. This is a good four **centuries** before the architectural style of the *Haunted Mansion* will be relevant, and over four **decades** before Christopher Columbus will even "discover" the New World. What's the crypt of a French aristocrat even doing in America?

The Bluebeard story is widely believed to be based on a notorious serial killer of French medieval history known as Gilles de Rais. Gilles was tried and executed for his crimes in 1440, so somebody at WED was reading their history books. Amongst the charges against de Rais, which are numerous and gruesome, is that he had tried several times to summon evil spirits, and had used the innards of his victims to do so. We've got the actual death date of a legitimate maniac attached to the name he's known by in folklore, relocated, quite improbably, to the American colonies.

But is it *really* that improbable, in an attraction where we also have a mummy, a Roman emperor, and a portrait of Jack the Ripper? In many ways this is the final echo of Marc's concept that the *Haunted Mansion* can be a home for "history's famous villains", an idea which was heavily excised from the Disneyland *Haunted Mansion* but which rolled back around for Walt Disney World. At Disneyland, the *Haunted Mansion* is in New Orleans Square, in an area with a strong focus on American history. In Florida, it was relocated up the river to sit directly next to Fantasyland, and given a fantastical architecture.

The *Haunted Mansion* represents American folklore, yes, but I think, especially at Walt Disney World, it represents folklore generally. After all, this is the Magic Kingdom, where Cinderella can have a castle and the cottage of the seven dwarfs can be visited, so why can't Bluebeard, and Jack the Ripper, and vampires and werewolves and the Flying Dutchman all have a home too?

A home that sits at a bend in the river, a home which is like the hinge of a fulcrum between reality and history, myth and fantasy.

14. THESES ON THE HAUNTED MANSION

So here we are, you and I, standing at the exit of the ride. We've seen a lot and talked about more. What else can be said about the *Haunted Mansion* that hasn't been said already?

What makes the *Haunted Mansion* such a rich, such a satisfying experience? That has been the question this text has been driving towards, but quite apart from the thousands of macro-level details I've already expounded on here at length, I have five points - five theses - which explain its power.

It has uncommonly graceful conceptual organization.

The flow of the entire experience, from a menacing house at a bend in the river that's rumored to be haunted, to our lived experience of getting through a night in the place, has an economy of organization that's astonishing. Our movement through the house, from bottom to top, from public spaces to private chambers to forbidden rooms, structures an emotional response that's resonant and can be returned to again and again.

It has generations of cultural resonances built in.

From Barnum to Bluebeard, Victorian architecture, Gothic horror, Poe and Lovecraft, American folklore and European horror tales, the *Haunted Mansion* uproots and exploits the stories and fears we carry around with us every day.

It is visually unambiguous but open to interpretation.

Only *Pirates of the Caribbean* at Disneyland is so near the perfect dream state. What other attraction offers up images and gags which are instantly understandable yet simultaneously totally inscrutable? These images are as iconic and easily understandable as marketing logos, but refuse to offer up any explanation for themselves - dropping shocking image after shocking image into the laps of riders, leaving us to sort out the details ourselves.

It requires that you bring only yourself to the experience.

When we ride *Space Mountain*, we pretend we are astronauts. When we ride *Star Tours*, we pretend we are Jedi. Drawing on deep-seated childhood fears and rituals and pop culture clichés, the *Haunted Mansion* cuts past our defensive barriers. We are only ourselves, daring to venture into the dark spaces of chaos and disorder, and live to tell the tale.

It is a definitive work on a universal story.

Every culture has ghost stories, because every culture has ways of dealing with death. The *Haunted Mansion* is the ultimate haunted house, the ultimate ghost story. Even if you don't believe in ghosts, everyone wants to explore a haunted house. And since 1969, the *Haunted Mansion* has been confounding, enchanting, frightening, baffling, and reassuring us as we prowl its haunted halls, where candles flicker in the deathly still air.

It works every time, for everyone.

PART III: APPENDICES

APPENDIX A: HUMAN AND ANIMAL IMAGERY

Many attractions have details which fall under the category of "decor" and "theme", but it takes an exceptionally creatively organized endeavor for those fine-grain touches to coalesce into "motifs". The *Haunted Mansion* has three categories of what I call *decorative imagery* - decor which works through a specific set of themes.

The first and most obvious category is the "human face" decorative motif, which works in tandem with the architecture to create a feeling of unease even in relatively placid areas.

The human shape, and especially the face, is a pattern we are instinctively wired to recognize, even in places where shapes are placed more or less by happenstance. The *Haunted Mansion* preys on this tendency by placing abstract faces in many decorative details, especially early in the experience. Once we notice one, we see many more, even in areas where no faces have been intentionally placed. This helps create the sensation not only that we are being watched, but that the house is alive and aware of our presence, creating the haunted atmosphere before we even see so much as an item being moved by invisible hands.

The second category of imagery is that of predatory animals. Reoccurring animal imagery in the *Haunted Mansion* helps create the sense of possibly hidden peril — none so obviously as the portrait of a seductive lady in black who becomes a snarling tiger. Along with the obvious but less frequent weapon imagery - dynamite kegs, battle spears, maces, and especially axes - placing snarling lions and coiled snakes alongside abstract human faces brings to mind such notions as claws and sharp teeth, subtly suggesting that the *Mansion* itself is a predator, waiting to strike. The convoluted facade at Magic Kingdom suggests a swooping bat, and the bat imagery in the ride follows through on the concept.

The use of animal images in the *Haunted Mansion* is mostly limited to birds, large cats, and the mythical creature which combines them - a gryphon. Gryphons are used in heraldry to symbolize the combination of the lord of the land and the lord of the sky, in effect the king of all beasts. Gryphons look ferocious - notice in the Mansion their arms are often raised in a striking position. As a result they're often used to symbolize divine protection, especially for royal families and their claims to a throne.

It's the notion of a fierce sentinel which the *Haunted Mansion* draws on, positioning gryphons at the base of the staircase to the second floor to create the appropriate atmosphere of trepidation of what lies ahead. Certain gryphons, especially if they combine a snake with the lion and eagle, are considered emblematic of evil or the Anti-Christ.

The gryphons were taken in and out of the planning for Disneyland *Haunted Mansion* as budgets waxed and waned. When they returned they brought with them many of the fine details evident in the ride today, most of them sculpted by Ciro Rolando Santana y Arrite. Ciro worked many gryphon-like creatures into his sculpture as he worked, and even more are added at Magic Kingdom.

Yet is this not appropriate for a house constructed in the "castellated" style? The faux-medieval details would have been fashionable, and gryphons go together with heraldry to imply an imitation of old world wealth. Any country castle circa 1840 would have had suits of armor, shields, tapestry reproductions, and gryphons.

So what's interesting about the gryphons at Magic Kingdom is they offer insight into the image of the persons who built the drafty old place for themselves. Redolent of royalty of a bygone era, they built an absurd faux medieval castle on a hill out in the wilds of America. And now that they're gone, the gryphons remain behind, no longer regal, but menacing - ready to strike.

Humans - Faces, Skulls, etc.

- ❖ Wrought Iron Tall Figure - in trim atop facade
- ❖ Wrought Iron Small Figure - in trim atop facade
- ❖ Stylized face - fireplace grate in the Foyer

- Stylized face - grates near the floor in the Stretch Rooms*
- Skull face - at cornice on standard interior doors through the Mansion
- Stylized face - transom above standard interior doors through the Mansion
- Skull face - repeated in wainscoting throughout Load Area / Great Hall
- Smiling Face - in pattern on rocking chair in Library
- Abstract, Evil Face - on newel post at bottom of Grand Stairs
- Face With Sharp Teeth - above exterior door in Music Room
- Smiling Face - in pattern on armchair by Endless Hall
- Frowning Faces - on banners below Conservatory coffin
- Ghost Faces - carved into sides of Conservatory coffin
- Abstract Faces - in balcony railing dividing Doombuggies from Ballroom
- Skull Faces - repeated in wainscoting throughout Ballroom
- Snarling Face - in pattern on Ballroom rocking chair
- Eye-Like pattern on Ballroom staircase balusters
- Statue Shielding Face - in Attic
- Abstract Faces - in balcony railing overlooking Graveyard
- Skeletal Arms - holding torches in the Crypt and Unload Area

Predators

- Bat - atop weathervane
- Alligator - in "Tightrope Girl" Stretch Room portrait
- Tiger - in "Lady in Black" changing portrait
- Bat - decorative stanchion poles in Load Area
- Serpent - door handle of standard interior door throughout Haunted Mansion
- Lion's Face - in center of standard interior doors through the Mansion
- Bat - stylized cornice above arch in Load Area
- Black Cat - in Witch portrait hanging in Load Area

APPENDIX A: HUMAN AND ANIMAL IMAGERY   267

- Bats' Faces - blended into woodwork through the library
- Swooping Eagle - curtain rod located between Music Room and Grand Stairs*
- Serpent - arch finials dividing Endless Hall from Corridor of Doors
- Snarling Lion Profile - corbels on pillars flanking Conservatory
- Talons - pointing downward on pillars flanking Conservatory
- Eagle's Feet - on table supporting coffin in Conservatory
- Black Cats - Grand Ballroom fireplace andirons
- Bat Face - top center of great chairs at Ballroom table
- Evil-Looking Bird - profiles in woodwork at top of Ballroom table great chairs
- Snarling Lion Profile - corbels on pillars in Ballroom
- Bat - sheet music stand at Grand Organ in Ballroom

Mythical Creatures

- Sandstone gryphon - Family Plot near front door
- Leering gargoyles - candle holders in the Stretch Rooms
- Snarling Gryphon - at base of Staircase outside Load Area
- Gorgon - in Medusa changing portrait
- Large Gryphon - at base of Grand Staircase
- Bird-Headed Man - suit of armor by Endless Hall
- Bat-Winged Gargoyles - carved in Conservatory coffin
- Man-Eating Ivy - wallpaper pattern throughout Corridor of Doors
- Devil Creature - horned creature grandfather clock cabinet
- Clawing Gryphon Profiles - in woodwork at top of Ballroom table great chairs
- Gryphon Profiles - in woodwork swirl on lid of Ballroom Hearse coffin
- Snarling Bird with Sharp Teeth - below armrest on Ballroom table great chairs
- Gryphon Face Profile - corbels on pillars on Ballroom Doombuggy balcony

❖ Unicorn and Gryphon - "Touch" tapestry reproduction in Attic

*Added in 2007

APPENDIX B: PHANTOM MANOR

In Mansionology circles, *Phantom Manor* would seem to represent a conundrum. Since the 1990s, the drumbeat has been steadily increasing to regard the *Haunted Mansion* as *the* defining masterpiece of Disney theme parks. This is a purely grass roots movement of fans and fellow obsessives who, thanks to the unregulated courts of public opinion such as fan magazines, newsletters, newsgroups, forums, and internet sites, have stolen the mantle from Disney's chief thrill rides and bestowed it on a weirdo magic trick house with a sterling pedigree and a troubled production.

And yet almost simultaneous to this rise from cult item to cultural force, Imagineering cranked out an even weirder variant of the *Mansion* called *Phantom Manor* for European audiences.

Among *Mansion* fans, the verdict for most who have not seen it - most *Mansion* fans being Americans - is pointedly still out. Here's a ride which repurposes the *Mansion*'s dramatic effects for an entirely different kind of ride, but which simultaneously keeps calling back to the *Mansion* as the touchstone it is.

It's almost neither here nor there, it's all faintly... *disrespectful.*

Yet there's a whole group of European fans who grew up with *Phantom Manor* and who love it fully for what it is. And, I would argue, *Phantom Manor* is a milestone accomplishment in the development of modern Imagineering, and there's only one of them. Yet it laid the groundwork for the acknowledged masterpiece *The Twilight Zone Tower of Terror* and is an earnest attempt to create a *Haunted Mansion* that outdoes even itself.

Point by point, area by area, *Phantom Manor* flings caution to the wind and enacts crazy "*What If*" scenarios, sometimes apparently only for the satisfaction of seeing the idea out. I think this may be the reason the *Manor* is the recipient of suspicious glances from many a *Mansion* fan - given the opportunity and the wherewithal to create the ultimate *Haunted Mansion*, the *Phantom Manor* team decided... not to.

Many *Phantom Manor* fans will insist that the ride should not be compared to the *Haunted Mansion* at all - which is *almost* true, but also less than half of the story.

The moments when *Phantom Manor* tries to emulate the *Haunted Mansion* is when it is at its weakest; and yet it also doesn't quite successfully pull off its original effects in some cases.

Although I believe *Phantom Manor* is wholly deserving of its own book of analysis, I am not the one to write it, because *Haunted Mansion* is mapped too strongly onto my psychology. My psychology runs along *that* omnimover ride path, and not any other. Yet it's important to grapple with *Phantom Manor*, because it's as wildly impressive as it is faintly ridiculous. It's like the *Haunted Mansion*'s charismatic mutant brother. So I'm going to offer a brief overview of *Phantom Manor* and the key conceptual contributions of the ride as I see them.

I advise every fan of the *Haunted Mansion* to try to see Disneyland Paris and *Phantom Manor* for themselves. It's a remarkable place, and the *Manor* fits into *that* park like a hand inside a glove in a way it would not in any other Disneyland-style park which exists. That's what you're missing if you only watch pictures and video, is the *way* that park operates.

Disneyland Paris is the castle theme park which goes all in on "Fantasy". And while it's true that Disneyland and Magic Kingdom are often said to be about "Fantasy", that's really just a marketing convenience; doubly in the case of Magic Kingdom, because it's grouped with three other parks with much clearer-cut themes.

Fantasyland may be the conceptual and economic heart of these parks, but to over-emphasize the role of fantasy in these parks is to overlook the fact that the parks are also intended to be in some way *educational*. As a result, although stylization and romanticism are common to these parks, they're also realistic enough in detail, design, color, and presentation. When you're looking at, say, the *Jungle Cruise* boathouse, or a building on Main Street, they're executed just this side of realistically enough for you to suspend disbelief and say "yeah, this really is what this would look like."

Disneyland Paris totally ignores the educational part of the Disneyland equation; every area of *that* park operates under the rules of Fantasyland. As a result that Main Street, USA is *the Fantasyland of Main Street, USAs*. The Frontierland is the *Fantasyland of Frontierlands*. Everything, from the colors to the textures, the shapes and sizes of things to the landscaping, is *pushed*.

Waterfalls which would be quaint trickles at Disneyland or Magic Kingdom are thundering cascades. Signs which would be small and handmade at any other park are twelve feet across, brightly painted, and use the most intricate typeface possible.

Sometimes this results in weird contradictions because the impulse towards fantasy at Disneyland Paris is also paired with a terrific, almost reckless push towards intricacy. Quaint, colorful *Big Thunder Mountain* cars on a downscale mountain of stylized rock become realistically colored cars on an intricately sculpted, accurate representation of Monument Valley in an attraction with the most detailed, complex, and accurate representation of a mining operation possible.

It's in this environment of aesthetic overstatement that *Phantom Manor* thrives. Everything about it is the *most* of that thing possible. Instead of a neatly tended yard or the suggestion of an old rambling estate, *Phantom Manor* has an endless maze of staircases and terraces through a front yard of twisted, artfully tortured looking shrubs that borders a forest of the blackest, darkest pines possible. The backyard is torn apart by an earthquake. A ghostly wind blows through the cemetery behind the house. It isn't just gloomy inside: it's frequently *pitch black*, the darkness pierced by a luridly colored light. The ghosts of *Phantom Manor* don't look like transparent people; they're rotting, gruesomely tattered, and skeletal.

A pretty good example of how much further *Phantom Manor* goes may be to look at how long the *Haunted Mansion* makes you wait before you see what is unambiguously a ghost; it's Madame Leota in the séance room - up to that point we've seen invisible ghosts moving objects or causing illusions, but Leota is the first who is fully revealed to us.

Phantom Manor wastes no time with this. Even if we discount the foyer transforming as being in the same category of an "illusion" as, say, a changing portrait, we still get in our car and see the bride standing right there at the top of the staircase in front of us. A moment later she's frozen in time running down the Endless Hallway towards us, fading in and out of sight, so that there's no mistake that this lady is **dead**.

But in reality *Phantom Manor* spends almost no time being coy about its ghosts the way *Haunted Mansion* does. The opening sequences of the *Haunted Mansion* are intentionally staged in such a way to invite us to make excuses, to explain away things: that voice could be coming from behind a curtain or through a hidden tube, and nobody says that *has* to be a ghost playing that creepy old organ. It isn't until we get into the architecturally impossible stretching room that things really get serious, and even then we're still a long ways away from seeing a ghost.

Phantom Manor has no interest in all of that. The waiting area has us seeing and hearing things almost as soon as we try to walk up towards the creepy old house. We pass by a glass-walled gazebo and hear a music box, but no music box can be seen. There's a tea pot in there, but this house is supposed to be uninhabited, so who put it there? In the covered queue area, voices seem to carry on the wind. Then, once inside the foyer, we hear the bride singing and see her portrait transform, and the meaning is clear: her voice fills the room, and her presence does too.

When the Phantom finally speaks it isn't remotely like when the Ghost Host begins his narration in the *Haunted Mansion*, a voice in the darkness. The Phantom's voice booms and fills the room; seems to come from everywhere at once. The point is clear: this place is Bad, and we're **In For It**.

It really is the careful build of the *Haunted Mansion*, especially at Disneyland, that Mansionites fetishize, so perhaps right off the bat we can see this as a misstep, but frankly *Phantom Manor* has something else on its mind. It's one of the great ironies that it's become common and cliché to say that the chief difference between *Haunted Mansion* and *Phantom Manor* is that *Phantom Manor* has a clear story whereas *Haunted Mansion* is a disconnected series of vignettes.

This is **entirely wrongheaded**, and I wouldn't be surprised to learn that it's more typically inaccurate nonsense that originates from Imagineering in the 1990s. Compared to *Phantom Manor*, *Haunted Mansion* is a model of narrative economy: it's the story of how *you*, played by yourself, entered a haunted house and lived to tell the tale. Along the way, you learned that most ghosts aren't really all that bad. That's all there is to it.

Phantom Manor may have a story that we can *guess* at, and two leading, powerfully symbolic characters, but we **can never and will never** figure out what the heck is happening in that big old house on the hill because we are not supposed to.

The creators did have a clear plan and idea, but bit by bit through a combination of choice and happenstance a lot of what was intended got compressed, stripped out, and altered. What we have left is the sort of thing you can argue over drinks, but never really comprehend because *Phantom Manor* doesn't give you the necessary information to decode and make logical most anything that happens.

This is the *opposite* of the clear, direct logic of *Haunted Mansion*. In *Haunted Mansion*, the effects and illusions are unsettling because they imply that in some way *you* are seeing things, that your perceptions are faulty, at least until the séance occurs and the party begins. Even after that, the tension in *Haunted Mansion* arises from "*what will happen to me? How will I get out of this crazy situation?*"

The original 1992 version of *Phantom Manor* was remarkably tension-free because the Bride and the Phantom just didn't seem all that interested in you. The Phantom laughs and offers you a coffin, the Bride points to the way out, the Phantom tries to grab you. But up until that moment, they've been playing out their silent drama at *each other*, visual representations of purity and darkness. We just happen to be there to see all of this, but there was never really any sense that we were in peril, and at the very end when we are *supposed* to be in peril, the idea didn't have any force.

The 2019 revisions would seem to address this problem, most prominently in reinstating Vincent Price in the role of the Phantom, because honestly Vincent Price improves everything. Most importantly, besides making the Phantom a significantly creepier figure always lurking just behind the Bride, restored is a short quip where Price laconically drawls "It would seem that everyone is doomed at Phantom Manor - even you!". This restores the necessary force of threat to the experience, that key question of "How will I escape?"

I had long been familiar with *Phantom Manor* before I finally got to ride it, and found that my impression of the dynamics of the experience were quite different in person. I had previously interpreted *Phantom Manor* as a kind of gothic romance, with the Bride the identification point and the Phantom as the moustache-twirling villain. As with all classic gothic, then, the main component was *empathy* – as the Bride sings and suffers and the Phantom laughs - not too different, really, from the pre-Lloyd Weber versions of *Phantom of the Opera*.

What I discovered was that, in person, it's impossible to identify with the Bride; she's too darn spooky. She's constantly standing in pitch black rooms, lit in a menacing way which does not inspire trust. She's also a ghost who tends to appear and disappear and who invades our personal space in the final scene to creepily plead "*marry me?*", which again does not readily invite warm feelings.

Does the Phantom trap the Bride in the house or does she willingly spend the rest of her life in there? If the model is Miss

Haversham from *Great Expectations* - which it appears to be - then the Bride willingly stays in the house as the Phantom torments her. She would seem to poison herself in her boudoir.

In other words, she's crazy.

Is the story of *Phantom Manor* a tragedy or is it strictly symbolic? In the original stretching portraits, the Bride poses obliviously as supernatural menace descends on her from all directions. That menace is obviously the Phantom, a reincarnation of her father Henry Ravenswood, whose grave on Boot Hill implies was abusive.

The 2019 revisions to the attraction unambiguously peg Ravenswood as the Phantom, making the connection clear repeatedly throughout the attraction. This is probably what the original designers had intended all along. But if we can wipe that now-canonical fact from our minds, a host of other associations baked into the character tie him more firmly to the over-arching theme of Frontierland. Because with his trim, expensive clothes, death's head, and gloating laugh, it's clear that the Phantom is a *revenger* on the Ravenswoods from beyond the grave.

The family made their money from the gold in *Big Thunder Mountain*, and carved in the side of the mountain facing their house is a Thunderbird, a mythical bird of the American southwest whose wings could cause earthquakes. In the backyard of the house is a fissure from an earthquake which runs towards the mountain, and the haunted ghost town out behind the *Manor* somewhere has been ripped apart in a way which suggests tectonic activity.

If the Phantom is an agent of the avenging spirit of the Thunderbird, then his fancy dress and connection to the gold mine which made the Ravenswoods rich suggests that the Phantom is an embodiment of greed which strips the land of its natural resources. The wealth and hubris of the Ravenswoods, symbolized by their ludicrous mansion on the hill, is literally an affront to the Gods.

This is why Martha and Henry Ravenswood die in the same year, and why their daughter's wedding is interrupted and she dies a crazy woman in a haunted house. The Phantom terminates the family line.

One of those now-removed stretching portraits showed the corpse of a gardener clawing its way out of the earth, ready to attack the Bride. If the other portraits seem more abstract in their menace, the "corpse" portrait depicts areas of the Ravenswood estate we already know because *we have already passed them*: the gazebo, the covered pavilion.

To me this strongly implied that the event this dramatizes is the return of the Phantom. As we exit the manor through its wine cellar, we pass a small area near a grape press where a photograph of a young woman sits near an overturned wine glass and some dead roses. The voice of the Phantom echoes through this area.

My interpretation of all of this was that the Phantom could have been a servant of the household, like a gardener, who returned from beyond the grave to claim the Bride and enact his revenge on his employers. While no longer canonical, there's still enough in to Manor for us to question and re-interpret the basic story.

This mystery aspect of *Phantom Manor* is its absolute best thing. Much like Kubrick's *The Shining* or Joyce's *Ulysses*, it's full of puzzles, mysteries, and dead ends. Whether this was intentional is irrelevant; *Phantom Manor* has escaped thought and become reality, an incontestable whole. Fans will be arguing about it for the rest of time.

Yet in execution, *Phantom Manor* is almost as good as the ideas behind it.

Truthfully, to anyone who grew up with the *Haunted Mansion*, *Phantom Manor* is occasionally a shocking mess. I realize that faulting *Phantom Manor* for not being one of the five most brilliant rides ever built is unfair and foolish, but upon riding it I was so taken aback I regretted having seen it and did not recover a positive opinion until my second ride.

And to this author this is a big problem, because the places where *Phantom Manor* stumbles are the places where its effectiveness really suffers. I hope the preceding paragraphs suffice in conveying my appreciation for *Phantom Manor*, because we're about to really dig into its faults.

For experienced *Mansion* riders, maybe the biggest fault in the ride is the lack of Doombuggies. *Phantom Manor* runs a chain of pseudo-Doombuggies manufactured by Vekoma. It's widely publicized that they lack internal speakers and use a simple lowering bar in place of a closing shell, but that's irrelevant compared to their limited functionality.

Doombuggies are remarkable precision instruments; they can turn in any direction and stop on a dime. They can tilt forwards or backwards, meaning they can ascend or descend slopes while keeping the cars oriented upright.

Compared to these, the *Phantom Manor* pseudo-buggies are amateur night. Their turns are sluggish and imprecise. Often they seem pointed in no particularly significant direction. When they go up or down slopes of any kind, they must tilt backwards relative to the slope of the floor. Because of this, all of the inclines in the attraction have been minimized.

As a result, the precise and dramatic way the *Haunted Mansion* Doombuggies manipulate space is gone entirely. In place of the dramatic sweep up to the Ballroom in the *Haunted Mansion*, *Phantom Manor* has our wiggling, wavering pod slowly chugging up a mild incline. The descent into the earth isn't the exciting turn, tilt, and drop of the Graveyard Slope; again, it's a mild incline that those poor pods wiggle and waver down as they go. For experienced *Mansion* riders, this has the unfortunate effect of making every scene in *Phantom Manor* feel tepid and uncertain.

Phantom Manor is lacking many of the clever details which make the *Haunted Mansion* so memorable, especially in the way of decor: the classic skull panel moulding becomes plain geometric wainscoting, the chairs don't contain abstract faces, serpents don't hold up the arches between rooms. This isn't bad, but it does subtly alter the interpretation of the attraction as it unfolds. The *Haunted Mansion* encourages us to think of all of the distortions we see as the works of ghosts; numerous, invisible hordes of ghosts.

There are fewer distortions in *Phantom Manor* but an overall increased atmosphere of weirdness, so there really isn't any sense that there's more than three ghosts in the house: the Bride, the Phantom, and Madame Leota who's a sort of guest star. Everything we see seems to be caused by one of these three characters instead of various ghosts we aren't familiar with.

Is that the Phantom playing the piano and causing the doors to knock? Do the wedding guests appear and disappear because they're the Bride's *perception* or *hallucination*? I doubt very much this was intended by the attraction designers, but it's hard to escape the impression. As a result, *Phantom Manor* feels less like it's filled with ghosts so much as that something about the house is horribly, horribly wrong. The very wood it's made out of has a sickness upon it. It's the story not of possession, but of a curse.

Once we leave the house and get down into the Catacombs and Phantom Canyon, suddenly the "hey look guys, lots of ghosts!" notion returns, only increasing the impression that the old house isn't super-saturated with haunts. I think the Catacombs sequence marks the apex of the really remarkable stretch of the ride, where nearly everything works perfectly. *Phantom Manor* hasn't been this good since before we got on the ride vehicle. The official end of the winning streak is, predictably, something copied direct from the *Haunted Mansion*: the singing busts.

The inappropriateness of the singing busts at this moment in the ride is extraordinary. In the *Mansion*, the busts really fulfill the role that the three-piece Pirate Band in *Pirates of the Caribbean* - a solo act who introduces the signature song to come. There's no follow up to *Phantom Manor*'s singing busts - they're singing alone, and their appearance is the only time a traditional arrangement of "Grim Grinning Ghosts" is heard in the attraction, only increasing the impression they have nothing to do with the scene they're in.

Even the staging of the scene is wrong - the effect works in the *Mansion* because there's nothing to look at in that moment *but* the busts. In Paris there's a forced perspective cave-in behind the busts to imply that they fell underground in the earthquake and they're surrounded by capering skeletons, all of which distracts from the tableau and turn the few seconds you have to enjoy the effect into a fight for your attention.

It's a shame they're there, because otherwise the Catacombs has to be one of the most effective adaptations of continental traditions of the grotesque in the ride. This scene accomplishes in under a minute what the *Haunted Mansion* spends its entire length doing - introducing spirits who seem terrifying, but who, as it turns out, just want to have fun.

Holding back the coffin escape to make it into an entire tableau where rotting bodies pull themselves out of their graves to cavort merrily pays off terrifically well. It's based on Ub Iwerks's 1929 *Skeleton Dance* cartoon, a genuine Disney predecessor to the *Haunted Mansion* and to me still exactly the right amount of unnerving-to-funny. The gags here are, much like the *Skeleton Dance*, just right - the catacombs ghosts are engaged in clearly lighthearted but not exactly funny antics. We're amused but we don't laugh, which is exactly the right level of comedy for decaying bodies.

But it's also the Catacombs, and the Phantom Canyon sequence in particular, where we can really see what drags down *Phantom Manor* - it's plain old poor visual communication. The *Haunted Mansion* is as perfect a visual pattern as, say, "*Kind of Blue*" is a perfect aural pattern. The pleasure of the ride is in the way it drags your eye through a fascinating, shifting sequence of mind-boggling stimuli over and over again in the exact same way every time. You may say to yourself that this time you'll look at the ceiling or the floor, but you never do. *Everyone* since 1969 has been unable to resist looking down the Endless Hall for their prescribed eight seconds, and who can resist looking at the Grandfather Clock long enough to look up and behind them to see the four little claws spinning in front of a light above our heads? Almost nobody.

Phantom Manor simply does not command the same power. The ride vehicles almost never seem to be pointed in the correct direction, and even when they are you end up straining forward to look at everything. At the end, instead of the wholly clear, distinct nature of the Graveyard, everything in *Phantom Manor* seems perfunctorily placed. It takes multiple rides through to even figure out what's going on in that place, which isn't *bad* but can't hold a candle to the clear, unfussy signals *Haunted Mansion* sends out. Everyone rides *Haunted Mansion* and *Phantom Manor* multiple times, but one is ridden repeatedly to discover new details and absorb a compelling visual sequence while the other is to try to figure out what in the hell you just saw.

And the trouble is, it just can't stand up to that kind of scrutiny. The more you see it, the more you suspect that there is *no real logic* holding the whole thing together, that the secret can't be uncovered because there isn't a solution.

The internal consistency is weird. What is Madame Leota doing in the house? Why does she have to summon spirits who we've been seeing in a very solid form since we entered? Why is there a party? The *Mansion*'s party is because the spirits have finally materialized, and they're happy and excited. In *Phantom Manor*, it's because there's a party in *Haunted Mansion*.

Was it the Bride who begged us to "hurry back" at the end? If it was, why does she speak with the face and voice of Madame Leota? If it isn't, why is Leota suddenly wearing a wedding dress? What about the Bride skeleton in the Catacombs? Is she connected to all this?

As we waltz out the exit door amid a swirl of these questions, there is a sense that the ride designers were not in control of their loaded imagery. Why confuse matters by introducing multiple brides to a narrative involving only one? And what was the deal with that ending? Yet the ride is a gigantic, elaborate sign pointing to a void where there should be an answer. Phone in at home if you know the solution!

The 2019 revisions went a long way towards knocking this unruly ride on the head and sorting it out without killing the mystery or atmosphere, which is honestly a remarkable feat. The story is set up for us immediately, as we enter the Foyer and immediately see a portrait of our two main characters - the Bride and her father - standing in front of the house you just entered. The Bride is mysteriously veiled, her father jealously holds her shoulders, scowling out at the intruders. As his voice fills the room, the portrait returns to a happier time - they are both younger, the house is new, and suddenly the room transforms back to its pristine state around us as the Bride's voice fills the air. That's far too big of an effect for that point in the Haunted Mansion, but it sets exactly the right note for Phantom Manor - XXL-sized visual and aural flourishes.

Every time we see the Phantom, he is literally shadowing the bride with glowing red eyes. This turns him from less of a mustache-twirling villain and more into a frightening, demonic figure - in the Endless Hallway scene, the implication is now less that the Bride is endlessly pacing the halls of the house and more that she's fleeing from the ghost! This increases the threat level of the character considerably, which pays off well when the Phantom returns to offer us a coffin at the end of the ride. Gone entirely is the conceit that the Bride and the Phantom decay as the ride progresses, making the situation clearer and punchier.

Perhaps even more interestingly, the revisions help clarify that the Bride is not exactly a figure of innocence. In our first view of her, her portrait in the foyer, in the mid-ground there is a tree with the initials of her suitors carved into the trunk - the four suitors we see in the new stretching portraits in the next room. Yet she vanishes from these portraits, one by one, and the room expands to reveal their gruesome deaths - all at the hands of the Phantom, of course. At the end of the ride, as the Phantom offers us a coffin, the Bride appears in your car with an offer to "Marry me?", making the cycle complete - it's a set-up, a homicidal double act. They're both crazy, murderous ghosts.

None of this is exactly subtle, but when the baseline of the attraction is so confusing, I feel that these changes, for viewers with a fresh perspective, make better on the promise of the attraction than the original version did. Now, instead of riding through and idly wondering what the hell is going on, they key figures' motivations are spelled out in the kind of big, bold-type characterizations that the ride-thru attraction demands. Whereas previously Phantom Manor was a night of weird wanderings with many questions left unresolved, there's now a clear narrative hook that pulls you through the experience and into a trap that you nearly avoid. This was the intent all along, of course, it's just that the previous finale, with the Phantom clinging to the back of your ride car, never quite worked as well. It's the same cluttered visual communication that sunk the digital Hitch-hiking Ghosts... the gag only works when a ghost *sits in the car with you*. That joke was repeated ad-infinitium in other haunted houses around the world for a reason.

Of course to look at it in another light, would the ride be as beloved if it were more accomplished? Perhaps not. In the absence of perfection, weirdness has always sufficed to distinguish ambitious art. It's maybe the best compliment to both rides that *Phantom Manor* damns the torpedoes, swings for the fences, breaks all of the rules, tries its damnedest over and over again to be different... and yet still can't quite escape from the *Haunted Mansion*'s shadow.

APPENDIX C: MARC, CLAUDE, AND THE MANSION

What *can* we say about Marc Davis and Claude Coats based on their work on the *Haunted Mansion*?

In a traditional scholarship mode, one would retort: quite a lot. But I've been a *Haunted Mansion* fan for long enough to know that it's never that simple. I've seen sacred cows torn down and common assumptions proven to be wrong too many times to simply say that we know the whole story, or even part of it. In many ways it's remarkable how much history is contained in the development cycle of just one ride. I have no doubt that some of the information printed in these pages will eventually be shown to be wrong.

This book is, as has hopefully been apparent to everyone since the start, a specialist text. Producing such a text has been my intent from the start, but there are pitfalls in taking on such an endeavor of limited focus. One of these perils is pervasive in *Mansion* fandom, and has unfortunately skewed a lot of discussion about the ride - questions of authorship and intent.

I've never met anybody who has a genuine interest in the design of the parks who has not been taken in by this game, and it's a tempting one. Prior to the development of EPCOT Center, a relatively small group of people were the real movers behind Disneyland and Magic Kingdom, and seasoned researchers can sniff out traces, pet interests, key touches these men left behind in their work.

Here's the thing about WED Enterprises. There isn't really a good word in English for what it was, but every so often through history a small group at the height of their accomplishment gets together and they accidentally create the future. Nintendo Research & Development 4 were one of those groups. The Beatles were another. The men and women at WED - they were one of *those*. They didn't always plan things out and they didn't always get along, but this group of about fifteen people set the standard. Herb Ryman, Collin Campbell, Marc Davis, Al Bertino, Bill Evans, Mary

Blair, X. Atencio, Yale Gracey, Claude Coats, Bob Gurr, Marvin Davis, Blaine Gibson, Fred Joerger, Buddy Baker, John Hench, and Dorothea Redmond all did what they could with their time and their names have become legendary.

But this activity is simultaneously subversive, because Disney and Imagineering has always had a closed door policy against such attribution - as Walt was fond of saying, there's only one name on the door to the Studio. As such, it's a delicate balance to strike, between assigning "credit" to these key artists and designers while also keeping in mind that Marc Davis, Claude Coats, X. Atencio, Emile Kuri, Yale Gracey and others were merely key players in a wide company employed in a vast array of disciplines. No one designer built the place alone, which means that there can be no true signature, no true credit attached to the place besides Walt Disney, WED Enterprises, and MAPO.

Yet perversely, there is a strain inside the park pushing in the opposite direction. In the early days of Disneyland - according to Harper Goff - in order to disguise areas of the park which had not been finished in time for opening Walt ended up hanging curtains in windows with signs saying things like "Mr. Goff is going to open his shoe store here soon". This eventually led to the famous Main Street windows, as well as little jokes hidden by Imagineers throughout their rides - a Spanish crest in the Magic Kingdom *Pirates of the Caribbean* reads "Marci Davisoso". Was Marc signing his work?

Haunted Mansion has always invited such speculation due to its mysterious and esoteric nature, and also because of the "credit" gravestones outside the front door, which just happen to be many fans' first encounter with the idea that these places were created by specific persons.

So what, really, can we say that we know about Marc Davis and Claude Coats?

Marc is a bit more of an open book. To begin with, Marc continued to talk about his career at Disney until his death in 2000, at fan conventions and in publications, often expressing his distaste for recent projects, especially *Splash Mountain*, which cannibalized what he felt was his best work at Disneyland (*America Sings*), and singling out the changes wrought on attractions like *Pirates of the Caribbean* at Disneyland Paris as off the mark.

Marc also talked quite a lot to fans and admirers about his Disneyland work, and sometimes he even spoke about his collaborators, often in somewhat odd ways. Of Claude Coats, Marc said "his work was very commendable", (Jeff Kurtti, *Disney's Legends of Imagineering*, p.58) which seems to be an understatement.

But it's important to remember that Marc quit in 1978 over frustration with WED Enterprises management. When you look at his later work for WED, especially for abandoned projects like *Western River Expedition* or *Enchanted Snow Palace*, you see an increasing obsession with detail in almost every regard. Very often his art would include specific instructions regarding speaker placement, special effects, mechanical means of animation, and even specify construction materials. As Marc lost support for his new ideas, he retaliated by working up increasingly fully thought-through concepts, including their technical realization.

Marc Davis was one of Walt's key men. He's famous for being one of the "Nine Old Men", but that designation ignores the context of Walt's sarcastic joke. Certainly, while guys like Frank Thomas and Ollie Johnson continued at the Disney Studio for their entire lives, simply being part of the "club of nine" was not instant immunity. Ward Kimball, who Walt had trusted with larger and larger projects through the 50s, eventually buckled under pressure in the lead-up to the creation of *Babes in Toyland* in 1961. Walt blamed the film's failure on Kimball's breakdown, and Ward spent the rest of his career at the studio doing odd jobs.

In contrast, Walt uprooted Marc from animation, threw him into the fray at WED, and Marc thrived. He moved into increasingly important roles on the 1964 World's Fair attractions, then to *Pirates of the Caribbean* and the *Haunted Mansion*, and Marc likely expected his responsibilities to increase, not decline.

In later years, Marc characterized his time at WED Enterprises as the part of his professional career where he was truly satisfied. He was, I believe, the first of the Imagineers to really take a critical look at what made Disneyland tick. After Walt sent him out to look at the place and gather ideas, he made it a habit: careful observation of how people acted and reacted inside the parks. The lessons learned in *Enchanted Tiki Room* he carried over to *Country Bear Jamboree*. Lessons learned in *Country Bear Jamboree* he carried on to *America Sings*. The enjoyment he took in this new medium, and level of serious thought he devoted to it, is evident in much of his work. You don't come up with powerfully communicative, funny stuff like the Trapped Safari at *Jungle Cruise* without putting a lot of thought into how to pull it off.

This played into his workaday persona as well. Practically everyone who worked with Marc described him somewhat wearily as "extremely serious". As he grew older, even to fans he could come off as cantankerous. As a fine art trained artist, Marc considered his ideas to be the most important thing he could offer, and until Walt died this is pretty much how it worked out. Marc's seriousness and his observations are manifestations of his belief in the theme park art form - his chosen field.

Claude Coats is a harder man to peg. A quiet giant of a man, Claude died before the fan press community really got going in the mid-90s and as such there is much less of a body of interviews and quotations to draw on. Judging from his work and what others said about him, Claude was as much of a willing collaborator as he was a temperamental artist. Working quietly as a background painter for much of his career at Disney, Claude was quietly given the keys to the Disneyland show and ended up inventing the art form.

Claude's art is as gorgeous and straightforward as Marc's is detail obsessed and elaborately wrought. Accustomed to decades of quietly supporting the animation with atmosphere and gravity, Claude's extravaganza is the haunted grottos in *Pirates of the Caribbean*, an entrancing plunge into pure atmosphere for its own sake.

Imagineers Bruce Gordon and David Mumford wrote in *The Nickel Tour*, first published in 1995, that Claude Coats was responsible for the "scary" first half of the *Haunted Mansion* and

Marc Davis was responsible for the "funny" second half (p.265). Gordon and Mumford seem to be repeating basically bad information which first appeared in *Disneyland: Inside Story* by Randy Bright (p. 204). Bright quotes Marc Davis, who said:

> *There were too many people. I think we had a lot of confusion because Walt had not been gone all that long. I think there were a lot of great ideas, but when you have too many people of equal clout, nobody's about to say, 'Hey, wait a minute! Let's do it this way', which Walt would have done in a moment.*

Here Marc seems to be repeating his wish to be allowed to design shows independently, a wish which was truly only fulfilled with *Country Bear Jamboree* and *America Sings*. But make no mistake: practically everything in the *Haunted Mansion* was designed by Marc.

Eventually Bright's supposition became rumors of discord in WED Enterprises after the death of their leader, with Claude arguing for shocks and Marc arguing for laughs. *The Nickel Tour* and *Disneyland: Inside Story* inadvertently gave rise to speculation which continues today.

The fact is that Marc Davis was fully capable of creating atmosphere, and drew quite a lot of pieces of art unused for the *Haunted Mansion* which range from eerie to disturbing. Starting from *Pirates of the Caribbean* forward, Marc worked on increasingly atmospheric attractions, having internalized what Claude Coats was so skillful at. Following the *Haunted Mansion*, Marc oversaw the Magic Kingdom *Jungle Cruise*, which is the version of that attraction most fully dedicated towards realizing a mysterious, spooky atmosphere.

Claude Coats was perfectly capable of working on attractions with strong characters. Coats's work on EPCOT Center's marvelous *Horizons* still contained Coatsian reveals and depth tricks but absolutely radiated human warmth and compassion in depicting a bright future for humankind. His version of *it's a small world* for Magic Kingdom doubled down on the attraction's charm but added a new layer of visual complexity.

Why *Haunted Mansion* works so well is because what you see in that attraction is every arm of WED Enterprises moving together perfectly, like a Swiss watch. And the more art we see of how their collaboration worked the more obviously off base *Disneyland: Inside Story* and *The Nickel Tour* are.

To cite one extremely tiny example, let's take the case of the famous "Donald Duck Chair" which sits near the Endless Hallway scene. For decades this exotic little detail was attributed in fan circles to the influence of Rolly Crump, who had designed a similar talking armchair for his much-publicized *Museum of the Weird* attraction. This particular piece was available for viewing early on because Rolly had thought to reproduce much of his *Museum of the Weird* art for his own personal use before leaving Imagineering, and thus was able to show fans his efforts.

From there, logic implied that since Crump was responsible for one of these abstract faces, perhaps he was responsible for *all* of them, and for some time fans credited Rolly as the source of so much of the alarming interior of the *Haunted Mansion*.

And yet in recent years, pieces of art by Marc Davis have appeared which feature swirling faces inside doors and even on the back of chairs which are **far closer** to what is in the final attraction than what Crump had drawn for the *Museum of the Weird*, seeming to occlude his earlier "Talking Armchair" as primary source.

This does not serve as evidence to exclude Rolly Crump from the pantheon of artistic contributors to the *Haunted Mansion*, but it does place his contributions in their proper context. Rolly was just one of many artists who left impressions seen and unseen upon the final text. In 1967, Dorothea Redmond painted a number of extremely atmospheric surreal pieces of the *Haunted Mansion*, with eyes shining out of wallpaper and blending into furniture, or screaming faces formed out of cobwebs and gnarled tree roots.

Redmond was an interior designer for WED at the time, and art of hers which was made explicitly for attractions is uncommon. It's almost as if somebody was directing people to come up with concepts in which faces and eyes could be hidden inside the attraction decor. That person was Claude Coats.

The fact is that practically every aspect of the *Haunted Mansion* as it was built has some origin in something Marc Davis or Claude Coats drew or painted. It's extremely likely that they both appropriated and refined ideas from other artists before proceeding with the design of the ride. Therefore, the "credits list" as it was handed down through official Imagineering sources and through word of mouth is correct after all: Marc Davis was the lead designer, Claude Coats was the overall attraction producer or manager. Their collaboration created what we enjoy today, yet neither man is wholly responsible for what we see, nor did they create in a total vacuum.

Readers need to keep this in mind while consuming *Boundless Realm* due to the severe speciality of the text. Throughout, this author draws parallels between the attraction as it exists in Florida and as it exists in California, as well as less concrete *Haunted Mansions* which may have existed in the past, or even at some point before the design of the attraction was finalized - thoroughly speculative places, to be sure.

In Florida, the Grandfather Clock is painted deep brown; in California, it's dark grey. It's tempting to ascribe this change to Claude Coats, who oversaw the show installation out in Florida.

But there's *no compelling proof* that Claude Coats, an actual historical person, saw, changed, or even especially cared about this particular detail. It could have been anybody in the scenic shop or construction crew who made the change. In this case we're not ascribing authorship of that particular color of that particular prop to Claude Coats, the man, so much as "Claude Coats", the name of the entity who is the presumed author. It's the same way that *Pirates of the Caribbean* or *The Jungle Book* is "Walt Disney's". It's the name on the door, but the room that door opens into contains many different people.

And Imagineering, being fans of all of these attractions as well, play this game too. In 2012, as part of a general refurbishment, the look of several figures in *Country Bear Jamboree* was altered to more closely resemble Marc Davis's concept art. Liver Lips, especially, had a totally different look than he had had in the 41 years since debuting. Yet in attempting to reproduce Marc's art, the fans in Imagineering had not taken into account his wishes.

Which is, they ignored (or forgot) the fact that Marc himself **had overseen** *Country Bear Jamboree*, and so almost certainly had to have approved the version of Liver Lips which appeared in the show in 1971.

In other words, Imagineering had fixated on one specific phase of the design of a character at one specific point in its development cycle instead of looking at the whole pattern. They failed to take into account that intent can change between projects or over time, and in trying to pay tribute to Marc, they ended up obscuring an actual approved design.

In speaking about "intent" in a project as complex as the *Haunted Mansion*, we can only possibly hope to recover intent as it existed at extremely specific points in time in the evolution of a project. Film restorers go through the same motions: what is the best, "approved" version of a work of art to preserve for posterity? Is it the film as it existed on the first night it opened? What if the director considered that a bastardized version? Is more always better? Some directors have furnished "Director's Cuts" both markedly shorter and inferior to their alternate versions.

My position throughout this text is to work from the assumption that Marc, or Claude, or Yale got the results they wanted. I've done this despite the fact that we know this **actually isn't the case** - that effects malfunctioned, were removed, or were in a state of flux. But it's the only way to fix the variables in place to make comparison possible, and to do otherwise is to open the possibilities for an endless cycle of "yes, but" responses.

In reality, it's arbitrary and insane to even consider the two *Haunted Mansions* as distinct experiences. They were both created by the same team at the same time, and have the same events in the same order with the same result and same meaning. We can consider them both "source texts" which are only hints of a third, imaginary text - a version of the ride given no resource limitations, a version which was never built.

All of this makes the *Haunted Mansion* a dangerous place to go rooting around for "intent" in, and even more dangerous for a published book, where errors cannot easily be corrected.

As readers and fans we must be careful when we speak about "Marc Davis's design for" or "that Claude Coats touch in". Remember the case of Bruce Gordon and David Mumford. Design intent and authorship is a slippery slope and can lead to some pretty ugly places, and readers are cautioned, even in reading this otherwise carefully crafted book, to not always believe everything they read.

APPENDIX D: THE SINISTER ELEVEN

Hanged Man

Also known as the "Hatchet Man", this painting depicts a gaunt, pop-eyed old man in tattered clothes. He has a noose around his neck and is holding a hatchet. It's based on a piece of concept art which Marc Davis explicitly labeled "Ghost Host", so this is it: until 2007 this was the only authorized visual representation of our invisible narrator in the attraction.

It's also the largest canonical clue that Master Gracey is not intended to be the Ghost Host, and it must be noted that the wardrobe of the "Hanged Man" figure above the Stretch Rooms is very, very close to the wardrobe depicted in this painting. The waist-up Florida portrait very nearly resembles an oval shaped full body portrait which has hung in the Disneyland Haunted Mansion since 1969.

Davis obviously modeled the face of the Ghost Host on the "Old Witch" from E.C. Comics in the 1950s. When this portrait existed in its "follow-you eyes" version, it was unique in that the pupils of his eyes were tiny black dots instead of painted full retinas.

The Hanged Man portrait currently hangs in the Load Area near the start of the loading belt. In recent years Magic Kingdom has been selling a shirt with a version of the "Aging Man" portrait and the words "GHOST HOST" - if you want to be one of those people you can lead anyone wearing this shirt to the real thing hanging in the Load Area and revel in your inconsequential triumph.

The Gorgon

This portrait depicted a snarling, pockmarked Medusa statue.

This is, of course, the second stage of a more famous Marc Davis changing portrait for the Disneyland Mansion which showed the transformation of a young Grecian woman. I've, personally, always found the use of the final "stone" version of the sequence to be a little weird... wouldn't it be scarier to show the middle stage where the woman is a snarling monster instead of a statue? Perhaps the change was not considered "strong" enough to read quickly as it flashed by inside the attraction.

The Gorgon, at least, is part of a "monsters of antiquity" motif that runs through the interior decor of the Mansion: gorgons, griffins, serpents, and skulls. As far as "things which could conceivably appear in the decor of a high Victorian country house" go, it's about the most ancient reference of all in the attraction, not counting of course the ghost of Caesar or an Egyptian mummy!

The piece as it hung in the Florida house for 36 years was an extremely faithful reproduction of Ed Kohn's Disneyland changing portrait. Since this portrait was replaced by a new changing one similar to Disneyland's, it was not displaced elsewhere in the ride. It's now part of the Walt Disney Archives and has been seen in touring exhibits around the country.

The Traveler

The most puzzling of the original batch of eleven, this mysterious stranger is directly descended from a Marc Davis concept for a werewolf changing portrait. The eleven portraits chosen largely fall into the category "Famous Villains" or "Creepy People", but this one is honestly much stranger and hides an unexpected connection.

Davis' original shows a shadowy man in a slouch hat with a walking stick pausing by a country manor with a distant, moonlit castle visible over his shoulder. The man's head was to turn into that of a snarling wolf. Obviously, the version used in the ride did not change, so instead of the moonlit cliffs and castle, the manor house behind him is in flames! The bonfire was, and is, nearly impossible to detect under the dim lighting in the ride.

Thanks to the research of Dan Olson and some very good luck, we now know that Marc designed nearly all of his changing

The Haunted Mansion in the "Magic Kingdom" will be the "happy haunting grounds" for 999 of the world's happiest ghosts, ghouls and goblins ... a veritable poltergeists' paradise.

Portraits above are of a few of the "creepy characters" that will call the foreboding stone-faced mansion their haunt. Workmen putting finishing touches on the Edgar Allan Poe-style "Haunted Mansion" have reported hearing strange noises, obviously made by restless spirits who already have moved into the cobweb corridors.

portraits to go through a six-frame progression. We know this because WED actually had Ed Kohn paint them for possible use in the Disneyland ride, including portraits that Marc only drew as two phases, such as the Skeleton Horseman. It's hard to imagine how a six-portrait version of this would unfold, especially coming ten years before *An American Werewolf in London*.

The appearance of this character, so unlike the jeans and red flannel shirted lycanthropes who stalk American popular culture, descends from an unexpected source - the character Scapinelli in the 1926 version of *The Student of Prague*. Played by Werner Kraus, Marc's werewolf character matches Scapinelli exactly in terms of wardrobe and even facial hair. But the similarities end there - there is no thematic link between the character presented in the Haunted Mansion and the character in the film.

Which is a shame, because Werner Kraus also played Dr. Caligari, and a direct link between the Mansion and history's inaugural terror film is rich meat indeed. In reality, *The Student of Prague* isn't a horror film so much as a bleak romantic fantasy in the style of E.T.A. Hoffmann, and Scapinelli as the devil character in this transposed Faust tale quits the scene halfway through. Still, a German silent film starring the two central actors from *Cabinet of Dr Caligari* - Werner Kraus and Conrad Veidt - is enough to keep *The Student of Prague* alive in posterity. The most famous thing about the film is a stark image of Kraus as Scapinelli standing atop a windy bluff with his umbrella outstretched behind him, his body posture perfectly echoed by a dead, twisted tree.

What we see here isn't influence, it's Marc's amazing capacity for research and to pull from any source that inspired him. Just as Lon Chaney's legendary *London After Midnight* makeup is clearly the basis for the Hatbox Ghost, Marc recognized the look of Scapinelli was a perfect visualization of a shady, mysterious stranger and went his own way on the idea. The mere presence of Conrad Veidt and Werner Kraus is enough to merit the republication of stills in reference books and magazines, and it's a near certainty that Marc picked up plenty of those in his research for the subject. Was he thumbing through *Famous Monsters of Filmland* looking for inspiration?

If you'd like to see Scapinelli in action, be sure to seek out the 1926 version of *Student of Prague*, not the 1913 version. Both are excellent, but Scapinelli in 1913 is quite a different type of devil, and the seething malevolence of Werner Kraus in the role is clearly what Marc was responding to.

The Traveler is currently on display in the Great Hall.

Miss December

This is a very slavish recreation of Ed Kohn's rendering of a Marc Davis piece of art for a Disneyland changing portrait, showing a young woman shriveling into an old crone. In the upper right hand corner of the portrait as originally painted is the title "April"; when she ages it becomes "December".

Kohn did paint a six portrait version of this sequence for use at Disneyland, as April became June, then September and December, which would have been awesome in motion. Frozen on the last phase as it is, this is maybe the least interesting portrait of the eleven, and today December hangs on the lower landing of the Stairwell scene, just a few yards away from her original location.

Rasputin

Descended, albeit loosely, from a Davis concept for a Rasputin portrait, in the original version Rasputin's hypnotic eyes were to grow larger and larger until a single gigantic eye filled the picture frame. Davis' art for this may be seen above his desk in the "Imagineering Workroom" sequence of the Disneyland Tencennial *Wonderful World of Disney* show.

The version that was in the *Haunted Mansion* actually did not depict Rasputin - instead showing a broad-shouldered bearded man with wild grey hair. Legend has it that Walt Disney himself was concerned that living descendants of Rasputin could sue!

At Tokyo Disneyland, the "Sinister Eleven" - a scene which still exists there - are all hung at crazy angles, as one may do when she is building a haunted house. The Florida originals, however, hung perfectly straight and flat on the wall - except Rasputin. He leaned forward towards the Doombuggies, a slight but noticeable pitch.

I've spoken to some who believed that at one point the painting was or was intended to actually animate and lean forward and back, as if the man in the portrait were straining out to glare at passing cars. I never saw it move nor saw any proof of the mechanism, but the distinct forward tilt of this particular portrait did give it unique power.

Rasputin may today be found in the Great Hall.

The Sea Captain

Here's a piece which both is and is not a piece of concept art for a changing portrait, but more about that in a moment. There are two components here which must be discussed individually to make sense of, but first I'd like to discuss for a moment what this one portrait implies.

When WED decided to move the *Haunted Mansion* across the country, they moved it not just from California to Florida, but from New Orleans to New England, and I think this was only natural. The interior of the Disneyland *Haunted Mansion* has next to nothing to do with its exterior - we think of Southern manses as open, gay, and airy, not dismal, dark, and heavy-paneled. New England, home of Sleepy Hollow, Salem, H. P. Lovecraft, Nathaniel Hawthorne, Spiritualism, Stephen King, Henry James, and untold legions of dead, is the gothic capital of the United States. Yet despite all of that, there was precious little actually done to the attraction to make it feel at home in New England, and our very drowned Sea Captain here is one of the only distinct links.

In the background of the Sea Captain portrait - besides a rockbound coast and stormy sea not unlike any found in the region - we can see the remains of a storm-tossed ship; this is our link to a changing portrait which appeared at the Disneyland Mansion. It showed a schooner at sea suddenly transforming into a ghost ship, illuminated by lightning and sails tattered. This, however, was just two stages of a more elaborate progression that was originally planned.

In the full version, we saw a schooner at sail on a windy ocean. In the second image, the waves subsided and storm clouds began to build. The third showed the same ship lost in fog with slack sails; the doldrums.

The fourth image is the familiar one of the ship with tattered sails being tossed by a storm; the fifth showed the boat, now stripped nearly bare, floating on the ocean. Unnatural glowing forms are gathering on its decks, and St. Elmo's Fire, a kind of natural ball lightning which maritime tradition said spelled doom for all aboard, gathered amid the rotting masts.

The final image showed those glowing masses on the decks forming into the spirits of dead sailors, flying towards the viewers, their eyes made of St. Elmo's Fire and their hands white lightning. The waves and swells of the ocean now resemble frightened faces and eyes.

For my money this full sequence is the most bloodcurdling concept Davis worked up for the attraction, and the main ghost seen rising off the wreck in the concept art bears a striking resemblance to the one seen in this portrait, floppy rain hat and all. But the idea of a doomed sea captain is not wholly Marc's alone.

It was one concept worked up by Ken Anderson for the *Mansion* in the late 1950s; in his version, the new bride of the master of the house discovered he was a pirate and he disposed of her by throwing her down a well.

When Yale Gracey and Rolly Crump began working on the attraction in the mid-60s, they actually mocked up an elaborate special effect sequence involving the sea captain and his wife, who in their version had been buried in a wall. This apparently impressed everyone in WED Enterprises so much that Davis kept drawing various ghostly sea captains through the 60s, hoping to find a way to include the effect in the ride. He even included the exact same dead sea captain in concept proposals for the *Treasure Island* attraction at Walt Disney World, hoping Yale's show stopping effect could finally be seen. The "sailing ship" changing portrait, pointedly without the sea captain that motivated it, was the only thing to make the cut.

The portrait instantly calls up lost sea captains, lonely brides left behind, ghost ships, and the Flying Dutchman, and an entire imagined history of doomed seafaring in the old house. The associations conjured up by this character are so strong that he received a souvenir Magic Kingdom action figure in 2004 and his own special crypt outside the attraction in 2011.

Besides the size of the portrait, by far the best thing about the Sea Captain was his position above the exit door of the Portrait Hall; while every other portrait's eyes slid side to side to follow you, his eyes seemed to lower to watch you pass below and out of sight. The Sea Captain prominently hangs in the Great Hall today.

The Witch of Walpurgis...

...Or so she is labelled on her Davis concept art, was another "bad guy's head turns into an animal" changing portrait idea. A dark haired, menacing lady in a cave holding a black cat, originally her head was to turn into a goat's head.

The final portrait, besides giving her two skulls with knives in them, adds a circle to the upper right hand corner of the frame, which I spent a great deal of time in high school trying to transcribe from a blurry photograph. Thanks to Brandon Champlain and Dan Olson, the circle and source text for the art's details haves been identified: a 1929 book by Émile Grillot de Givry called "*Le musée des sorciers, mages, et alchemists*". It turns out it's a slavishly copied pentacle for summoning evil spirits!

Walpurgis, of course, is a transliteration of the German Walpurgisnacht, the night at the end of April in which the Witch's Sabbat is traditionally supposed to have been held. This is, therefore, a distinctly old-world witch. Her presence, however, cannot help but remind us, appearing as it does in an ancient-looking New England mansion, of the witchcraft mania of the American Puritan era.

Being, as she is, the only vestige of genuine supernatural belief in the *Haunted Mansion*, some may be inclined to view that spirit pentacle in the corner less than favorably. Personally, I see the Witch of Walpurgis, along with the Hanging Body and the bride in the Attic, as part of the darkness to balance the light necessary to a dramatic story. Fears of black cats and moons may seem silly to us, but for our ancestors they held genuine power and this is what ghost narratives seek to remind us of.

Less poetically, I'm pretty sure this one got bookmarked for inclusion in the hallway just because she's holding a cat. The cat's follow-you eyes were green and had feline slits. Two sets of eyes in one painting! It looked pretty awesome. The Witch now hangs in the Great Hall.

Jack the Ripper

I've heaped praise on Marc Davis throughout this book, but here's an example of a time I think Marc miscalculated badly.

Some early *Haunted Mansion* promotional materials referred to its residents as "famous ghosts, and ghosts trying to make a name for themselves". Indeed, at Disneyland, the Ghost Host confidently states "we have several prominent ghosts who have retired here from creepy old crypts all over the world." And as promised, when the spirits become visible, we see generic upper-high Victorian ghosts and ghosts from across the Old World - banshees, mummies, even a Caesar. So why does Jack here stick out so badly?

It's because it's a vestige of an idea that Davis was nursing which begins way back with Ken Anderson's ideas for Disneyland's Ghost House back in the late 1950s. Anderson included such figures of fantasy as the Headless Horseman, Frankenstein's monster and the Phantom of the Opera amongst his attraction's ghosts. Over time, this concept was gradually weeded out of the attraction concept until only Marc Davis was really still pursuing it.

Marc's idea was that the Mansion could be a retirement home for "famous villains" and he drew up ideas for Nero, Dracula, Jack the Ripper, Guy Fawkes, Rasputin, Attila the Hun, Bluebeard, and Ivan the Terrible.

The trouble with Jack here is, I think, the thin veneer between Jack the Ripper and our own anxieties in the era of the modern serial killer. Nero burning Rome is only an abstracted atrocity to us, but Jack seems somehow out of place amid all that pseudo-Gothic romantic revival monsters and ghouls. Furthermore, Jack doesn't even fit very well alongside Constance, the Mansion's other serial killer, because while Constance murdered for money, nobody's ever figured out what the inexplicable, brutal Whitechapel murders were all about.

Davis himself drew plenty of pieces of wives murdering husbands, but he was always careful to show the husbands as blundering idiots and their wives as getting their triumphant revenge. The humor arose not so much from the murder as her delight in the accomplishment and his blustered, shocked reaction. No matter how comic Davis tried to make him look, Jack the Ripper is still Jack the Ripper, and he's even got his knife out.

Of course, we don't know to what extent Davis culled art from his archives to present in the 1971 Mansion or if it was just selected for being a recognizable character and worked up as a finished painting. All we have is a pencil piece of Davis's art, where Jack has a human foot stuffed in his jacket pocket! Below the art, Davis has labeled his art "Talking Face", meaning that Jack was meant to appear alongside Guy Fawkes, Nero, and Ivan the Terrible in some sort of gallery of famous villains.

It's worth noting here that Marc pitched a concept for the Tokyo Disneyland *Haunted Mansion* in 1978 as an enhancement to their Unload area as a "burial crypt of famous villains". His 1978 lineup included Nero, Dracula, Jack the Ripper, Medusa, Attila the Hun, and Bluebeard. The crypts would push in and out and "try to open with horrendous sound effects - there are moans, groans, and screams". It's hard to imagine this working in the Haunted Mansion as we have it, but who knows.

Love him or leave him, Jack's portrait migrated to the Load Area in 2007, where he hangs today.

Lucretia and George

The tallest portrait in the group is of a seated gentleman with a handlebar mustache and a severe looking lady in a high collared dress standing behind him. Back when this was a changing portrait, the lady would remove her hands from the man's shoulders and reach up to throttle his neck! Besides their generally spooky appearance, the single point of interest here would appear to be the framed painting on the wall behind them: a landscape view of a haunted house. So inside a haunted house in a haunted portrait is a portrait of a haunted house... weird, right?

The seated gentleman is practically identical to a character we've already seen before: George, whose tombstone the old lady in the Stretch Room portrait was seated on. This is evidently a portrait of George in younger days, based on the copious amount of hair he has.

Today, it's a bit fussier to identify this guy as George because now there's another George vying for identification as the guy in the Stretch Room portrait: George Hightower, the last of Constance's doomed husbands, whose wedding photo we see up in the Attic.

To even further complicate things, George Hightower is supposed to be part of the same family as Harrison Hightower, himself a member of the Society of Explorers and Adventurers, or S.E.A. - S.E.A., of course, is the conceptual framework which ties together Tokyo DisneySea, wherein one may find a *Tower of Terror* which tells of Harrison Hightower's fate.

Confused yet? Let's simplify. Both Stretch Room-George and Portrait Hall-George came out of Marc Davis's pen and were there many years before Constance appeared, so I think it's okay to identify this as the "real" George and Attic-George as the "fake" George.

The lady standing behind him is rendered in the final portrait as "Aunt Lucretia", a character Davis drew repeatedly in the *Haunted Mansion* and modeled on, I believe, Martha Mattox's role as a creepy maid in *The Cat and the Canary* (1927). We know she's named Aunt Lucretia because Davis labeled her, along with other characters who kicked around the Haunted Mansion development cycle like Rollo Rumkin and Phineas Pock, in a series of concept sketches supposedly done for singing graveyard busts.

What lends this credibility is that Lucretia did indeed end up in the ride. In fact, she can be seen in the Library next door, as a haunted bust. The same bust can be seen on the mantelpiece of the Ballroom with a ghost's arm around her shoulder.

So obviously both George and Lucretia were longtime residents of the old house. Lucretia and George now hang in the Stairwell scene, not far above Miss December.

The Opera Glasses Lady

My favorite of the eleven portraits also has the richest history. This in an eerie portrait of a willowy blonde woman whose hair blows ominously about her head. In one hand she holds a black cat, and in the other a pair of opera glasses, the kind that are on a long handle. Her eyes, the eyes of the cat, and a pair of eyes inexplicably appearing in her glasses all follow the cars as they pass by. Executed in a vivid, sharp-edged modernist style foreign to the other eleven portraits, Glasses Lady is both memorably weird and seriously creepy. She's second only to the Hanged Man (Ghost Host) portrait for evoking the heebie-jeebies.

Her origin story goes way back to the original version of the attraction conceived by Ken Anderson. Ken, no doubt, pored through volumes of ghost stories and lore and saw the most famous ghost photograph of all: the Brown Lady of Raynham Hall, an image of a wispy female figure gliding down a staircase. Ken drew up his own version of her for Disneyland's Ghost House, replicating the staging of the photograph nearly exactly - only Ken gave his ghost lady a candle.

Marc Davis seems to have seen Anderson's drawing and liked it, and worked up his own version. Davis kept Anderson's candle and gave the ghost lady a black cat. He kept working at the concept, evolving the figure until one of his candle-holding ghost ladies entered production as a figure known as "Beating Heart" - and dressed as a bride.

Just as it's impossible to guess when Marc and Ken's ideas for generic "ghost ladies" evolved into brides, the reasons why this pencil sketch was revived for use in a portrait gallery are impossible to guess. The position of the black cat is totally different in the final portrait, and the ghost lady's candle has become those silly opera glasses.

When the *Haunted Mansion* returned from refurbishment in 2007, not all of the Portrait Hall portraits were ready for re-hanging. The last to return was the Glasses Lady, and weirdly it was the only of the ten portraits to be subject to suspect alteration. Instead of simply painting normal eyes or empty glass lenses into the cut-out holes for her opera glasses, the scenic artist painted in a set of googly crossed eyes.

The Glasses Lady now hangs in the dark space between the Ballroom and the Attic, only visible from the light that creeps into this space from the Ballroom set below. It's one of the *Haunted Mansion's* most difficult to spot hidden details. Googly eyes or no, perhaps it's appropriate that she ended up so near the character who was created out of her basic concept - the Attic ghost bride.

The Vampire

A traditional vampire in perhaps more of the Christopher Lee than Bela Lugosi mold, this portrait has our undead Count hoisting a lantern high by his face and lurking about a castle.

An early and obvious stab at a changing portrait, Count Dracula here completes the informal trilogy of Halloween archetypes represented in the Portrait Gallery, one of them obvious, one subtle, and one unrecognizable: Vampire, Werewolf, and Witch (ghosts are well-represented and we'll meet a mummy later). In the changing portrait version, Drac's head and hand turned into a wolf's head and paw and bats flew out of the arch behind him.

It's interesting to note that all three of these "Halloween" portraits - The Traveler/Werewolf, the Witch, and the Vampire - used the same kind of transformation in their changing portrait versions - person's head becomes an animal head.

Besides the slightly comical effect of this, the only version of this gag that actually made it into any of the *Haunted Mansion*s was extremely different in design and effect - at Disneyland, a changing portrait shows a seductive young woman lying on a sofa who turns into a giant black panther. Originally, only her upper body turned into a cat, resulting in an implication more in line with the goat-head the Witch was supposed to show: this lady may look nice, but she's actually a killer.

And yet, like the April-December changing portrait, the idea here seems to be more about the gap between appearance and reality, the realm of prophecy and parable, much like the young man in the Foyer who deteriorates into a corpse. There was something appealingly ambiguous about the "Panther" version of the portrait, a subtlety that all three abandoned "Animal People" portraits miss out on entirely.

Who knows, maybe Marc was just a big fan of the film *Cat People*?

The Vampire is currently the very last portrait the Doombuggies pass in the Load Area. One fun detail to point out to fellow passengers is the background behind the Count: it's his coffin, sitting inside a stone arch on a checkerboard marble floor with a single candle lit on top of it. It's impossible to see it in the ride context and not think of the coffin sitting in the Conservatory upstairs, even sitting on a similar similar black and white checkerboard marble floor. Coincidence? Premonition? Is the guy in the coffin upstairs a vampire?

APPENDIX E: FOUR OTHER HAUNTED MANSIONS

It's hard to say what the most influential Disney ride is. There are many imitations of *Space Mountain*, and in the 60s and 70s most American regional amusement parks had their own variations on the *Jungle Cruise*. For a long time it probably was the *Jungle Cruise*, in fact, but most of those cheap Junglelands are now gone while the *Jungle Cruise* lives on.

Pirates of the Caribbean is another good choice, but the thing about *Pirates of the Caribbean* is that the attraction exists within its own self-contained sets of references. There was nothing like it before the ride opened and that's still the case. And none of those attractions hold a candle, in terms of modern influences, on the *Haunted Mansion*. Because the *Mansion* synthesizes generations of popular culture ghost lore and mythology into their ultimate form, there's leeway to create riffs on the *Haunted Mansion* material while still finding demonstrably unique variations.

Of course maybe the ultimate example of this is *Phantom Manor*, which is at its most successful when up to its own thing and pointedly less than successful when it's trying to be a *Haunted Mansion*. That alone perhaps should grant it full independence from the *Mansion*, which is an attractive option as it tends to stress its best qualities, but that success was won only on the back of a superior predecessor. I've split the difference in this book by choosing to discuss *Phantom Manor*, but as a wholly separate entity, in Appendix B.

Outside of *Phantom Manor*, Disney hasn't really made much of an effort to go back to the *Haunted Mansion*'s pool of influences. There's *Tower of Terror*, which is a sort of upgraded 90s blockbuster thrill ride take on the same basic "spooky doings in a big decaying building" concept, but in effect it's a wholly different animal. Sometimes included in discussions of the *Haunted Mansion* is Hong Kong Disneyland's charming *Mystic Manor*, which includes a few direct tips of the hat to the old dark house. But really the connections are so few as to make such a claim to connection unenlightening, and disrespectful to what a fun, interesting fantasy the *Mystic Manor* design team actually *did* create.

In perhaps a different book I could conceivably include the Walt Disney World expanded queue area and Memento Mori gift shop in this section, for they *are* riffs and takes on the *Haunted Mansion* concept to variable degrees of success. But since they are physically connected to an actual *Haunted Mansion*, we must think of them as parts of the "*Haunted Mansion Universe*" instead of separate entities.

Most of what's left in the Disney bag amounts to weird references and lame punnery. In an early version of the show that became *Fantasmic!*, at one point ghosts were supposed to fly out of the house and glide across the Rivers of America. The Mickey's Not-So-Scary Halloween Party at Magic Kingdom is centered on the *Haunted Mansion*, which has a dedicated series of parade floats and has the Ghost Host narrating the special Halloween fireworks.

Interestingly, two of the least loved Disney dark rides ever opened included prominent *Haunted Mansion* references. *Journey Into YOUR Imagination*, replacing the beloved original 1983 ride, offered a corner tableau of a magnifying glass distorting a series of office hallways. The effect was accomplished with cutaway painted flats, and included Eric Idle as Dr. Nigel Channing saying: "Is this looking glass actually magnifying, or is it your imagination?"

After a record 14 months of operation, the ride closed to be retooled due to overwhelming guest complaints (the *Mansion* reference had nothing to do with this). Then, just two years later, the equally short-lived *Superstar Limo* attraction at Disney's California Adventure featured Melissa Joan Hart's head in a crystal ball intoning "Execs, producers beyond, give us a sign the green light is on!".

But if we widen our scope *beyond* Disney we will find a rich and complex web of relationships between traditional spook trains, the *Haunted Mansion*, and inspired and appreciative riders all over the world. The *Haunted Mansion* has launched thousands of home haunts, craft projects, and dark rides unable to replicate its slow burn majesty but willing to improvise on the material. Knoebel's *Haunted House*, a brilliant dark ride in the traditional Bill Tracy mode, still shows a *Mansion* influence by providing an elaborate Victorian facade with a landscaped front lawn and disembodied, ghostly wolf howls. Inside, a face is projected on a blank form, a figure plays a colossal pipe organ, and doors slam open and closed, not to mention the cars visiting a library, attic, and roll past spooky portraits. It could be coincidental, but I seriously doubt it.

So I'd like to profile four of the most interesting *Haunted Mansion*-inflected attractions. Some of them truly are imaginative, others less than inspiring, but they all reflect a tradition that this book is part of: a tradition of inspiration, imitation, flattery, and marginalia which have sprung up around the "source text" of the *Haunted Mansion*.

Some Disney fans, perhaps, would argue that such "imitation productions" are déclassé. But I spent many years of my young life building slavish seasonal tributes to the *Haunted Mansion* and still I managed to create my own ideas and spins on the material all the same. To me these are fascinating, valid, and essential parts of the story of the *Haunted Mansion* and how it moves us even today.

Ghost Castle (Geisterschloss) - *Europa Park, Rust, Germany*

Those who feel that the *Haunted Mansion* and *Phantom Manor* just have too much conceptual unity may be interested in Europa Park's completely bananas *Ghost Castle*. Probably the most baldfaced *Mansion* imitation in this section, *Geisterschloss* manages to attain its own unique character through pure lack of restraint. If *one* ghost can appear playing a double bass, then there's no reason there can't be *six*, all in different costumes and heights (one with their leg in a cast), plus a seventh bass for good measure being played by a disembodied arm. And there needs to be an irrelevant mural behind them while the cars roll backwards down a hill. It's that kind of ride.

Europa Park in general is noteworthy for being one of the key reasons why Imagineering departed so radically from their traditional designs for Disneyland Paris. This is the park that has a smaller reproduction of *Spaceship Earth* with a *Space Mountain*-style coaster inside it. They also had their own Skyway, Pirate ride, and *Universe of Energy* dinosaur ride.

Nobody will ever accuse *Geisterschloss* of being high art, but it has its own rococo charms. What's most interesting about the *Geisterschloss* is the way that it repeats ideas and images from the *Haunted Mansion* but in a way that seems as if the person who designed the ride was relying on faulty memory, or got confused as to which ride at Magic Kingdom was which. For example, there is a "night watchman" with dog and lantern very much like the cemetery caretaker at the *Haunted Mansion*, but the dog is now growling at the passing cars! Later in the ride, grave robbers lurk outside the gates of a cemetery looking scared as three busts sing inside the cemetery. It's as though the one figure has been split into six, with non-overlapping roles.

Opened in 1982, *Geisterschloss* sits behind an attractive facade in the "Italy" section of the park. Stylized to resemble an Italian villa, riders are greeted outside by a towering animatronic figure in a dark hood. Inside, moving past portraits showing things like pop-eyed ghouls eating eyeballs, the line passes through a gigantic Italianate hall, with a ceiling fresco made up of devils instead of angels, stained glass windows, and a chandelier made of skulls. From there the line passes a small window diorama where far below a cemetery in the snow - including three miniature singing busts - can be seen. Stopping in a dimly lit octagonal room, a menacing voice speaks as the walls move and portraits stretch, and a hung body drops down through a hole in the ceiling. Moving past more gruesome portraits, riders climb up and up before descending into a huge circular load area where the chain of black "ghost cars" endlessly circle into the ride. Statues line the walls, organ music plays, and the central chandelier spins in circles.

If you're a fan of Disney you're imagining something far more atmospheric and impressive than this really is. It's really quite a tawdry imitation of the *Haunted Mansion*, and repeats ideas for no discernible reason: the stretching room portraits look like normal renaissance portraits, but when they stretch we see the subjects aren't wearing pants... *and have ugly legs!!!!!* It's as though the designer saw a photo of the "Dynamite Man" stretching portrait only 2/3 revealed and assumed that's exactly what his version would be like.

The ride itself is almost totally nonsensical. Cars pass a table where various ghosts drink wine around a severed head. A waiter nearby raises a plate with another head on it. Behind him is a skeleton in a coffin. Both the lights inside the room and outside the windows flash randomly. Above the scene, hooded figures lurk menacingly. That's just one scene.

It's clear that Europa Park has invested in the *Geisterschloss* every year, adding and replacing scenes but with often no real regard for what it all means. Anything that's deemed good enough can go in the ride, wherever it can be fitted in. The final result is much nearer the kind of crazy quilt chaos typified by a Bill Tracy *Whacky Shack*. There is, of course, a guy in an electric chair, a mad scientist laboratory, and a torture chamber.

But it would also be wrong to suggest that the *Geisterschloss* doesn't also have its inspired moments. The ride at one point makes a corkscrew around a central chamber, the ride's equivalent of the *Mansion*'s ballroom. There's no attempt at a Pepper's Ghost effect, but instead the room is based on the principles of a renaissance music box, where figures twirl and turn around a man playing a harpsichord. As the cars climb higher and higher, passing the central skeleton-draped chandelier, the movement of the cars, figures, and music coheres into something special.

There's a later moment where, after passing the uninspired mad lab and torture rooms, cars sweep past the mysterious figure of a woman in a billowing gown looking out a window. The scene then transitions to a graveyard under a heavy blanket of snow - the same graveyard we saw through a window while entering. The effect is strangely poetic. These moments where ideas and execution cohere stand out amongst the rest like plums in a pudding.

Interestingly, the ride seems to have been a much more coherent, serious attempt at a ghost house prior to 1996. All of the paintings in the entrance area were grotesque parodies of specific

Renaissance portraits. The facade was not decorated with axes and carnival lights as it is now. The figures on-ride all had specifically sculpted faces and period appropriate renaissance costumes. Obviously lacking the artistic genius of Claude Coats and Marc Davis or the resources of the Walt Disney Company, this version of the *Geisterschloss* - then called the *Spukschloss* - nevertheless appears to have hung together in a significantly more coherent way.

Too genuinely weird to ignore, but too scattershot to truly work, *Geisterschloss* may not be good, exactly... but it's memorable, and in my opinion anything so bizarre can't be truly *bad*, either.

Ghost Rickshaw (Geister Rikscha) - *Phantasialand, Brühl, Germany*

If Europa Park's *Geisterschloss* never quite escapes the shadow of the *Haunted Mansion*, then let's take a trip across Germany to Phantasialand, a charming park with an eye for reworking Disneyland ideas into a new form. For example, the entrance of the park represents Old Berlin, before it was destroyed by social upheaval and two world wars. Most regional amusement parks, especially in the United States, thoughtlessly repeated the Victorian gingerbread architecture of Main Street at their entrance without taking into consideration what it actually means. Phantasialand's ornate and intricate Old Berlin finds a uniquely German expression of the *idea* of Main Street USA, and in doing so is starting to speak the coded language of theme parks.

Their in-house *Haunted Mansion*, called the *Ghost Rickshaw*, is much less of a direct imitation of the *Mansion* than it is "loosely inspired". It's located in the "China Town" section of the park, which is very elaborately conceived and landscaped with shops, cafes, a "Houdini Swing", koi ponds, and gardens. It's actually a good deal more elaborate than the China pavilion at EPCOT's World Showcase, for an example most readers of this book will be familiar with.

The *Geister Rikscha* is located in a large building which resembles an ancient Chinese fortress, with a large stone Buddha located near the entrance. The queue moves through narrow, torchlit passages where here and there displays of exotic potions and offerings sit in lit alcoves. Eventually the stonework columns transition into twisting tree trunks and the endless chain of three person "ghost rickshaws" come into view, chugging along silently underneath a canopy of artificial trees. Once past the load belt, the cars slide down into the underworld - the ghost rickshaw is located almost entirely underneath the China area of the park!

A long, mysterious, visually rich and sometimes quite unsettling journey, the *Ghost Rickshaw* none the less has no shocks. What it does have is beautifully sculpted scenery. While most haunted house style attractions take place entirely in enclosed environments, the mysterious specters of *Ghost Rickshaw* haunt beautifully elaborate indoor forests, caves, and oceans.

As the cars descend to the underworld below dimly illuminated branches, mysterious, evocative music can be heard. The first scene comes into view, as a gigantic demon can be seen with three henchmen. Then, monstrous bandits lurk on a Chinese mountainside, peering out of caves and hiding places. Dragon-headed warriors practice martial arts and sharpen their weapons in their cave hideout. While passing a country graveyard strewn with bones, hands reaching out of the earth claw at the air. Three skeletal ghosts hover inside a crypt, while near a Buddha shrine gravestones rock and tilt. Across the way, three statues rise out of a misty pond, their projected faces moving, suggesting souls trapped in the underworld. The pond is overseen by a colossal, living stone face.

Cars pass a huge waterfall and wrap around a Chinese merchant ship being tossed to and fro in a rainstorm. The tattered sails whip in the wind, lightning flashes on the horizon, and a projected face in the sky seems to taunt the boat. It's steered by a skeleton, while below deck a group of four more skeletons play cards. Terrified sailors cling to the rails on deck while another sailor opens a hatch in the hull to peer out at the passing rickshaws. This entire scene is accomplished with a full sized Chinese junk, wind machines, and surrounded with a moat of real water. The boat pitches to and fro in the storm. Although clearly indebted to *Pirates* of the Caribbean, in scale and execution it's one of the most impressive dark ride scenes ever put together.

In the next scene, royals are removing a hoard of treasure scattered with skeletons and guarded by a ghost, which flies around the room over their heads. Next, supplicants approach the throne of a gigantic, four-armed goddess. The rickshaws begin to ascend back to the surface, wrapping around this scene. Then, the biggest scene yet: a two-level Imperial court overseen by a six-armed Emperor. Female ghosts play instruments, while below ghosts (in Pepper's Ghost reflection) dance and a man appears and disappears while playing a stringed instrument. The Emperor appears to command it all from his elevated throne.

The rickshaws then pass into a cave where three troll-like creatures seem to "hitch a ride", appearing in the cars in ultraviolet light reflection. Finally, the rickshaw pass a gigantic ogre - twenty feet tall - who wears a necklace of moving heads and is being attacked by five men with ropes. The rickshaws return to the load area after this eventful and mysterious journey.

Nothing in *Geister Rikscha* makes any sense, but this is the absolute best kind of dislogic. Nothing in Europa Park's *Geisterschloss* makes any sense either, but in that case there's clearly *no sense to be uncovered* - everything in that ride is there for no other good reason than that it can be. In *Geister Rikscha*, there is a strange sense of the abandonment of reality, and that every scene *means something*, however opaque. The fact that my summary of events above itself contains a great deal of guessing and interpretation should signal the extent to which *Geister Rikscha* succeeds at creating a hushed, heavy atmosphere, where it feels as if anything could happen and mysterious forces are at work. It's a compliment to the designers that the overriding impression of a trip through *Geister Rikscha*'s underworld is that we are very fortunate to have passed by these mysterious creatures without being noticed, an impression deepened by some genuinely freaky designs, especially the menacing four-armed goddess who marks the ascent back to the surface.

Geister Rikscha's figures appear to be largely animated by simple cams, levers, and in many cases cables. It would be tempting incredulity to imply that they are at all realistic or impressive, but much like the simple figures in the *Haunted Mansion*, they are extremely appropriate for the spooky, stylized atmosphere represented by this attraction.

Ride documentation predating about 2004 shows that the show once made extensive use of custom-sculpted faces for its Chinese ghosts, created to resemble the faces in traditional Chinese artwork. At some point the ride was "refurbished" and much of this custom work was removed. Videos from the late 2000s show that all of the paper mache faces had been replaced with generic Halloween masks, and all of the Chinese garments had become standard "spooky" textiles.

Recent coverage from 2014 and 2015 shows that some new custom sculpted faces, especially the alligator-faced bandits, have been restored and the garments and details in the costuming are much more appropriate and specific. Unfortunately the ride still has a number of plastic skeletons, axes, and scythes that could have come direct from the sale rack of Party City. To say that these undercut the artistry of the ride is a severe understatement.

It appears that not all of the "rubber mask" figures have been upgraded yet, but hopefully this will be an ongoing project. Phantasialand has recently seen a lot of investment, and it's one of the few parks where their imitation of a recent Disney ride - *Maus au Chocolat* - is head and shoulders above the original *Toy Story Midway Mania*.

Geister Rikscha is a case where imitation also came with a lot of inspiration. It doesn't always work that way, and it's worth celebrating it when it does happen.

Besides the design of the vehicles - and let's be fair, designating those scalloped black pods as "ghost rickshaws" is far more creative than the *Haunted Mansion*'s "Doombuggies" - *Geister Rikscha* is at its weakest when it's imitating the *Haunted Mansion*, which it does very rarely.

But then again, there is that pond of statues with moving faces overseen by a glowering stone face. Obviously inspired by the Singing Busts, instead of levity it serves up a nightmare image. At its best *Geister Rikscha* pulls off those sorts of transformations. The ride may be physically gentle, but there's nothing safe about its scenes and their implied meanings.

Many rides have riffed and ripped off the *Haunted Mansion* and ended up with just a lot of "stuff". *Geister Rikscha* went to the well and brought back a phantasmagoria of alarming images and surprising dignity. It's a classic in its own right, and an excellent example of what can be done with ambition, imagination... and only a *little* money.

The Haunted House - *Alton Towers, Staffordshire, England*

One of the most impressive haunted houses ever attempted outside the walls of the "big three" theme park operators, *The Haunted House* is one of the most effective combinations of the illusionistic and atmospheric effects of the *Haunted Mansion* and the traditional spook house trappings of the American fairground. And - at least in its original incarnation - it was entirely steeped in the traditions of European gothic.

Alton Towers is a unique kind of theme park. It originally began as an adjunct to an 18th century Gothic manor house, which like many historical houses in England was eventually opened to the public as a tourism attraction, eventually adding fairground rides and a boating lake. In the 1970s the house and grounds were purchased by a millionaire, who paved the way for the current theme park by installing a number of themed structures, rides, and amenities such as an enclosed steel coaster modeled on *Space Mountain* called *The Black Hole* and a sedate boat ride, *Around the World in 80 Days*, clearly inspired by *it's a small world*.

Among these attractions was a walk-through haunted house called *Doom & Sons*, based on a traditional fun house. Ostensibly a tour through a mortician's shop, signs throughout the house intentionally misled visitors; a sign reading "Don't Look Up" would cue you to see a hanging body, another sign on a cupboard reading "Don't Open This" of course encouraged everyone to go open it and see a man's body falling towards them. Skeletons popped out of coffins and one room had a soft, spongy floor. A ghoul played an organ with a familiar bat-shaped sheet music holder.

In the early 90s, Tussands Entertainment purchased Alton Towers as their first major theme park acquisition - this is the same company that would also purchase and open several Legolands, the London Eye, and is today known as Merlin Entertainment.

In the 90s throughout Europe, the push was on to meet the threat of the imminent opening of Disneyland Paris head-on. Many regional amusement centers had spent the last few decades imitating things they had seen at Walt Disney World and Disneyland through research trips and postcards, with little fear of direct competition from a theme park empire oceans away. Disneyland Paris spurred development of elaborate attractions throughout Europe, and one of the initial wave of attractions intended by Tussands to strengthen the profile of Alton Towers was *The Haunted House*, opening in spring 1992 and designed by John Wardley.

Located at the back edge of the park, connecting two new roller coasters, *The Haunted House* sat alone in an area known as Gloomy Wood. Modeled on an 18th century country seat, a front facade of considerable size hid a gigantic show building. A stone vault sat near the front door, a tall tombstone leaning against the vault displaying the attraction's name.

Proceeding through the front door, guests came across an entry hall featuring spooky portraits and a mounted animal head made of bones. Turning down a short hallway, cross-stitch "mottos" on the wall warned: "Remember: Wherever You Are In Ye Haunted House, Hidden Eyes Are Watching You" and a child's cross-stitch alphabet depicting a skeleton and devil with the words: "Gaze Notte Into The Fire Ye Have Been Warned Emily Alton Age 9".

From here the line moved into the pre-show room, easily the most impressive scene in the attraction. Designed to resemble a drawing room, the entire chamber was built at a slight pitch, adding to the disorientation. A lavishly dressed interior set - including a fireplace, furniture, doll's house, and windows illuminated by moonlight - it was the show piece of the ride. Propped up on an armchair, a book's pages turned by themselves, passing illustrations of menacing figures, and a title page inscribed "A True Relation Of Sir Hugo Alton Who Engaged In Divers Satantic Practices". A fire flickered in the fireplace, actually a reflection of a television hidden below a nearby table, which allowed the face of Sir Henry Alton to appear in the flames, warning riders of the dangers that awaited them.

In the nearby doll's house, the tiny Pepper's Ghost figure of Emily Alton appeared in a downstairs room with her cat, and appeared to walk around a table to write a math sum on a tiny prop blackboard, accompanied by the eerie singing voice of a child. Nearby, a wooden rocking chair horse would move back and forth, and on a small table a severed hand underneath a bell jar would occasionally twitch.

The ride through the *Haunted House* was accomplished in carriages resembling Gothic woodwork which could be sped up or slowed down as needed, resulting in an unusually dynamic dark ride experience. Once out of the load area, the house itself more strongly resembled a haunted castle instead of a country mansion but there were still many surprises and unique ideas in the *Haunted House*.

Cars initially entered a room where the walls were appearing the break apart and float. Initially pointed towards a wooden door, a turntable rotated the cars 90 degrees and sent them off towards a long, pillar-lined Grand Hall. A stately Georgian-style room with chandeliers and floor lamps, what appeared to be two free-standing pillars about halfway down the room actually disguised mirrors - the rest of the room was a reflection of itself. This allowed a gigantic horned ghost to suddenly lunge from behind the pillars, seemingly appearing out of thin air. As the cars swerved to avoid this, the ghost appeared on the right, holding a tea cup and apologizing for frightening riders! And with a terrific illusion right off the bat, the *Haunted House* was off running.

Inspired by the climax of the 1987 film *The Witches of Eastwick*, one section of the ride had gigantic fingers crashing through arched windows attempting to grab riders. Passing a huge Gothic window, riders could see half of the face and eye of a giant outside the windows, intent on catching the little car. In another section, the car approached a door far too small for it to fit through, part of the door and wall swinging away at the last second as the car approached. The cars were sent down a spinning barrel, the front of it resembling the mouth of hell with a nearby sign reading "Abandon Hope, All Ye Who Enter Here".

The Haunted House really took off once the cars "left" the house and proceeded outside, through a walled garden out back. At the end of the garden a phantom coachman stood by a crashed hearse, its wheels spinning in the mud. As the coachman gestured, Pepper's Ghost spirits rose eerily out of the hearse. A wide-mouthed maniac attacked the cars while in a stone gazebo the Grim Reaper stood silently. What appeared to be Roman-style columns would spin to reveal creatures hidden inside them, which could lunge and attack the car.

A bit further down the track, a forced perspective model of the house suggested that riders were out *behind* it somewhere, while lightning appeared to strike a tree and send it tumbling down towards riders. Walls and a garden trellis swayed and tilted dangerously as riders tried to pass under them. Lost in a swamp behind the house infested with leaping dragon-like creatures, cars approached a gigantic head that split in half, revealing tiny, screaming heads inside it. A creature leapt up out of nowhere, blocking off access to a bridge which offered possible escape.

As a ride experience, *The Haunted House* was a peculiar blend of danger and charm. Not all of its scare effects were especially intense, but especially by the end of the ride something would leap out every five feet, making *The Haunted House* a classic of its kind. Not even the very best of the Bill Tracy dark rides in the United States made quite as much time for as rich of a blend of scenic complexity, frightening imagery, and good old-fashioned illusion. The garden graveyard, foyer, hallway, and drawing room are a pocket *Haunted Mansion*, impressive in their care and attention to detail. The ride itself is an uncommonly cleverly worked out ghost train, managing to come up with at least a dozen new variations on the dark ride bait and switch.

If anything, the Alton Towers *Haunted House* was almost *too* ambitious, because a lot of what was in it didn't last long. After the first season, park managers decided they didn't like the ultraviolet lighting of most of the ride and requested it to be changed to incandescent lights, spoiling some of the best effects. The Grand Hall show scene was declared to be "too bare" and was given a warped tile floor, chairs, tables, and curtains, partially spoiling the cleverly worked out reflection effect. The unique giant scene was declared to be "boring" and the giant's fingers were re-dressed as screaming ghouls, leaving the colossal head outside the window at the end of the scene unexplained. Another scene, where a ghost would fly over rider's heads and vanish around a corner, broke down constantly. The idea was that the ghost would turn a corner ahead of the cars, and when the cars would make the corner they'd see the ghost had slammed directly into a wall! The mechanism to dispatch the ghost never synched with the cars correctly, so the scene was replaced with some skeletons. At one point cars passed a skeleton sitting on a toilet, then another throwing a cartoon bomb, the scene ending with the skeleton and toilet on the ground in pieces!

For a ride that seems almost universally fondly remembered by Alton Towers patrons, the *Haunted House*'s prime lasted a mere ten years. In 2002, it was closed for refurbishment and became a light gun shooting game. Reopening as *Duel - The Haunted House Strikes Back!*, ghosts had been evicted in favor of zombies. The sound of Emily Alton's singing in the drawing room was silenced and Sir Henry Alton's face in the fireplace flames was removed. All of the scenes in the ride were relit with amber, red, and green lights, revealing some of the mechanisms that powered the illusions. Everywhere in the ride, illuminated yellow targets litter the walls and show scenes, spoiling the carefully crafted scenery. The entire final sequence in the swamp, with its uncommonly ambitious attempts to create a sense of spatial relationship with the house and unique shocks, was removed and replaced with zombie figures popping out of metal barrels. It was a particularly undignified fate for a wildly ambitious ride.

Interestingly enough, the removal of a miniature railroad attraction prompted Alton Towers to expand the Gloomy Woods section of the park by reopening what was previously a scenic stretch of rail line along a lake as "Haunted Hollow" in 2007. Primarily a long, scenic walk alongside such attractions as the skyway ride and log flume, Haunted Hollow also includes some special elements that connect it to the *Haunted House*. A crypt has a prominent crack running through it, with a sign, calling back to *Doom & Sons*, instructing pedestrians: "Warning! Do Not Look in this Crypt!" The view inside the crypt is a mirror effect where a bare skeleton flashes back and forth with a decaying body covered with snakes and spiders.

Further along, headstones of two gentlemen - Bernard Grumblebum and Edwin Mutterson - carry on their tedious conversation from beyond the grave. A crypt contains a mirror inside which a hideous face appears, and further along a small plot of five music-themed tombstones can summon ghostly music from beyond the grave by standing on the inscribed sarcophagi lids. Nearer the *Haunted House* along a twisting path, four statues of household servants - a cook, a maid, a butler, and a gardener - moan ominously. About halfway through the area, a crashed hearse offers a photo opportunity.

Haunted Hollow may be dead simple as an attraction, but it's very interesting to *Haunted Mansion* fans for being a far more effective version of the "interactive queue" from the Florida *Haunted Mansion*, done four years earlier, much more simply, and for a fraction of the money. There's nothing especially noteworthy or accomplished about the epitaphs of the tombs or the quality of the sculpture, but the effects and illusions are simple and low tech, and all the stronger for being so.

Outside of the regional cadre of fans and supporters of Alton Towers, *The Haunted House* is not recognized around the world as being a seminal attraction the way the *Haunted Mansion* is, so it's unlikely to get the kind of careful renovation and restoration that it should.

Which is a shame. It's easily the best ride ever funded by Tussauds/Merlin, with a healthy respect for setting, detail, and invention. Now that the craze for light gun games and zombies is on the wane, it'd be respectful and appropriate for a full restoration of the original Alton Towers *Haunted House*, a classic of its kind in a genre more often noted for rote repetition.

Haunted Castle (Spookslot) - *Efteling, Kaatsheuvel, Netherlands*

While the three previous attractions profiled in this section have ranged from unusual to noteworthy, with *Spookslot* we arrive at the only other haunted attraction ever built which rivals the Disney *Haunted Mansion* in genius, artistry, and execution. Designed by Ton van de Ven and opening in 1978, Efteling's *Spookslot* is an honest to goodness masterpiece. Efteling is the reason why Tony Baxter fought for Disneyland Paris to be as rich and sumptuous as it is, and *Spookslot* is *the* reason he was determined not to repeat the *Haunted Mansion* in Marne la Vallee.

Efteling began as an early example of an attraction that proliferated along roadsides in the United States in the 1950s and 1960s: the fairy tale forest or "Mother Goose Land". Generally these were small businesses located near regional destinations featuring handcrafted cement or fiberglass standalone set pieces in an area of open woodland and accessed by trails or sidewalks. The "Mother Goose Land" category of attraction took advantage of the availability of postwar modern building supplies and added native American aggressiveness and creativity. Some local American examples include Storytown USA in Queensbury, New York; Mother Goose Land in

Canton, Ohio; Enchanted Forest in Salem, Oregon; and Mother Goose Gardens in Utica, Illinois.

Besides providing safe, unthreatening local entertainment for the baby boom, Mother Goose Lands stimulated local economies, sometimes developing into full amusement parks of their own, but they scratched the itch of midcentury Americans to escape in a world of make believe - the same impulse that gave rise to tiki bars, shopping malls, Disneyland, and Cinerama.

Efteling was different from the start. Carved out of an existing nature park, Efteling features tableaux and decor designed by a famous Dutch illustrator, Anton Pieck. The park was given a dramatic layout and clever devices to animate Pieck's designs by a Dutch filmmaker, Peter Reijnders. Reijnders and Pieck's park was executed on as carefully crafted a scale as possible. Instead of the crudely pieced together mannequins and concrete toadstools common in the United States, everything in Efteling was carved, built, and decorated to the highest possible standards. From an original slate of ten fairy tale stories, Efteling now hosts twenty-five in its *"Sprookjesbos"* Fairy Tale Forest.

The real predecessor to the *Haunted Castle*, Efteling's *Indian Water Lillies* opened in 1966. Officially part of the Fairy Tale Forest, the *Water Lillies* is a complete experience where groups enter a lavishly appointed far-east courtyard with a flowing reflecting pond. Proceeding through a cave, the *Water Lillies* is a standing room attraction simulating a view across a pond in a dense jungle dotted with the titular water lilies. In the distance, an Indian palace can be seen against a starry sky. As the show starts, music begins, a sorceress rises into view, the lilies open, and faeries inside begin to dance. Shortly, a frog band appears, then a chorus of three geese. After several minutes of synchronized dancing, the music stops, the faeries and animals vanish, and the sun rises. Although it's not fair to say that it's *exactly* like the *Tiki Room*, the overall effect is very similar.

The *Haunted Castle* marked the start of a period of expansion of Efteling as well as the ascension of Ton van de Ven as the new head designer of the park. Officially located outside of the Fairy Tale Forest, *Spookslot* was built in a stand of old trees not far from the original boating pond, and even with the addition of a bobsled run and promenade nearby, to this day it's unusually isolated for a theme park attraction. In 1978, it must have felt absolutely desolate. Some of that effect can be enjoyed today on an isolated path that runs behind the *Spookslot* through a forest. Basically unpaved and demarcated only by logs, it's one of the least "theme park" experiences you can have inside a theme park on the planet as you trace a rambling path behind the decaying, haunted castle.

The *Haunted Castle* sits at the back of a cobblestone courtyard dotted with crumbling Celtic gravestones. The marquee hangs from a crooked gibbet near an old covered-over well. To the left of the entrance, the bottom of a tower has crumbled away, the holes in the stonework resembling the eyes and mouth of a screaming face. An intricately carved stone arch entryway appears to be a mouth, with two windows above it acting as eyes. One of the "eyes" has a hole in the stonework and is an exit path for the show building's drainage system, allowing the face to "cry" during rain storms.

After passing through a rustic stone antechamber - with some unusual highly themed warning signs - the queue passes into a dark tunnel. An unmarked wooden door, when attempted to be opened, is slammed shut while barking dogs can be heard from behind it. Off to the right, a semicircular niche in the wall is filled with skulls, who move back and forth and roll their eyeballs. The low, dark chamber is filled with moaning. Near the end of the hall, a low barred window looks down into what could be a dungeon where the moans seem to be coming from - a man without eyes is in chains seated in a chair.

The hall empties into a tall, eight sided chamber where the line pivots around a central pillar. Leering gargoyles hold two candles at each corner. On each wall is the bas relief image of a goat-headed satyr holding the family crest - a shield of skulls and hearts. From the center of the room, a chandelier hangs from what appears to be a monstrously large arm. The ceiling is painted in patterns which appear to be decorative swirls, but on closer inspection are the heads of horned demons. If spectators linger in this room, eventually they will hear unsettling sounds as the lighting begins to dim. The central chandelier starts to sway, and the ceiling starts to become transparent, behind which strange fluttering shapes and movements can be seen. Finally the lights extinguish and three tusked, bat-winged creatures can be seen hovering above. They descend towards the viewers and vanish as the lights in the room return.

The queue snakes upwards into a holding room. While waiting for the next show to begin, guests can see a tall, shadowy form sitting in a curtained niche in the wall. Mysterious music plays, and the figure is revealed to be a Persian demon. Under his hands is a crystal ball, in which appears the face of a young girl. As the sitar music builds, the girl's face fades into a skull. The demon looks up at the audience as his laughter echoes through the room and he vanishes.

Upon entering the main show, the look and feel of the *Spookslot* changes. The main show is viewed through windows from a three-tiered balcony, similar to the pre-show area of the *Enchanted Tiki Room* at Magic Kingdom. As the show begins, the scene beyond the windows brightens. It's a full size elevated view of a dilapidated monastery. An overgrown graveyard can be seen far below, tall grasses blown by winds. Part of the earth has collapsed, affording a view into the crypts below the monastery.

The show begins as a demon perched high on a balcony overlooking the churchyard appears, ringing a funeral bell. After a few moments that bell is joined by another chiming bell, and a window illuminates in a monastery, revealing that a man has been hung from the bell-pull.

Eerie music begins as, inside the monastery, an arched window is illuminated as a procession of ghostly monks pass, each bearing lighted candles. The monks pass out of sight, then the light is extinguished as the sound of a slamming door announces the start of the festivities.

A floating violin, bowed by a disembodied hand, appears in the churchyard, playing Saint-Saëns' *Danse Macabre*. As it plays, moonlight illuminates the graveyard. The tombstones begin to rock and sway, and the earth begins to bulge in time with the music. The graves start to open, and ghosts can be seen chasing each other through the crypts below the monastery.

In a far window of the monastery, a ghoulish young lady appears, tied to a stake. As the music builds, decaying bodies can be seen prying off the lids of their coffins as the young lady in the monastery appears to be burning up. Finally, a peal of thunder and flash of lightning end the manifestations at the height of the music. The phantom violin returns, playing the final notes of the *Danse Macabre*, then vanishes as the show ends and the exit doors open, leading back to the front of the *Haunted Castle*.

As my description above hopefully indicates, in my opinion Efteling's *Spookslot* comes nearer to recapturing the specific magic of the *Haunted Mansion* than any other haunted attraction ever built - a list that pointedly includes *Phantom Manor*.

After decades of thought and thousands of rides I've realized that it isn't the scale of the *Haunted Mansion* that makes it so special. If ambition and scale were guarantors of excellence then the *Mansion* would have been long surpassed by such impressive, cutting edge extravaganzas as *Harry Potter and the Forbidden Journey*. That's an amazing ride, but it isn't the *Haunted Mansion*.

What makes the *Mansion* is its specific, heady blend of illusion, design, and impenetrability. We see and understand so much, and those things throw deep-seated switches in our brains, but we cannot account for them. The *Haunted Mansion* constantly provides complex, inscrutable images and inadequate explanations for them.

Spookslot is similarly extremely elaborate and bizarrely, weirdly incomplete. The void that sits at the center of the *Haunted Mansion* and *Spookslot* is "what does this all mean?" *Spookslot*'s blend of frightening demons, witchcraft, oriental spirits, and crumbling ruins richly evokes a story we can only guess at.

This cuts to the heart of the traditional ghost story as a precursor to the detective novel: the dead have returned to the realm of the living, a situation we know is not natural, but if we follow the clues we can uncover the reason for the return and end this violation of the natural order of things.

Consider the way the archetypal ghost story maps onto the contours of the detective novel: the phantom hitch-hiker. The vanishing girl in the back seat of the car opens a mystery that the visit to the house of her parents resolves. The chill in the phantom hitch-hiker story comes not from the girl's disappearance, but the belated revelation that she was *not alive to begin with*.

Spookslot and the *Haunted Mansion* circumvent this logic. We never find out *why* the Mansion is Haunted or what the meaning behind the girl who burns away in the crumbling monastery is. In this sense they violate the complicity of the standard ghost story and open a place for the viewer to inhabit. The end of the eventful stay in the *Haunted Mansion* leads not to comprehension, but ever-increasing cycles of speculation.

Spookslot goes heavier on the menacing imagery than Disney would dare to - the eyeless man, the suggestions of Satanism, and the burning witch are all stronger images that WED would have offered - but the attraction arrives in a similar place anyway - lighthearted, almost comic.

Since the form was invented, the haunted house attraction has sought to reassure us that the worst isn't the worst, even when it happens - that even death is survivable. While Ghost Trains and *Laff in the Darks* aplenty whisked patrons past car headlights bearing down on them and screaming women sawed in half, Disney's *Haunted Mansion* and Efteling's *Spookslot* have offered us a portal to another place beyond life - where our reflections wink back at us. The real chill comes later, when you're alone - and you realize just how scary some of those ideas actually were.

NOTES

Part 1

1. Stephen King, *Danse Macabre*, p.265
2. New York Times, "*DISASTROUS FIRE.; Total Destruction of Barnum's American Museum*", July 14, 1865
3. David J. Skal explores this concept fully in *The Monster Show*, Faber and Faber, 2001
4. Much of the information that follows in these next three paragraphs is indebted to the marvelous research of Bill Luca and George LaCross at their superlative website, Laff in the Dark. http://www.laffinthedark.com
5. There may be no more comically alarming image of female sensuality in Disney than this brief moment, which explodes both propriety and common sense.
6. It's impossible to know if *The Mad Doctor*'s coffin clock is directly responsible for the one in the *Haunted Mansion*. What can be said is that the version in the cartoon closely resembles a model that Rolly Crump designed for the Museum of the Weird, but neither is very close to the final version in the attraction, besides all three being scary clocks.
7. J.B. Kaufman, *The Fairest One of All*, p.116
8. This grisly detail comes from the scene's animator, Bill Justice, in his book *Justice For Disney*.
9. Tim Lucas, *Black Sunday* Audio Commentary Track, Image Entertainment DVD, 2000.
10. Thanks to Mike Lee for noticing this for the first time.
11. I heard this one working as a Cast Member and never forgot how absurdly specific it was - only to discover years later that Silver Dollar City in Branson, Missouri operates a fun house called Grandfather's Mansion. For the record, those of us who worked the Mansion most often called it "Spooky House".
12. First identified, to my knowledge, by former imagineer Justin Jorgensen at his website ThusJustin.Com
13. Published in 1950 by Bonanza Books, this is not hard or expensive to find online and worth buying for a dedicated Mansionite.
14. Lichten, p.61

15. In our imaginations! Speculation of this type is unavoidable but always conceptually tedious.
16. Tony Baxter remembers this in a late-90s video produced for Imagineering in which he walks the Mansion and talks; this readily circulates online and has been available in fan circles since at least the early 2000s. Sadly he spends most of his time talking about Phantom Manor.
17. This from an interview published in *The E-Ticket Magazine*, n.30, Fall 1998.
18. David Koenig, *More Mouse Tales*, p.111
19. See Appendix C
20. The rediscovery of the traveling light effect is not something I can take credit for, but I was a witness. Morning in the Haunted Mansion break room often meant discussion of this or that relating to the attraction, for no other reason than that fans of the attraction tend to want to work at it. The traveling light effect was brought up as a subject for discussion. Some swore that there was no traveling light effect, but that matter could be put to rest easily: by going up there ourselves. Today access is restricted to the innards of the attractions, but I worked at Magic Kingdom at a time when the long arm of potential litigation had not yet removed all of the "residual benefits" of bumbling around attraction interiors. About five of us went up through the interior of the facade, inching our way along the narrow walkways between the facade's outer shell and the moving walls of the stretch room. Once we had squeezed around the top of one of the stretch rooms, the interior door to the Conservatory was in reach. From here, we could have, if we chose, opened the outside door to the Conservatory to step out onto the Haunted Mansion's exterior terrace, which is always a fun place to be - provided you don't get caught. The view from the Mansion's "Front Door" - which is barely tall enough to stand up in - is gorgeous. We didn't go outside today. The light mechanism is located in the center and rear of the Conservatory, and had been maintained over the years in the respect that the lightbulb inside it had always been replaced. We could all agree that the weird coffee-can looking thing was supposed to do something. The other three moving lights on the bottom floor were easy enough to find, and as the group pressed on I found myself wedging my way slowly underneath the stairs which led up to the facade's front door. Down there, among all the old sawdust, was an Orlando Sentinel, neatly folded in thirds, with the Used Cars

section facing outwards. I turned over the paper and saw it was from 1974. At that point sunlight flooded the wooden interior with the sound of screeching hinges. The fellow who suggested we all go up into the facade to check it out had climbed up one of the vertical ladders and had pushed open one of the facade's upper windows, perhaps for the first time in more than three decades. He had found the upper light mechanisms, too. From there all we had to do was pass the word on to Maintenance that yes, those light fixtures up in the facade were supposed to do something, and one by one they slowly began to get repaired. The long-forgotten effect was brought back to life. In the grand scheme of things, a pack of Cast Members out on a jaunt isn't a really important contribution to Disney history, but by bending the rules we did get a very effective gag restored. That was a long time ago, but every time I see that spooky orange glow creep past one of the windows of the Haunted Mansion, I imagine Claude Coats or Yale Gracey smiling down from heaven.

21. Joseph Citro, *Weird New England*, p.35
22. Joseph Citro, *Passing Strange*, p.278
23. The E Ticket, No. 32, p.8
24. Ken named his pirate Captain Gore and his virginal bride Priscilla, and structured most of this version of the ride on *Bluebeard*, which we will revisit later in this discussion.
25. Devil's Elbow, at the northern tip of the Rivers of America, is mentioned by Twain in Chapters 25 and 29 of *Life on the Mississippi*.
26. He didn't; the interior treatment was devised by Dorothea Redmond.
27. Those who are tracking ironies through this text now have a whopper: Albany is indeed on the Hudson - upper Hudson, not lower, and all of this after I have bent over backwards arguing that the Mansion should be thought of as seaside - an argument I still support. Don't go driving thru Albany looking for the Rathbone house - it was supposedly torn down less than 20 years after being built. Downing wrote another book, *"A treatise on the theory and practice of landscape gardening, adapted to North America"*, which features an illustration of the rear of the Rathbone villa, practically unrecognizable. Both of A.J. Downing's books can be read full length at Archive.Org.

Part 2

1. Interestingly enough, years later I shot footage of these upper floors for a student film, and many people claimed to be able to see a face looking out of one of the windows. I seem to be unable to see it, myself.
2. I learned this by being able to see a construction schedule for the Rivers of America as a Cast Member.
3. Rubens, a less versatile approximation of the authentic Victorian typeface WED used for the attraction plaque, was uncovered by Mansion fan Tim McKenny in the late 90s and it spread rapidly outward through the much smaller Disney fan internet from there.
4. The face on the tombstone bears so little resemblance to the character "Madame Leota" that when the Memento Mori shop opened in 2014, a portrait inside tried valiantly to merge the gravestone image and in-ride projected face to mixed, but fascinating, results.
5. The cables that hoist the stretch rooms were originally theatrical ropes and did on occasion break, resulting in the upper part of the room slumping off to the side with a terrific crash.
6. So far as I know, Marc Davis is the only designer to come up with a use for the Stretch Room concept in a new way. In the late 70s he designed an attraction for Fort Wilderness called *Adventure House*, a kind of deluxe fun house which was never built. In one room, a bear is asleep in a guest bedroom. As the bear snored, the ceiling was to raise and lower in time with his wheezes!
7. Certain Maids and Butlers use the blackout as a moment to sneak up alongside a temporally distracted guest to provide a quick scare; for those who can pull this off, I tip my hat - as it's totally in keeping with the hammy quality of the blackout gag. I myself would sometimes, after the blackout, be found laying facedown on the stretch room floor, apparently dead.
8. MAPO, short for MAry POppins (really, you can't make this stuff up), was the manufacturing division for WED Enterprises from 1964 to 1990.
9. Thanks to Mansionologists Brandon Champlain and Dan Olson for reconstructing what was intended here.
10. Of course nobody actually experiencing the attraction in the intended way could ever note this detail, but it's a fun one.

11. Dan Olson, *Famous Ghosts and Ghosts Trying To Make A Name For Themselves*, Long Forgotten, March 2011
12. In this version of the ride, you could look down the well as you exited and see that the water inside it is blood red! Gruesome!
13. "Disneyland's Ghost House", *The E-Ticket*, Issue 41
14. George is bald-pated in the stretch room portrait, which I don't think signifies anything more than making it easier to show the axe stuck in his head.
15. S.E.A. itself is a conceptual outgrowth of the Adventurer's Club at Pleasure Island, and supposedly part of the Jungle Navigation Company, the shipping business that runs the *Jungle Cruise*. If any of this means anything to you, you either are in deep with the Disney parks or write for Imagineering.
16. Brown ladies, White ladies, Blue ladies and more are traditional haunts of English manor houses, and rare indeed are the ancestral homes that don't claim some manner of supernatural haunt as their own - after all, it's good for tourism.
17. Van Eaton Galleries, *Collecting Disneyland*, Fall 2015
18. I may not be convinced by the "ghost boy" photograph, but my friend Tim McKenny did take a photo of a very strange swirling vortex of smoke outside the front gates of the attraction in 2002.
19. Bruce Stark, *Black Sheep in Tokyo*, p.82
20. One of these embellishments, "Ron V.", was photographed by one zealous fan and published online, leading to the infamous comment that somebody had "gotten jiggy with a Sharpie". I worked with Ron V., and his reply to this is not printable.
21. When the *Haunted Mansion* got her big refurbishment in 2007, the three dead trees outside the window were replaced. For the first few days of operation, some mischievous Imagineer snuck a hanging noose into the top-most branch of the center tree.
22. One of the few Atencio concepts to have come close to realization was his idea for an agrarian American farm destroyed by a dust bowl. This was actually painted by Ed Kohn and prepared for use at Disneyland, but didn't make the final cut.
23. One easy way to give your own home a "Haunted Mansion" feel is to find and restore some Gone With the Wind lamps yourself. They can be found for less than $100.
24. That griffin was so dark in the 90s that I once bought a disposable camera at the park just to take a flash photo of it and see what it

actually was. Honestly, the entire ride was unacceptably dim through the 90s, only really improving in 2003 and then 2007.
25. When I say skull-spiders, I mean that Tracy made the figures by sticking spider legs into foam skulls, like that crab-head monster from The Thing (1982).
26. Ginger Honetor was responsible for providing guided tours of the Mansion for groups of Cast Members; walking tours of the house are the common team-building "bonus" offered by various labor units around the Resort.
27. Nesler also mocked up a scene intended to be installed in the Jungle Cruise between the Elephant Bathing Pool and Trader Sam; a parrot on a tree stump mocking some encircling crocodiles attempting to eat it. In this case, we have multiple pieces of Marc Davis art of the scene and several diagrams indicating it is to be installed "in year 2". Apparently somebody decided the scene would be better used alongside the Walt Disney World Railroad. Marc Davis redesigned the scene and it was installed along the "back stretch" on the railroad, where it can still be seen today - a large frog replacing the stranded parrot on the stump.
28. As Cast Members we used to joke that it was "neither grand, nor a staircase", which is true - it's just a big ramp.
29. Dan Olson, *Does Size Matter?*, Long Forgotten, January 2013
30. The wallpaper in this short section is original wallpaper left over from the show installation in 1970 - it was discovered rolled up in a storage room.
31. The debate over which version of *Sgt Pepper's Lonely Hearts Club Band* - the Mono version directly overseen by the Beatles or the Stereo version produced by George Martin - best represents the album is a debate which is still believe it or not, going on. And this was only two years earlier than the opening of the Mansion!
32. Bob Thomas, *Walt Disney: An American Original*, p.155
33. You can hear the effect on the "Story and Song" Haunted Mansion LP.
34. I'm not saying it's bad, but it's always struck me as weird to have a glossy armchair just hanging out there like it's totally normal to have chairs be glossy.
35. The chair removed from the Music Room was the one all the way over on the right, near the table with the flower arrangement. Thankfully I'm around to remember important details like these, right?

36. At Disneyland when you go through this arch there's a bump as if the track didn't settle right. I only put this here because it baffles me greatly.
37. Identified as such throughout the industry, nobody seems to know where this name comes from.
38. Jason Surrell, *The Haunted Mansion: Imagineering A Disney Classic*, p.24
39. Private correspondence, Summer 2015
40. Victorians often had bodies laid out for days, and they did creepy things with them like posed them in chairs and took photos. Those darn Victorians!
41. For a particularly spectacular reported example of this, check out the ghost story compilation *Weird Hauntings*, p.31, "The Man of the House" featuring figures made of billowing smoke and a screaming Civil War general.
42. Mike Lee once suggested that had WED found a *third* place to stash those dancing candles - say, in the dark turnaround between Load and Unload - it would've been hard to walk along at Unload knowing those infernal candles were right behind you. I've been trying unsuccessfully to get that image out of my head for years.
43. At least, not dramatically different in the way that paddling a low raft through the *Jungle Cruise* river - something I've done a few times - makes you realize just how different it is to see these things from up in a boat.
44. One could argue that the new 2007 scene of the eyes becoming the wallpaper is a pretty transparent sop to fans, and if it is, then it worked. Of all of the changes wrought on the attraction during that refurbishment, everyone seems to agree that that scene is a winner.
45. Hat tip to Melody Vagnini for digging this up at D23.
46. Dan Olson, *The Ghostland Around Us, Beneath Us*, Long Forgotten, May 2012
47. Charlie Hass, *Disneyland is Good For You*, New West, December 1978
48. That clock used to be outside the Elgin clock shop, but it remained after the store was closed. Notice that every Main Street has one of those free standing clocks whether or not they ever had a clock shop.
49. Passport to Dreams Old & New, *The Theme Park Trope List*, March 2015
50. E.A.J. Honigmann, *Othello*, Arden Third Edition, p.68

51. p.118
52. Joseph Citro, *Passing Strange*, p.49
53. You can read this entire text online through Project Gutenberg and see if, like me, you find it as strangely puzzling as Olcott did.
54. This again is from that walkthrough video with Tony.
55. Or at least it isn't unless you're at Disneyland, who replaced their ectoplasm effect with a projection effect based on a sort of swimming light.
56. Dan Olson, *The Duelists*, Long Forgotten, January 2011
57. Growing up, my parents had a 1920s reclining chair not at all unlike the one in the *Haunted Mansion* that was in pretty poor shape. It sat in an awkward spot in our summer cottage, right near the TV that only picked up the public access channels through a crappy pair of rabbit ears. As an indoor kid there was little for me to do at the cottage, but I was able to wake up early, sit in the old recliner, and try to tune the TV to Channel 6 and watch *Garfield & Friends*. I always felt uncomfortable sitting in the old chair, and one day my Mom informed me that my great, great grandfather died in the chair! Every time I see the *Haunted Mansion*'s old lady ghost, I think of Grandpa John.
58. I'm fairly sure that Disneyland lost their cobweb because it complicated the installation of *Haunted Mansion Holiday*.
59. It's done with an identical chair painted flat black that's in there under the Doombuggy track with the dummy legs. WED's commitment to pulling off the Pepper's Ghost gag in this scene is amazing.
60. We used to make lots of weird Hidden Mickeys and then remove them once word leaked onto the internet - there's a cluster of three rocks I placed on the pebbly beach of the "Trapped safari" scene at the *Jungle Cruise* and destroyed once I saw the rocks had made it into the Hidden Mickeys book published by Steven Barrett.
61. What is true is that most of the plates on the table of the *Haunted Mansion* have photographs underneath them. This is a tradition begun by Ginger Honetor in the 1980s when two guests approached her outside the attraction with a photograph of their mother who had recently died. Since she had loved the *Haunted Mansion*, Ginger placed the photo underneath a Ballroom plate. Much to the credit of Imagineering, none of the photographs have - to my knowledge - been removed. Don't ask to have a photo of your own loved one placed under a plate; at least as of my tenure at *Mansion*, we were out of "vacant" plates and Ginger has retired on any account.

62. Much of my appreciation for this is indebted to Dan Olson, who saw the Haunted Mansion with Hatbox Ghost in August 1969 and so was able to appreciate the original intent here.
63. It's worth noting that the Disneyland Attic was stocked exclusively with antiques and items from the studio prop warehouse; I remain convinced that the distinctive plaster "statue" still kicking around the Attic can be spotted in the background somewhere in *The Happiest Millionaire*.
64. Or at least prior to 2015, there was an identical screen upstairs on the Disneyland facade, until the furniture was recently replaced.
65. Unfortunately, WDI decided to replace her head with a stock women's head - and it was the same head as Jane, the teenage daughter from the final act of the *Carousel of Progress*.
66. This, incidentally, made it possible to ride though the Attic without seeing a single pop-up, which I managed to do a few times.
67. This is where the set dressing really falls short for me, and even more absurd is the presence of an actual wedding cake near her, and not a decayed, moldy one like *Phantom Manor* has. All hail the invincible 120-year-old cake!
68. The Hatbox Ghost returned to Disneyland in 2015, and while the figure is amazing, he's now up on the roof in his own little scene, technically part of the Graveyard Jamboree. This means than any connection he has to Constance is, officially, entirely hypothetical, and should not reflect on our interpretation of the Constance bride tableau. Which, to me as a fan of the Attic's original conception, is a huge disappointment.
69. *Disney Family Album*, "Marc Davis", The Disney Channel, 1984
70. Bob Thomas, *Walt Disney: An American Original*, p.312
71. Those cloud projections also provide the moving fog effect, which they never quite got right at Disneyland and excluded at Magic Kingdom except for two very small patches directly in front of the opera singers and behind the tea party. It's supposed to look like long wisps of fog crawling along the ground in front of the ghosts, but in practice it mostly just looks like a bunch of confusing lights projected on a screen for no good reason. You can see what it's supposed to look like in the stock footage of the attraction captured in 1969 and shown on "Disneyland Showtime" in 1970, that venerable Disneyland program where the Osmonds tour the Mansion with E. J. Peaker. Early interior photos of the Disneyland *Mansion* reveal that they appear to have tried

to spray-paint wisps of fog on the scrims at first, perhaps to give a similar impression that the projections did. So far as I know, Magic Kingdom has always simply had the curtains.
72. He could also do gags that took two or three glances; along the *Rivers of America* at Disneyland, until the area was re-thought, there was a classic Davis gag of a native american boy standing on an overturned canoe fishing in the river. His trusty dog was by his side, but looking the other way, because right behind the kid's back, a fish keeps jumping out of the water. Davis was able to combine stock situations - a boy and his dog, fishing - with a surprise sting in the tail like nobody before or since.
73. Check out Chapter 5 in *The Decorative Art of Victoria's Era* for a lot of info on this.
74. Joseph Citro, *Weird New England*, p.220
75. *Spook-A-Rama* at Coney Island had a "behind the waterfall" gag, but really we need look no closer than Knoebel's *Haunted House* for a great example.
76. One of the last places to see operating Pretzel Amusement Company stunts is the *Laffland* attraction at Sylvan Beach Amusement Park in upstate New York. Get there before it's gone!
77. p.45
78. You'd think that the Constance storyline would add some contradictory information to this, but it doesn't - she married her last husband, George Hightower, in 1877. We don't really need to try to explicate her story with the Graceys' story.
79. This is only a problem within the Magic Kingdom's "story" setting if you let it be. *The Haunted Mansion* is stylized to fit Liberty Square and so it does, an area which also incorporates the American Revolution (1776), the current U.S. President, Mark Twain's days as a Riverboat Pilot (1850s), Mark Twain's nostalgic remembrance of his youth in Mississippi (1840s), plus Frontierland, the Gold Rush, and a Pacific Northwest music hall dated 1898 and filled with bears singing songs from the 1920s and 1960s. It's called The Magic Kingdom for good reason.
80. To the list above of "unsavory hitchhikers" today we would likely add "serial killer", but remember that the *Haunted Mansion* was designed in the mid to late 60s, before the crimes of Charles Manson's "family" propagated the notion that mad killers could be everybody's next door neighbors. The extent to which the generation that designed the

Mansion took the notion of serial killers seriously can be seen in the fact that they put up a portrait of Jack the Ripper as a generic boogeyman.
81. The reference to "final arrangements" is deleted at Disneyland, where the Ghost Host ends his spiel with "-if you insist on lagging behind, you may not need to volunteer!". Now that it is understood that WED expected to have an actual show in the Picture Gallery with five portraits going through six-stage transformations, it's possible that what still plays at Disneyland is a truncated version of the intended spiel, dropping the words that set up Little Leota. That's a long setup, even for the *Mansion*!
82. Dan Olson has demonstrated that Little Leota originally wore a dress with a hood and held a bouquet of lilies, making her a kind of living piece of funerary statuary, a tiny, eternal mourner. At some point they changed her to wear a bridal outfit, and Olson believes this was done intentionally, to increase her ambiguity and hint at ties to the Attic bride. If this is true it certainly fits with her role in the show to add a note of ambiguity to the end of the ride.
83. What Florida's exit hallway doesn't really pull off is the illusion of being underground that's so successful at Disneyland, with its numerous roots and deeply felt ascent back to the surface. Directly across the park, Pirates of the Caribbean actually does convey the impression of being underground and riding back to the surface in much the same way Disneyland did: showing you roots coming in through a rock wall and having riders move past them on a Speedramp.
84. Dan Olson, *To Find A Way Out*, Long Forgotten, April 2013
85. Outside the entrance to the attraction, a circle of rocks marks the spot where a circular planter once stood, removed in 2000 for the implementation of Fastpass. Guests began to circulate the idea that this was a "fairy circle" and by standing inside it at midnight and chanting the name "Madame Leota", her spirit could be summoned. I saw this happen a few times. I probably don't need to point out that this is completely insane.
86. Of course, it's now several meters from the house and most improbably placed for a suicide. Maybe the Bride got a running start off the roof??
87. As it pertains to the Haunted Mansion, the most likely source here is the 1944 MGM film *Gaslight*, which kicked off a whole cycle of women's film melodramas which traded in weird and frankly Gothic

atmosphere, occasionally getting close to semi-horror territory. *Gaslight* began a popular thriller tradition of a husband plotting to kill or drive a wife crazy, which continued all the way into the 1950s when it suddenly pivoted into a more horrific mode with Herni-George Clouzout's film *Les Diaboliques*. That 1955 film was a new high-water mark for both terror and sadism, and its international success begat a new wave of horror films, reflected in *The House on Haunted Hill* and *The Tingler* directed by William Castle, as well as *Psycho* by Alfred Hitchcock. This meant that when Ken Andersen and Marc Davis were coming up with ideas for a Haunted Mansion in the 50s and 60s, plots to kill wives and husbands were a much stronger component of thriller culture than the supernatural itself - and would remain so until the devil-film craze of the 70s started by *The Exorcist*. This is why this motif runs so strongly through the Haunted Mansion, as ever a reflection of its era.

Bibliography

Allan, Robin, *Walt Disney and Europe*, Indiana University Press, 1999
Baham, Jeff, *The Unauthorized Story of Walt Disney's Haunted Mansion*, Theme Park Press, 2014
Bright, Randy, *Disneyland Inside Story*, Harry N. Abrams, 1987
Doctor, Pete and Merritt, Christopher, *Marc Davis In His Own Words: Imagineering the Disney Theme Parks*, Disney Editions, 2019
Fjellman, Stephen M., *Vinyl Leaves: Walt Disney World and America*, Westview Press, 1992
Gottdiener, Mark, *The Theming of America*, Westview Press, 2001
Hench, John, *Designing Disney: Imagineering and the Art of the Show*, Disney Editions, 2003
Koenig, David, *More Mouse Tales*, Bonaventure Press, 1999
Koenig, David, *Realityland*, Bonaventure Press, 2007
Lichten, Frances, *Decorative Art of Victoria's Era*, Charles Scribner's Sons, 1950
McCullough, Edo, *Good Old Coney Island*, Charles Scribner's Sons, 1957
Rhodes, Gary D., *The Birth of the American Horror Film*, Edinburgh University Press, 2018
Skal, David J., *The Monster Show*, Faber and Faber, 2001

Surrell, Jason, *The Haunted Mansion: Imagineering A Disney Classic*, Disney Editions, 2015
Thomas, Bob, *Walt Disney: An American Original*, Hyperion, 1994
Walker, Lester, *American Homes*, Black Dog & Leventhal Publishers, 1996
Walt Disney World: The First Decade, Walt Disney Productions, 1980

Luca, Bill and LaCross, George, *Laff in the Dark*, 1999 - 2020, http://www.laffinthedark.com
Olson, Dan, *Long-Forgotten Haunted Mansion*, 2010-2020, https://longforgottenhauntedmansion.blogspot.com

The Adventures of Ichabod and Mr. Toad. Walt Disney Productions, 1949.
The Bat. Directed by Roland West, United Artists, 1926
The Cat and the Canary. Directed by Paul Leni, Universal Pictures, 1927
Les Diaboliques. Directed by Henri-Georges Clouzout, Cinédis, 1955
Das Cabinet des Dr. Caligari. Directed by Robert Wiene, Decla-Bioscop, 1920
The Haunted House. Animated by Ub Iwerks, Walt Disney Productions, 1929
The Haunting. Directed by Robert Wise, Metro-Goldwyn-Mayer, 1963
The Mad Doctor. Walt Disney Productions, 1933.
The Skeleton Dance. Animated by Ub Iwerks, Walt Disney Productions, 1929
Snow White and the Seven Dwarfs. Directed by David Hand, Walt Disney Productions, 1933

Photographic Plates

The images in *Boundless Realm* are presented under Fair Use for educational and historic purposes only. Neither the author nor Inklingwood Press claim any rights of ownership, which remain with the respective rights holders.

1. "Barnum's American Museum, New York." LOC PPOC LC-DIG-ppmsca-05604
2. Coney Island postcard, Luna Park ca. 1910 - Authors Collection

3. Pretzel Ride: "Joyland Park; midway with confectionary, 1930" Lafayette Studios Collection, University of Kentucky Special Collections.
4. Sleeping Beauty Castle Under Construction, Walt Disney Productions 1954, Author's Collection, © Disney
5. Riverboat Behind Landing circa 2015, Author's Collection
6. Joel Rathbone Residence, Albany NY, from "Decorative Art of Victoria's Era", Author's Collection
7. The Haunted Mansion Facade, 1999, Author's Collection
8. Joel Rathbone Residence, "Cottage residences, or, A series of designs for rural cottages and cottage villas, and their gardens and grounds: adapted to North America", Hathi Trust Digital Library, book digitized by Google
9. Liberty Square Under Construction, Disney Depository, Orange County Library System, © Disney
10. Haunted Mansion in 2007, Author's Collection
11. 'Queequeg Pursuing Moby Dick', Marc Davis, 1956, "The Fine Art of Marc Davis", Forest Lawn Museum 2005
12. Family Plot in 2002, Author's Collection
13. Family Plot in 2002, Author's Collection
14. Foyer Scene in 1999, Author's Collection
15. Stretching Gallery in 1999, Author's Collection
16. Load Area in 1999, Author's Collection
17. Bat Stanchion Topper Rubbed Smooth in 1999, Author's Collection
18. Portrait Hall in 1999, Author's Collection
19. Webbing the Music Room, from "The Walt Disney World Story" 1972, Walt Disney Productions, Author's Collection, © Disney
20. Painted flat outside the Music Room window, Courtesy of Dave Ensign
21. Giant Spider Animated Figure in 2003, Courtesy of Dave Ensign. Note speaker against rear wall.
22. Armchair Prop in 1999, Author's Collection
23. Haunted Mansion Maintenance Diagram showing Speaker Placement, 1971 - note "Traveling Sound" in Endless Hallway. Courtesy Mike Lee.
24. Conservatory Scene in 1994, Author's Collection. Some early documents call this the "Viewing Room".
25. Mrs. Fish and the Misses Fox, engraving by Currier and Ives, Library of Congress Prints and Photographs Division, pga 09494
26. Haunted Mansion Ballroom Table in 2009, Shot by Dan Warren, Courtesy of Martin Smith
27. Organist Without Hat, Early 1971, Walt Disney Word Postcard, Author's Collection, © Disney

28. Magic Kingdom Attic in 1993, Courtesy of Mike Lee
29. Graveyard Band Postcard, 1971, Walt Disney Productions, Author's Collection, © Disney
30. Hitch-hikers Souvenir Slide, 1969, Walt Disney Productions, Author's Collection, © Disney
31. Exit Hall in 2006, Author's Collection
32. Bluebeard Crypt, Vacation Slide ca. 1971, Author's Collection
33. Haunted Mansion Advertisement, April 1971, from "Walt Disney World News", Walt Disney Productions, Author's Collection, © Disney

Acknowledgments

Many thanks to the early Haunted Mansion web pioneers: Jeff Baham, Jared Grey, and Tim McKenny.

For research, fact checking and general support: Mike Lee, Dan Olson, Tom Morris, Chris Merritt, Michael Crawford, Brandon Wane, Steven Vagnini, Brice Croskey, Dave Ensign, Cory Doctorow, Martin Smith, Steven Curler and Jon Plant.

Also thanks to my parents, Bill and Dee, for raising a weird kid.

ALSO FROM INKLINGWOOD PRESS

Over the past century, theme parks have created worlds where pirates still loot Caribbean towns, where daring adventurers explore booby-trapped temples, and where superheroes swing from New York skyscrapers - and allowed us to step into them too. This is a book about how to design those fantastic places, and the ingenuity that goes into their creation.

This is a handbook for the practicing designer, a textbook for the aspiring student, and a behind the scenes guidebook for the theme park fan, building on hundreds of interviews with accomplished designers from Walt Disney Imagineering, Universal Creative, Merlin Entertainments, and more. *Theme Park Design & The Art of Themed Entertainment* explores everything from the stories, themes, and characters that theme parks bring to life, to the business models, processes, and techniques that allow them to do it.

From rocket ships to roller coasters, fairy tales to fireworks shows, and dinosaurs to dark rides, never before has a book dived so deep into the art form of themed entertainment.

Written by David Younger
Foreword by Tony Baxter, Afterword by Joe Rohde

"This is the most thorough book on theme park design I have ever seen. One that quotes real designers with priceless knowledge."
Peter Alexander, lead designer of Universal Studios Florida

"This book captures in one document the greatest collection of turning points, philosophies, and ground rules that have sprung to life since the birth of the theme park. I can't imagine a person contemplating a role in themed entertainment not coming out of this immersive experience inside David Younger's mind without the equivalent of a Master's Degree in the psychology of the themed experience."
Tony Baxter, lead designer of Disneyland Paris

"David Younger has created one of the finest studies of the themed entertainment industry ever attempted. It is a comprehensive and thoughtful analysis of every aspect of this most complex design discipline from the micro to the macro levels without once becoming heavy handed. Congratulations on providing both the novice and the grizzled veteran with this wonderful compendium!"
Steve Kirk, lead designer of Tokyo DisneySea

"Authoritative, entertaining, and fascinating, *Theme Park Design* is a themed entertainment aficionado's dream. David Younger has created a one-of-a-kind work that is both a scrupulously researched reference and a jolly good read; an excellent encyclopedia on its subject, and a 'bathtub book' one can open to any page and have a wonderful time exploring."
Jeff Kurtti, lead designer of The Walt Disney Family Museum

"The art of theme park design involves more alchemy than it does art or science, and much of the secret sauce resides behind the obvious surface. Perhaps that's why so little has been written about the subject, let alone anything of practical value. David Younger's book is the first to break down many of these illusive and temporal theories into distinct, understandable, and enlightening observations."
Tom Morris, lead designer of Hong Kong Disneyland

"Expertise is real, and, at least in part, quantifiable, as David Younger's magnum opus demonstrates. By amassing the communal knowledge of this disparate and diverse group into a single opus, David Younger has provided us all with a landmark in our intellectual space."
Joe Rohde, lead designer of Disney's Animal Kingdom

www.ThemeParkDesignBook.com

www.ingramcontent.com/pod-product-compliance
Lightning Source LLC
Chambersburg PA
CBHW020416010526
44118CB00010B/275